D0009687

MIND
MATTERS

Teaching for
Thinking

Dan Kirby and Carol Kuykendall

Boynton/Cook Publishers
Heinemann
Portsmouth, New Hampshire

LB 1590.3
K57
1991

Boynton/Cook Publishers, Inc.
A Subsidiary of
Heinemann Educational Books, Inc.
361 Hanover Street, Portsmouth, NH 03801–3959
Offices and agents throughout the world

© 1991 by Dan Kirby and Carol Kuykendall. All rights reserved. No part of this book may be reproduced in any form or by electronic or mechanical means, including information storage and retrieval systems, without permission in writing from the publisher, except by a reviewer, who may quote brief passages in a review.

The following have generously given permission to use quotations from copyrighted works:
    Pages 111–12: Reprinted with permission of Charles Scribner's Sons, an imprint of Macmillan Publishing Company from *All the Strange Hours* by Loren Eiseley. Copyright © 1975 Loren Eiseley.
    Pages 112–13: From *The Immense Journey* by Loren Eiseley. Copyright © 1946, 1950, 1953, 1955, 1956, 1957 by Loren Eiseley. Reprinted by permission of Random House, Inc.
    Page 115: Excerpt from *Pilgrim at Tinker Creek* by Annie Dillard. Copyright © 1974 by Annie Dillard. Reprinted by permission of HarperCollins Publishers.
    Every effort has been made to contact the copyright holders and students for permission to reprint borrowed material. We regret any oversights that may have occurred and would be happy to rectify them in future printings of this work.

Library of Congress Cataloging-in-Publication Data

Kirby, Dan.
    Mind matters: teaching for thinking / Dan Kirby and Carol Kuykendall.
        p.   cm.
    Includes bibliographical references (p. 231).
    ISBN 0–86709–276–9
    1. Thought and thinking—Study and teaching—United States.
    2. Interdisciplinary approach in education—United States.
    3. Cognitive learning—United States. I. Kuykendall, Carol, 1933–
    II. Title.
    LB1590.3.K57 1991
    370. 15'2—dc20   90–27201
                                                                                 CIP

Prepress production by PC&F, Inc.
Printed in the United States of America.

91 92 93 94 95   9 8 7 6 5 4 3 2 1

137727

Contents

N. L. TERTELING LIBRARY
ALBERTSON COLLEGE OF IDAHO
CALDWELL, ID 83605

Preface

Writing is like putting a note in a bottle.
—Clifford Geertz

Going public with five years' thinking about thinking does indeed feel like putting a note in a bottle. We can only hope that this extended note will find its way into the hands of those for whom it's intended, practicing and prospective teachers who share our interest in matters of the mind and our struggle to create more thoughtful classrooms.

To us, inserting this preface offers an opportunity to stuff a postscript into the bottle. We welcome the chance to say what we hope we've brought to this book and what we hope readers will take from it. We also welcome the chance to say a bit about what the book is and—perhaps more importantly—what it is not.

Admittedly, we approached the writing of this book with more questions than answers. As teachers of language turned teachers of teachers, we've spent much of our professional lives puzzling over thinking and how it can be developed. As we discovered very early, reading and writing—and indeed teaching—are special ways of thinking. During the last few years, our questions have become more focused and our search for answers more systematic. Emboldened by our reading of a proliferating body of literature and encouraged by experimentation in classrooms as well as workshops, we began what might not be too grand to call our own research. To say the least, we became immersed in reading, writing, and thinking about thinking. This book is the most recent product of that work.

Like other work we've done together, this book reflects a dual perspective that we count among the major advantages of a partnership that is as rich as it is geographically inconvenient. Ideas on the following pages have been generated, tested, and refined in Dan's language education classes at the University of Georgia as well as in his writing classes during a year's guest stint at the University of California, Santa Barbara. They have also been stimulated and shaped by interaction with colleagues across the country as Dan has conducted workshops and served as consultant. Carol's work in Houston public schools, on the other hand, has kept her much closer to home. There, she has borrowed classrooms and worked with teachers on all grade levels and in all subject areas to find ways of developing the thinking of students that could hardly be more diverse. Action research in Carol's multicultural, Texas-size school district has been an abundant source as well as a tough testing ground for ideas advanced in this book. Borrowing once more from our favorite anthropologist, Clifford Geertz, we like to think that our work—while informed, we hope, by current theory—is grounded in local knowledge.

What we hope you as a reader will take from this book is not too different from what we've brought to it. We hope that *Mind Matters* will prompt as many questions as answers, that it will engage you in your own continuing research into how minds work and how to work more powerfully with young minds. We also hope that you'll put some of our suggestions to the test in classrooms, your own or those you borrow. Furthermore, we hope that you'll go us one better and find even more promising ways to teach for thinking—in other words, make your own local knowledge.

Now, a few claims about what this book is and a few disclaimers about what it is not. Let us acknowledge right up front that *Mind Matters* is not a how-to book; certainly it offers no compendium of one-size-fits-all activities that can be lifted for lesson plans to fill an otherwise empty Monday morning. To us, scripted lessons in thinking would be a contradiction in terms; only thinking teachers, we are convinced, can nurture thinking students. For that reason, you'll find no facile formulas. You'll find instead assisted explorations into the territory of thinking and lots of models to spark ideas for your own one-of-a-kind classroom.

Let us also acknowledge that this book is not a scholarly treatise. Though steeped in theory and research—our own and that of the best experts we could find—*Mind Matters* is really a conversation with colleagues. Its tone is that of the teachers' lounge rather than the lecture platform. We unabashedly speak in first person and distinguish our respective points of view by using first names. Besides being right for us, such informality seems helpful in deflating some of the rhetoric that has so often obscured more than it has revealed about thinking and how to develop it.

One final point about what this book is and what it is not. Though filtered through the minds of two people, the book is more than a dialogue: It features a chorus of voices—scholars we've studied but never met, colleagues we've learned from, and students we've both taught and been instructed by.

Though we could—and probably should—acknowledge many of these collaborators, let us single out just a few. First, we'd like to implicate Bob Boynton in everything this book is and is not. We'd also like to thank him. Without Bob—our editor, publisher, and friend—*Mind Matters* would never have happened. The same goes for the Houston teachers in Carol's "Growing Thinkers" program, many of whom you'll meet on the following pages. It was these teachers who shaped this book by becoming researchers in their own classrooms and finding ways to translate theories and hunches about how to teach for thinking into Monday-through-Friday reality.

We'd like to give one of these teachers the last word in this preface. Bill Pisciella, whose voice you'll hear often on subsequent pages, wrote this as he reflected on a year-long series of shared explorations into thinking: "If we leave here satisfied with what we have accomplished, we will have failed."

By Bill's standard, this book should be a success.

UNIT I
What's the Matter?

These first two chapters invite you to survey the landscape of thinking—
to stake out that territory and make it your own. They encourage you to
do so by exploring some of the big questions that drew us into this territory in the first place.

You'll notice right away that these chapters are long on questions and
short on answers. That's partly because the questions are so big: Why
the swelling chorus of demands to teach thinking? What's really being
demanded? What *is* thinking anyway? Can it really be taught in school? If
so, how?

Despite the proliferation of research into matters of the mind and the
spate of articles in educational journals, we don't believe such questions
have ready answers. Besides, the only answers that make much difference are those we construct for ourselves. That's why we encourage
you not just to *read* these chapters but to *participate* in them—to do
the activities, to record your thoughts and talk back to us in a journal, to
try out ideas in your classroom and on your colleagues.

As teachers, we need to claim thinking as our primary territory. It's
much too important to be left to white-coated researchers or arm-chair
theorists. What's being learned about thinking needs to be filtered
through the minds of real teachers and translated into practice in real
classrooms. We hope that working through these first two chapters will
help you get started doing just that.

1

What's All This About Thinking?

Attempting to operate one's own mind, powered by
such a magical instrument as the human brain,
strikes me as rather like using the world's biggest
computer to add columns of figures, or towing a
Rolls-Royce with a nylon rope.

—Lewis Thomas

Four or five years ago, when this book was little more than thoughts on
yellow notepads, a perfectly awful commercial was running incessantly on
television. In the commercial, a man, who apparently acted the part of a doctor on some daytime soap opera, stood behind four or five different bottles of
cough syrup and said, "I am not a doctor, but I play one on television." This
self-confessed bogus doctor then proceeded to "play one" for the duration of
the commercial, offering advice about which bottle to take for which symp-
tom. About that same time, some of the talk we were hearing from cognitive
scientists about thinking sounded a little like the phony doctor: "I am not a
teacher, but here's what you ought to do in your classrooms." Discussions in
journals about what thinking was and how it might be taught were mostly between cognitive psychologists and educational researchers.

Beginning a book on thinking had us feeling uncertain and a bit self-
conscious about our credentials for entering that dialogue. We were, after all,
teachers and writers and mentors of teachers, not cognitive psychologists,
learning theorists, or educational philosophers. We were fearful then that the
lofty models and theories those folks were using to discuss matters of the
mind might prove to be alien territory for practitioners whose concerns were
centered more on classrooms than computer models of the brain, but we
didn't like what we were hearing and decided to get into the action.

We had dabbled a bit in the thinking business earlier, writing a book for middle school students,[1] and we were working with classroom teachers, who in turn were trying some of our ideas with students. But we remained uncertain about our ability to distill the murky prose and the conflicting claims of cognitive psychologists into clear and potable strategies for teaching and learning. At some point, however, our decision to write this book was made for us. In a matter of a few short months during 1984 and 1985, articles about thinking and models for teaching it exploded onto the pages of influential journals such as *Educational Leadership* and *Phi Delta Kappan,* appeared overnight as hastily packaged materials at publishers' exhibits, and became a hot topic among educators and curriculum specialists at conventions. There was serious talk in some school districts of major curriculum revisions based on this or that list of thinking skills. A few articles even suggested the development of separate courses in thinking: Thinking 101, perhaps.

This flurry of activity, much of it wrongheaded, made us worry that discussions about the "whats" and "whys" and "hows" of teaching for thinking might bypass teachers altogether and flow directly from the minds of cognitive psychologists into schools and curriculum guides. We were afraid that teachers might once again find themselves victims rather than coauthors of innovations. We were certain that discussions regarding the teaching of thinking and decisions about what schools might do to foster intellectual development—not to mention what roles teachers ought to play—were far too important to leave to cognitive psychologists and educational researchers. It was not that we believed those theorists were untrustworthy or that their assumptions and models were inherently wrong; it was just that we found their articles and packaged materials lacking in sensitivity to learners and classrooms. We felt that many of the assumptions and pedagogical approaches in the articles we read lacked a sense of classroom reality or what Ulrich Neisser has called "ecological validity."[2] This theoretical work needed to be shared with teachers to see if it had the ring of truth about it—true to kids and classrooms. We knew that real learning theorists live in classrooms, and we wanted teachers to take an active part in discussions of the nature of thinking and how it is taught.

So this is our book about thinking, filtered through the minds of real teachers, a book to inform and enlist both practicing and aspiring teachers in efforts to place thinking at the center of schooling. Our book may not look or sound like other books on matters of the mind. We try to be honest about our uncertainties. We admit that our conclusions are tentative, still forming as we continue to try things with teachers and students.

We think the questions about how young people grow intellectually and what teachers might do to enhance that growth still outnumber the answers. We're reassured by D. N. Perkins, whose book, *The Mind's Best Work,*[3] suggests that creative, productive people work more at the edge of their competence than at the center of it. As teachers and writers, we know what Perkins means. Some of our very best teaching and writing has come when we had more questions than answers. Some of our very best teaching and writing still happens when we take intellectual risks, confessing our uncertainties in front of students and readers and joining them in seeking to construct hypotheses and to find solutions. We have tried to write this book in that way, and the process has been an intellectual odyssey for us. We want you to join us on this journey of discovery by exploring the workings of your own mind, by thinking about your own teaching, and by considering what you can do to nurture the growth of young minds.

WHY THE SUDDEN INTEREST IN TEACHING THINKING?

If you've survived a few years in the old schoolhouse, you've seen some educational fads come and go and come again. The "New ____"(Fill in the blank with "English," "Math," etc.), Post-Sputnik rigor, the curriculum of relevance, phase electives, and back-to-basics have all blown into the schools, been featured in a few in-services, lingered for a few years, and blown out again. (May accountability in the form of ill-conceived statewide testing, models of effective teaching, and mastery learning soon go with the same winds!) Each fad has left its own special residue. In a few cases, these fads have actually had a cosmetic effect on classrooms, and in some rare instances they have triggered wholesale revision of curriculum guides.

Several years ago, some educational critics were suggesting in the usual forums for such criticism, *Newsweek* and *Time,* that the new concern for teaching thinking might prove to be just one more fad, and that writings about thinking were mostly rhetoric. Those critics maintained that even if the schools taught thinking, only the smart kids would benefit from such attention.

At about that same time, Jim Moffett raised an even more sinister possibility. "When the public asks schools to teach its children to think and create, it does not entirely mean it. At least they don't mean the same kind of thinking we're talking about because it is impossible to both indoctrinate and teach students to think for themselves."[4] Implicit in Moffett's concerns, and perhaps in the popular news magazines, was the suspicion that what the general public was looking for from schooling was not the empowerment of young thinkers who might challenge and even transform the culture, but rather the transmission of values and information that support and perpetuate the perspectives of the privileged culture. Thinking and curricular "rigor" were linked in some articles, and it sounded as if thinking might be a matter of more difficult content or higher expectations for students in Advanced Placement classes.

We think Jim's hunch proved to be right, particularly with the ensuing rise of cultural literacy as curriculum. We should point out that this elitist revival of anything having to do with Western civilization comes at a time when student populations are rapidly changing from predominantly white to culturally and ethnically diverse. We also suspect that concerns for teaching thinking may have been largely cosmetic among educational leaders themselves, but we still believe that defining thinking in school settings, developing models for intellectual growth, and convincing teachers and administrators to experiment with promising strategies in their schools can improve learning for all students regardless of IQ or cultural heritage. We're convinced that the teaching of thinking has never been more important than it is right now.

The federal government has been strangely mute on the thinking issue, as it has been on most other important educational issues. After eight years of presidential silence about schools in general, recent proposals from the Bush administration seem only slightly less vacuous: broaden Head Start (with what?), lower the dropout rate (how?), test kids more often (when will we have time to teach them anything?). None of these proposals takes notice of the fundamental problems of schools. Most observers of public education agree that something is wrong, very wrong with schools. To our way of thinking, it's not just that kids can't find Albania on a world map or that they haven't read *Hamlet*—the kind of stuff newspapers so love to talk about. What's wrong in schools today is that kids are not becoming independent thinkers who know their own minds and know how to use them.

In short, we suggest that the most serious problem in education today is that kids have to leave school to learn how to think. Maybe the current interest in teaching for thinking is another fad, soon to dissipate. That's all the more reason to capitalize on the current debate and engage teachers in it. Tinkering with trivia and riding the waves of short-lived innovations will not right the wrongs. What schools need is a dramatic restructuring around matters of mind; we believe that practicing and aspiring teachers like you, armed with knowledge about current research in the teaching of thinking, might just lead such a reform.

Exploration

Before plunging further into the book, take time out to see where you stand on some key issues involved in the nature and nurture of minds. This exploration invites you to take an inventory of your preliminary assumptions about thinking and how—indeed whether—it can be taught.

FIGURE 1.1

	Strongly Agree	Somewhat Agree	Somewhat Disagree	Strongly Disagree
1. Intelligence is primarily de-termined by heredity and remains constant throughout life.	4	3	2	1
2. There are different kinds of intelligence; in fact, we all have *intelligences*.	4	3	2	1
3. Thinking includes feeling.	4	3	2	1
4. The mind is mainly an infor-mation processor.	4	3	2	1
5. Thinking involves a hierarchy of skills, applied in a simple-to-complex order.	4	3	2	1
6. Even very young children use higher-level thinking to make sense of their world.	4	3	2	1
7. Thinkers can be classified as left-brained or right-brained.	4	3	2	1
8. Thinking is a holistic process in which different mental operations work in concert.	4	3	2	1
9. Intelligence can be learned and taught.	4	3	2	1

The nine items in Figure 1.1 represent a continuum of assumptions. Find the point on each continuum that best indicates your position right now. As you do so, jot down the number closest to that position.

Share your assumptions with someone else who is also interested in thinking and explain your point of view. We also suggest that you keep a jour-nal or notebook to use throughout your reading of this book. We'll be provid-ing many opportunities for you to think with your pencil or pen.

CAN THINKING BE TAUGHT?

When we plot our own assumptions on the chart shown in Figure 1.1, it's clear that we strongly agree with numbers 2, 3, 6, 8, and 9. We strongly disagree with every other assumption. That's not where we started, but we find increasing confirmation both in the literature and in our own teaching that all students can become better thinkers and that teachers can help them to do so. In the course of writing this book, we've even warmed up to Arthur Whimbey's audacious assertion that intelligence can be taught.[5] While we would never support a further bloating of the curriculum with a subject called "thinking," we don't see a problem there. Thinking has a natural home in the various disciplines. As Bruner has long insisted, "There is nothing more central to a discipline than its way of thinking. There is nothing more important in its teaching than to provide the earliest opportunity to learn that way of thinking—the forms of connection, the attitudes, hopes, jokes, and frustrations that go with it."[6] While we believe that thinking grows best as it is nurtured in specific disciplines and rich contexts by teachers who model ways of thinking, we do not reject the possibility that general strategic knowledge that transcends subject matter boundaries—things like heuristics and general problem-solving strategies—might also be useful to students as thinkers. As the work of Perkins and Salomon suggests, an "intimate intermingling" of general and context-specific practice may prove to produce the greatest growth in thinking.[7]

We'll talk more about some of the assumptions about thinking later in the chapter. Meanwhile, regardless of where you presently stand in your assumptions, we hope you will reject the idea that teaching thinking is just another fad, something you might just as well wait out. Momentum is building out there for significant reform of schools, and we would like to believe that teaching for thinking could lead that reform. Thinking has moved to the top of the educational agenda during the past eight years. Goodlad's extensive study, *A Place Called School*,[8] found that more than 50 percent of parents and teachers surveyed placed intellectual development first on their list of goals for the schools. The National Assessment of Educational Progress and The College Board echo this call for the centrality of thinking in the curriculum.[9] Sizer's widely read and quoted report of several years ago stated categorically that "education's job today is less in purveying information than in helping people use it—that is to exercise their minds."[10]

Despite such widespread calls for schools to teach thinking, there is still no clear consensus on what that means; in fact, the debate seems to be sharpening. As recently as February, 1990, the ASCD *Update,* the newsletter of the Association for Supervision and Curriculum Development, reported continuing disagreements among key theorists about the significance of context in learning to think and the value of generic thinking abilities as opposed to thinking abilities learned through the study of specific subject matter.[11] As teachers, we know who reads those publications and attends to those issues: administrators and curriculum directors who want to be sure their school districts are on the cutting edge of innovation. Even though there is still no clear consensus on how to develop and deliver a thinking curriculum, one of the most promising directions to date comes from Grant Wiggins and others who have begun to focus on developing *habits* of mind. As Wiggins points out, good thinkers are characteristically curious, open-minded, persistent, and willing to take risks. Though such dispositions cannot be "taught," they can be developed—indeed deliberately cultivated as habits, as what Wiggins calls "virtues of mind."[12]

Other sources of support and direction for deliberate teaching of thinking focus on *processes* of mind. Some of these studies examine how the same modes of thought are applied in different fields. The findings of such studies, which typically contrast the thinking of novices with the thinking of experts in a field, have been used as the basis for teaching students to think like thinkers in various fields—for example, scientists, artists, and historians.[13] This epistemic approach allows students to discover through personal experience the key ways of working that are characteristic of thinkers within a particular field. Lauren Resnick has recently supported such an approach because it "turns our attention away from the traditional educator's problem of how to construct lessons that teach specific skills or knowledge to the new problem of how to create cognitive work environments that are capable of providing true apprenticeship experience."[14] Resnick has coined the term "cognitive apprenticeships" to describe the kinds of interactions that can exist between students, teachers, and the knowledge-makers in a field of study in such environments. Later in this book, you will be invited to undertake several brief apprenticeships of your own within different intellectual environments.

Though theorists and educators alike are far from unanimity on how to foster intellectual development, most echo a growing criticism of the workbook mentality and the bits-and-pieces curriculum found inevitably in schools that overemphasize "testable knowledge" and "mastery learning." Most join Goodlad in decrying the "relentless monotony of telling, questioning, textbooks, and workbooks so characteristic of classes from the fourth grade up."[15] Yet it is Robert Root-Bernstein who articulates the problem most eloquently:

> What is wrong, of course, is that … students have learned to copy paths of reasoning worked out by others, but not to recreate or create for themselves a line of reasoning on their own. Their acquired skills are the skills of the forger or plagiarist, not those of the artist, writer, or inventor. They have not been taught to think for themselves …. They have not learned to ask questions but only to give answers. They do not invent, but only repeat.[16]

Root-Bernstein is a scientific historian whose research has traced the development and work of a number of successful scientists. His warning that schooling turns students into copycat automotons is a sobering one. This country has always prided itself on its "Yankee ingenuity," its ability to solve complex problems through scientific and technologic breakthroughs. If Root-Bernstein is correct, American scientists and inventors of the twenty-first century may not be able to deliver on such expectations. Certainly the progressive movement of the thirties and the reformers of the sixties sounded some of these same notes about the hum-drum of skills and the anti-intellectual quality of workbook-driven instruction.

What is new, however, is this growing science of cognition, still largely speculative, and a constantly enlarging body of research and knowledge about how the brain works and how learning occurs. Without making too much of this coincidence of concern for growth in thinking voiced by the general public and a proliferating body of research and inquiry into the nature of thinking, let us suggest a parallel to the unprecedented emphasis on writing and the scholarly work with writing instruction during the past few years. The fortuitous marriage of researchers and teachers of writing in the sixties and early seventies has given rise to a remarkable and enduring change in the attitudes and practices of many classroom teachers. The teaching of writing has changed, and that change is more than fad and more than tinkering with curriculum.

We remain optimistic that the current smoke and heat over teaching for thinking may also give way to light and change. We're convinced that it will not do so unless classroom teachers bring to the dialogue their own unique experiences and indeed the confidence of insiders. We're also convinced that transforming schools into thoughtful places that nurture young minds to their fullest will take more than business as usual. In fact, it will require those three *F*'s that Rosabeth Moss Kantor claims American businesses will require if they are to regain their competitive edge. In the first place, Kantor believes, change requires *focus:* vision, clear goals, a set of shared values—in our case, a real commitment to placing thinking at the center rather than at the edges of classrooms. It also requires *flexibility,* a willingness to break free of routinization, to follow new leads, and to risk whatever approaches seem most promising in nurturing individual minds. Change also requires what Kantor calls *friendliness,* a willingness to form partnerships and networks with other professionals rather than go it alone.[17] These are themes we'll revisit in the chapters that follow.

TALKING ABOUT THINKING

Given all of the above, where do we begin in this dialogue about thinking, and how do we talk about something as mysterious as the mind? That task is complicated by the plethora of different terms and labels researchers use to describe operations of the mind. You may already be experiencing that difficulty while reading this text. Developing a shared vocabulary of terms, finding just the right language to explain what we mean by "thinking," has been problematic. In this chapter, we have already used the terms *think-*

ing, intellectual development, reasoning, exercising the mind, cognitive appren-ticeships, and *habits of mind.* That's not counting terms like *skillful thinking, cognitive development, intellectual skills training, intelligent behavior, and cognitive growth,* all of which get thrown around in the books we read. Part of the difficulty in talking about complex and mysterious things like the mind lies in the nature of language itself. As Bruffee has suggested, words about thinking are social constructs rather than universal, objectifiable terms. As constructs, they represent attempts to reify "unconfirmed and sometimes un-confirmable inferences about what happens in the 'black box' of the mind" and to justify those beliefs about thinking to those around us.[18] Said a different way, the words one uses to talk about thinking reflect an underlying set of values not just about the mind but also about teaching and learning. If, for instance, we see the teaching of thinking as essentially a series of training exercises, then Sternberg's model for intellectual skills training will be help-ful.[19] If we see the learning of thinking as intellectual growth, more a matter of behaviors or habits or inclinations, then we are likely to find Costa's term "intelligent behavior" more to our liking.[20] There are many more models out there, but we have yet to find one that fits exactly the way we talk about thinking. One thing is certain: How people talk about thinking will inevitably shape how they come to understand and act on their knowledge.

METAPHORS FOR THE MIND

Since thinking is invisible and difficult to describe in words, terms for thinking may be less useful than metaphors and analogues. To keep this talk about thinking from becoming too abstract and to connect it to common experience, let's look at some metaphors for thinking. Bruner says we can learn much about what people believe by examining the "metaphoric crutch-es they use to climb mountains of abstraction."[21] Metaphors structure our conceptual systems, which in turn structure our perceptions and actions. Your own style of teaching, for instance, is shaped and altered by the metaphors you use to explain what you do. If you think of yourself as a "professor," you may be primarily an information dispenser and lecturer. If you see yourself as a "coach," your instructional stance may be more as helper and mentor. This next exploration will help you discover some of your metaphors for thinking.

Exploration

Frank Smith calls metaphors "the legs of language."[22] He's right: Metaphors are more than models in our heads. They keep us moving in a certain direction. That's why metaphors for the mind matter so much. It's also why we'd like you to spend a little time finding and exploring your own metaphors. Maybe Lewis Thomas's somewhat playful metaphor of the mind as attic will help you get started. Can you see where this metaphor might take you? You might treat the mind as a handy if haphazard place to collect ideas worth holding onto—at least for you. You might find it an intriguing place to explore—to take a flashlight and go poking into hidden nooks and crannies to see what you can rediscover. You might reflect on how private and how idiosyncratic the mind is. You could go on and on, as Thomas does in his provocative essay "Attic of the Brain."[23]

In finding your own metaphors for the mind, think beyond what the mind is; think what it does, how it seems to work.

- Head a page in your journal, "My mind is like ...." or "My mind is a ...." Jot down as many promising comparisons as you can generate.
- Go back over your list, perhaps with a colleague who shares your interest in thinking. Which analogue seems to offer the greatest potential as a metaphor for thinking about thinking? In what ways does it represent the workings of your mind? In what direction would the legs of this metaphor take you as a thinker and as a teacher of thinkers?

What kinds of metaphors did you come up with: a fountain, a flower, a window, a television, an abstract painting, a Dagwood sandwich, a power line, a coffee pot, a black hole? Those are just a few of the images teachers and students have authored in our workshops, and they illustrate the diverse and idiosyncratic ways we can think about our own minds. Your choice of metaphors may also reveal something about the kind of thinker you are. Do you usually approach a problem in an orderly, step-by-step manner like an astronaut? Or do you plunge in, make a mess, and then sort it all out like a shark in a school of mackerel? You probably use both of those approaches and many others, depending on the kind of problem you're facing. We all have habits or characteristic strategies for approaching problems. Less successful thinkers have fewer strategies, fewer productive habits of mind, and may find themselves in the "Get a bigger hammer" mode when their repertoire of thinking strategies fails them. Continue to reflect on how your mind works as you read through this book. Add to and amend your metaphors as you come to know your own mind more thoroughly.

Mind as Computer

One metaphor you may have considered listing is the computer. If you chose a mind-as-computer metaphor, you're in familiar company. That metaphor has dominated much of the theory and research by psychologists and cognitive scientists. Focusing on the brain's ability to store and retrieve bits of information, these researchers have developed what has come to be called an information-processing model for thinking. Such a model explains thinking as the taking in of information bit by bit and storing it, first in short-term memory with its very limited capacity, and then organizing and shunting information into long-term memory through some kind of filing system. Information is then retrieved by accessing through a mysterious central processor somewhere in the brain. If you are computer literate and know about buffers and serial processing and such, you can understand why this metaphor has been attractive to some scientists, particularly those working with memory and artificial intelligence.[24]

We have big problems with the computer metaphor. While it does offer an explanation for some workings of the brain, it is woefully inadequate for others. It tends to limit, for example, the ability of scientists to explain such phenomena as intuitions, hunches, and gestalts—the sudden-discovery experiences we know are central to productive thinking. True, the computer is fast, relatively error-free, and certainly some of our thought processes are similar. Remembering phone numbers and addresses and social security numbers is computer-like, but reliving experiences through recollection and memoir is not. Certainly imagination and wonder can't be programmed any more than the endless variability and nuance of individual minds can be reduced to binary code.

Perhaps the most distressing thing about the computer metaphor is that its use tends to drive the wedge deeper between thinking and feeling. The mind-as-machine metaphor allows cognitive scientists to conduct most of their research in isolation, away from real human situations. Benjamin Bloom[25] and more recently Barry Beyer[26] have done schooling a serious disservice by developing learning models that depict cognition and affect as different kinds of thinking. We realize we're casting the information-processing, mind-as-computer crowd as the black hats of cognitive science even though their assumptions form the bases of much of contemporary cognitive theory. At least we're in good company in believing that hats matter. Anthropologist Clifford Geertz agrees with a vengeance. He cautions against taking our view of thinking from what he calls "rationalists wearing square hats sitting in square rooms thinking square thoughts."[27] We're convinced that it will take more than a few sombreros to redeem what seems to us the ultimately square way that the computer-as-metaphor enthusiasts go about explaining what goes on in the human mind.

After thirty years of working with the minds of the neurologically impaired (a field the Russians have labelled "defectology"), Oliver Sacks finds the computer metaphor entirely too limited. In his book *The Man Who Mistook His Wife for a Hat and Other Clinical Tales,* Sacks says this: "Of course the brain is a machine and a computer—everything in classical neurology is correct. But our mental processes, which constitute our being and life, are not just abstract and mechanical, but personal as well." He then goes on to caution against any view of thinking "which eschews the judgmental, the particular, the personal, and becomes entirely abstract and computational."[28]

That's exactly why we find the computer metaphor for matters of mind so distressing: It tends to create what Margaret Donaldson terms an "apartheid of the mind,"[29] an artificial separation of feelings and thoughts. We are convinced that thinking and feeling do not operate as independent domains, but rather wrap themselves around each other in helical fashion. In Nelson Goodman's words, "Emotion and cognition are interdependent: Feeling without understanding is blind and understanding without feeling is empty."[30] That's why we want to use metaphors that picture the mind as human and not machine-like. We know from our own experience that thinking flourishes in an environment where thinkers are free to voice convictions and beliefs and feelings. Our primary assumption about *thinking* is that *thinking and feeling are one.*

Mind as Kaleidoscope

Ulrich Neisser's scathing criticism of his information-processing colleagues in his book *Cognition and Reality* represents a decidedly different metaphor for thinking.[31] Neisser contends that when new ideas and information enter the brain they encounter an already well-formed but constantly changing kaleidoscopic structure—a scheme, if you will. The brain makes sense of this new information in terms of mental maps or schemes or frames already in place. Sudden flashes of brilliance can be explained as newly formed maps or the recombination of existing information into new patterns. These mental maps are not stored permanently in the brain as hard data or chunks or as photographs in a gallery but rather as an elaborate group of lights that flash first one way and then another, creating patterns by altering the circuitry. While the human element is still missing in this metaphor, using flashing lights and kaleidoscopes to explain thinking ascribes to the mind great power to form understandings and create its own meanings. We like his picture of the human mind as a dynamic, ever-changing light board.

MIND OR BRAIN?

We seem to be tripping over words again. In our attempt to explain the metaphors for thinking, we find ourselves interchanging the words *mind* and *brain*. Even in the literature of thinking, the terms are interchanged. We understand that the brain is a physical organ with a particular chemistry and a definable, if mysterious, physiology. What that organ does, though—thinking—is not as easy to pin down. Lawrence Lowery once suggested that thinking is the ghost in the machinery of the brain.[32] Maybe the physical brain is machine-like, but it's the ghost of the machine we're after here, and a ghost may be better explained by a philosopher like Susanne Langer than by a neurophysiologist.

Langer suggests that the mind has a life of its own, carrying on a constant dialectic of sensory and imaginative activity—a making of scenes, acts, beings, intentions, and realizations. She notes that it's only human beings who can speak of such "experiences," and it's experience that makes up "the psychic background of each person's current consciousness and future envisagment. It's this structure that constitutes what we mean by 'life of the mind'."[33] The brain gives off electrical energy through chemical reactions; the mind lives and feels and experiences.

Surprisingly, the study of the mind has only recently been promoted to respectability in mainstream psychology. As Jerome Bruner[34] ruefully observes, it took the cognitive revolution of the fifties to make *mind* more than a four-letter word to be whispered or wrapped in quotation marks among serious scientists. Even though we wanted to avoid all four-letter words in this book, we did not choose to title this book *Brain Business*. Emerging research into workings of the brain is intriguing and useful, but it is the study of the mind that informs our work; thinking is what minds do.

Exploration

This activity is an invitation to tap the only primary source you have for thinking—your mind. Don't underestimate that source. Not only can it inform your work with thinking in the classroom, it can help you check out what you read in those secondary sources. Try tapping your own experience to see what you know intuitively about various mental operations. In your journal, free-write from these two leads:

1. The hardest thinking job I've had lately was ....
2. To work through that job, I had to do these kinds of thinking:

In following that second lead, keep retracing the way your mind worked through that hard intellectual task until you have a good full list of the kinds of thinking you had to do. If someone you know is reading this book, compare lists of mental operations. Together, how many different operations of mind did you list?

Lists of thinking words like the ones you just made have been popular with theorists; in advancing their own definitions of thinking, they seem inevitably to resort to them. Rudolf Arnheim is a case in point:

The cognitive operations called thinking are not the privilege of mental processes above and beyond perception, but the essential ingredients of perception itself. I am referring to such operations as active exploration, selection, grasping of essentials, simplification, abstraction, analysis and synthesis, completion, correction, comparison, problem solving as well as combining, separating, putting in context.[35]

D. N. Perkins, whose focus is creative thinking rather than perception, offers a slightly different but overlapping list:

Creativity—the mind's best work—involves no special processes, just special purposes to marshal familiar operations like noticing, remembering, looking harder, judging, doing, un-doing, problem-finding and—above all—selecting.[36]

While lists may be necessary for purposes of definition and emphasis, they do not really give us a picture of the mind at work. In the real world of the mind, the various processes work not in isolation but in concert. All are manifestations of what Anderson calls the "unity of human cognition," the belief that "all higher cognitive processes i.e. memory, language, problem solving, imagery, deduction and induction are different manifestations of the same underlying structure."[37] Even those who favor a theory of "multiple intelligences," like Howard Gardner, acknowledge that "the intelligences actually interact and build upon one another from the beginning of life. Complexes of intelligences function together smoothly, even seamlessly in order to execute intricate human activities."[38]

Bruner comes at the same point from a different angle. He acknowledges the differences between intuitive and analytic thinking but sees them as complementary rather than contradictory:

In contrast to analytic thinking, intuitive thinking characteristically does not advance in careful, well-defined steps. It tends to involve maneuvers based seemingly on an implicit perception of the total problem. Usually intuitive thinking rests on familiarity with the domain of knowledge involved and with its structure, which makes it possible for the thinker to leap about, skipping steps and employing short cuts in a manner that requires later rechecking of conclusions by more analytic means.[39]

Are we getting any closer to a definition of thinking? We think so. Of course, there are still a few obstacles to stumble over—obstacles like those ubiquitous references to critical thinking, apparently not to be confused with creative thinking, apparently not to be confused with higher order thinking. Are those kinds of thinking really so different one from another? If we scratched their surfaces, might they not look a lot alike? We're not sure, but we worry about classroom approaches that emphasize name-brand thinking. The labeling of kinds of thinking or types of thinkers smacks of the categorizing of complexities—the naming of parts—that has always plagued us as teachers. We've been told about left brains and right brains and Meyers-Briggs types, and we just don't find those kinds of categories much more helpful than reading our students' horoscopes.

Here let's be careful, though. To resist name-brand labels for kinds of thinking is not to say there is only one way the mind can operate. To the contrary, the mind has an amazing repertoire of operations. Even our students know that. Listen to Stephanie, a high school senior: "I don't often reflect on the processes and particulars of thinking. I think consciously, subconciously, out loud, and to myself. I reason, comprehend, memorize, assimilate, and create. All of these are modes of thinking which I use every day. I often feel that my brain functions like gears in a car. I can shift from lower to higher levels and back down again ...."[40]

Stephanie knows from consulting her own primary source on matters of the mind what Howard Gardner explains after years of research. Different operations of the mind—which Gardner sees as different intelligences or frames—work together harmoniously.[41] Here then, is another assumption: *thinking* is whole, not piecemeal, and yet *quite specific* to the *purposes of the thinker.*

What does all of this mean for teachers of thinking? Are we getting any closer to a definition we can use in our classrooms? Again, we think so. Separating cognition and feeling dehumanizes thinking; lists of discrete thinking skills and categories of mental operations, while perhaps attractive to curriculum planners, will lead us to a fragmented and trivialized approach to very complex processes. We don't think that dissecting the natural process of thinking into elaborate and artificial subskills or building walls between kinds of thinking labelled critical, creative, productive, etc., will help us develop thinking or thinkers. Our own experiences as thinkers and as teachers convince us anew that Ann Berthoff is right: Thinking is not mechanical, "not assembling parts into a whole, not filling slots and grids, not manipulating discrete elements like chessmen and Scrabble squares."[42]

Berthoff's caution should raise a whole flurry of red flags. Schools have always been masters of dissection. Despite what we should have learned from having shredded reading and writing and math into lifeless subskills, history seems to be repeating itself as thinking finds its way into the curriculum. We were especially dismayed by a recent article describing two programs as "integrating thinking skills and mastery learning." This "integration" was illustrated by a tidy grid displaying three sample lessons. "Thinking skills" (a term we don't use without quotation marks) were neatly sliced for discrete teaching—comparing in grade 3, evaluating evidence in grade 7, and determining the credibility of evidence in grade 12. Each lesson was further partitioned into four parts: instructional activity, corrective, extension, and assessment.[43] Although we understand the temptation to break complex wholes into discrete parts so that they can fill familiar slots and grids in curriculum guides and lesson plan books, we vehemently resist such dissection. Especially when it comes to developing thinking, we worry about taxonomies and curricular decisions based on such taxonomies.

That brings us close to the definition of thinking we promised earlier. What is it that really goes on in the mind? To us, it's nothing less than the making of meaning. And we mean *making* in its most literal sense—as in "making sense" and "making up our minds." We're convinced that every mind creates its own understanding by pulling things together in its own way, and "thinking" is what we call that process.

We like Frank Smith's metaphor of the brain as an artist with the capacity to create, select, and arrange experience. That's not too far from the famous image of the mind as an enchanted loom weaving the stuff of life into a one-of-a-kind tapestry of ever-changing meaning. Nor is it far from Ulrich Neisser's kaleidoscopic structures we mentioned earlier. We like these metaphors because they represent the mind as dynamic, complex, and—above all—human. Thinking is not a program or a text or a hierarchy of skills. Thinking is the essential human act. All of these metaphors reaffirm what we believe: that each mind must do its own creating, forming and inventing—indeed, make its own meaning. To us, thinking is just that, meaning-making, nothing less. And any attempt to teach thinking in some disembodied, decontextualized way where knowledge-makers are isolated from the messy processes of knowledge-making is inevitably doomed to failure.

Before you do some retrospective scanning of this chapter, we invite you to reflect on the following questions, which may help you gather your thoughts.

Exploration

In your journal, jot a few quick and candid responses to these questions:

1. Do I ever worry about whether I think as clearly or logically or quickly as others? About whether I am a competent thinker?
2. How can I tell when a relative, friend, or co-worker is "thinking straight"? Is it possible to think "crooked"? If so, should that be called "thinking"?
3. What evidence do I see that students need help with thinking?
4. What obstacles in my school would I have to overcome to teach for thinking?
5. What would I have to do differently in my own classroom to create a

climate in which students can make up their own minds, develop new and more successful habits of mind, and became apprentice thinkers?

Keep these questions in the back of your mind as you skim back through this first chapter. In your journal, jot a few quick and candid responses to these questions.

NOTES

1. Dan Kirby and Carol Kuykendall. *Thinking Through Language*. Urbana: National Council of Teachers of English, 1985.
2. Ulrich Neisser, *Cognition and Reality*. San Francisco: W. H. Freeman, 1976.
3. D. N. Perkins, *The Mind's Best Work*. Cambridge: Harvard University Press, 1981.
4. James Moffett, "Hidden Impediments to Improving English Teaching." *Phi Delta Kappan* (September, 1985).
5. Arthur Whimbey, *Intelligence Can Be Taught*. New York: Bantam Books, 1975.
6. Jerome Bruner, *Actual Minds, Possible Worlds*. Cambridge: Harvard University Press, 1986.
7. D. N. Perkins and Gavriel Salomon, "Are Cognitive Skills Context-Bound?" *Educational Researcher* (January–February 1989).
8. John I. Goodlad, *A Place Called School: Prospects for the Future*. New York: McGraw-Hill Book Company, 1984.
9. The College Board, *Academic Preparation for College: What Students Need to Know and Be Able to Do*. New York: The College Board, 1983.
10. Theodore R. Sizer, *Horace's Compromise: The Dilemma of the American High School*. Boston: Houghton Mifflin Company, 1984.
11. John O'Neil, Ed., *Update* (February 1990).
12. Grant Wiggins, "The Futility of Trying to Teach Everything of Importance." *Educational Leadership*. (November 1989).
13. Arthur M. Costa, "Teaching For, Of, and About Thinking." *Developing Minds: A Resource Book for Teaching Thinking*. Alexandria, Va.: Association for Supervision and Curriculum Development, 1985.
14. Lauren Resnick, *Education and Learning to Think*. Washington D.C.: National Academy Press, 1989.
15. See note 8 above.
16. Robert Scott Root-Bernstein, "Creative Process as a Unifying Theme of Human Cultures." *Daedalus* (Summer 1984).
17. Rosabeth Moss Kantor, "Becoming an Educational Change Master: Building New Organizations to Meet New Challenges." Keynote Address, ASCD Convention, March 1989.
18. Kenneth A. Bruffee, "Social Construction, Language, and the Authority of Knowledge: A Bibliographical Essay." *College English* (December 1986).

19. Robert Sternberg, "Criteria for Intellectual Skills Training." *Education Researcher* (February 1983).
20. Costa, Arthur L. "Teaching For Intelligent Behavior." *Educational Leadership,* (October 1981).
21. See note 6 above.
22. Frank Smith, *Essays into Literacy.* Portsmouth, N.H.: Heinemann Educational Books, 1983.
23. Lewis Thomas, *Late Night Thoughts on Listening to Mahler's Ninth Symphony.* New York: Bantam Books, 1984.
24. For a highly readable and even interesting account of the shift in cognitive science from bottom-up to top-down processing, see Howard Gardner's *The Mind's New Science.* New York: Basic Books, 1985.
25. Benjamin S. Bloom, Ed., with Max Englehart, Edward J. Furst, Walker H. Hill, David R. Krathwohl. *Taxonomy of Educational Objectives, Handbook I: Cognitive Domain.* New York: David McKay, 1956.
26. Barry Beyer, "Improving Thinking Skills: Defining the Problem." *Phi Delta Kappan* (March 1984).
27. Clifford E. Geertz, *Local Knowledge: Further Essays in Interpretive Anthropology.* New York: Basic Books, 1983.
28. Oliver Sacks, *The Man Who Mistook His Wife for a Hat and Other Clinical Tales.* New York: Summit Books, 1987,
29. Margaret Donaldson, *Children's Minds.* New York: W. W. Norton & Company, 1978.
30. Nelson Goodman, *Of Mind and Other Matters.* Cambridge: Harvard University Press, 1984.
31. See note 2 above.
32. Lawrence F. Lowery, "The Biological for Thinking." *Developing Minds: A Resource Book for Teaching Thinking,* Arthur Costa, Ed., Alexandria, Va.: Association for Supervision and Curriculum Development, 1985.
33. Susanne K. Langer, *Mind: An Essay on Human Feeling.* Baltimore: Johns Hopkins, 1972.
34. See note 6 above.
35. Rudolf Arnheim, *Visual Thinking.* Berkeley: University of California Press, 1969.
36. See note 3 above.
37. John R. Anderson, *The Architecture of Cognition.* Cambridge: Harvard University Press, 1983.
38. Howard Gardner, *Frames of Mind: The Theory of Multiple Intelligences.* New York: Basic Books Inc., 1983.
39. Jerome Bruner, *Process of Education.* Cambridge: Harvard University Press, 1960.
40. In 1987, Stephanie Harris was a student in Martha West's Advanced Placement English class and a senior at Parkview High School in Gwinnett County, Georgia.
41. See note 38 above.
42. Ann E. Berthoff, *The Making of Meaning.* Portsmouth, N.H.: Boynton/Cook Publishers, 1981.
43. Daisy E. Arrendondo and James H. Block, "Recognizing the Connections Between Thinking Skills and Mastery Learning." *Education Leadership* (February 1990).

2

Teach for Thinking? How?

[The master] begins from the center and not from the fringe. He imparts an understanding of the basic principles of the art before going on to the meticulous details, and he refuses to break down the t'ai chi movements into a one-two-three drill so as to make the student into a robot.

—Gary Zugav

In his book *Actual Minds, Possible Worlds,*[1] Jerome Bruner looks back across decades and remembers Miss Orcutt, one of his earliest teachers. He recalls the day she said in class, "It is a very puzzling thing not that water turns to ice at 32 degrees Fahrenheit, but that it should change from a liquid into a solid." As he further recalls, "She then went on to give us an intuitive account of Brownian movement and molecules, expressing a sense of wonder that matched, indeed bettered, the sense of wonder I felt at that age (around ten) about everything I turned my mind to…. In effect, she was inviting me to extend my world of wonder to encompass hers. She was not just informing us. She was, rather, negotiating the world of wonder and possibility. Molecules, solids, liquids, movement were not facts; they were to be used in pondering and imagining. Miss Orcutt was the rarity. She was a human event, not a transmission device."

You can see why we think Miss Orcutt belongs right up front in this chapter. More than fifty years ago, she was already what we are struggling to become: teachers of thinking. We share her penchant for puzzling aloud and aspire to her reach of mind. In this chapter, we'll follow the lead of this remarkable "human event" as we puzzle through what we know about how to teach for thinking and reach with our minds to discover more.

So far, in taking on the teaching of thinking and doing our homework to find out how to teach it, we have gained nothing more fundamental than an increasingly firm fix on conditions critical to intellectual development. Before getting down to Monday-through-Friday specifics, we need to sort through those conditions that foster thinking and consider ways of creating them in our classrooms.

The thinking classroom is a delicate ecosystem. To underscore this point, we resort to our all-time *un*favorite kind of research—the white-coated kind performed on laboratory rats. For several years, researchers into brain growth and plasticity have been studying the effect of highly stimulating but secure environments—in this case, cages—on the brains of the rats that inhabit them. Over and over, it has been demonstrated that enriched settings with lots of social-environmental stimulation and the security of what we would call tender loving care enhances development of the brain itself. Rats nurtured under such conditions actually develop brains with a thicker and heavier cortex than do other rats—brains with larger neurons, more and better interneural connections, and a greater supply of support cells—indeed potentially better brains for learning and remembering.[2]

Though wary of generalizing from rats to human beings—shades of B. F. Skinner's pigeons—we can't resist mentioning this phenomenon. That's partly because it's so dramatic and partly because it confirms so strongly the findings of parallel educational research. The fundamental point could hardly be overstated: When it comes to thinking and learning and growing, conditions count. That's why the next few pages will focus on the kind of ecosystem that nurtures intellectual development.

A CLIMATE FOR THINKING

Classrooms can be lively places. They can also be deadly. The difference is not so much a matter of glass, paint, and bulletin boards as it is a matter of atmosphere. Carol recalls having learned this firsthand in the discarded home economics lab she inherited as a rookie teacher. As she remembers, there were good days and bad days in that awkward L-shaped hall darkened by pine-oiled floors and broken by blocky islands indented with dry sinks. Since there were good days, the bad ones couldn't have had much to do with the room itself. The difference must have been in that elusive thing called atmosphere, that feeling created by the people who live in a classroom—and more to the point, as we have learned over the years, by the teacher whose job it is to see that people really do *live* there, that they find it a safe, supportive place to be themselves and do challenging work.

These days, we're heartened to find just that kind of atmosphere in the classrooms of many teachers we know. A montage of images comes to mind: a second-grade room where life-size cutouts of each child hang from the ceiling, under which the children themselves work so intently in small groups that they don't even glance up when a visitor enters; a middle school computer lab in which some students busily enter various drafts of a composition while others confer with an editing committee in the corner and still others bind finished texts into booklets or create graphics for covers; a biology room bulging with specimens ranging from fossils to live fish, amidst which students seated around cafeteria tables design the next day's lab experiment.

We think particularly of classrooms in which the teacher faces a special challenge in creating and maintaining an ecosystem for thinking and learning. James Claypool's social studies classroom provides a case in point.[3] James—a blue-eyed blond who hails from the Northeast by way of Williams College—could hardly differ more starkly from his predominantly Black high school juniors in inner-city Houston. James's challenge was to make the classroom theirs, not just his. To create an environment in which those students can do more than go through the motions of studying American history, James has invited community culture into the classroom, which now spills over into a double room adjoining the library. There, walls are adorned with murals donated by noted artist John Biggers, who has visited the class. These murals depicting the history of Black America surround archives organized and maintained by students who now open their little museum to other students. It is indeed a place of their own—a research center in which they learn first-hand to think as historians think, but also a place in which to feel comfortably at home—a place, in James's words, "sort of like a womb."

Although classrooms charged with such an atmosphere don't all look alike, they share some key characteristics. Walk into any secure but stimulating classroom, and you will see busy but comfortable students. You probably won't see the teacher front and center but rather first at one elbow and then another, doing what Dan likes to call coaxing, coaching, and consulting. You will sense both energy and ease. That's the feel of the nurturing climate now identified as crucial for intellectual development[4]—the warm, vibrant, trusting environment that encourages young thinkers not just to soak up "facts," but to ponder and to wonder and to take risks.

Most of us are at least on nodding terms with such an environment. Now what? Just how do we go about making that climate for thinking everyday K–12 reality?

Let's begin with what teachers always do: ask questions and make assignments. For starters, we must swear off short-term, highly defined tasks and questions with easy, stock answers. As Dennie Wolf points out, dealing with such questions and tasks simply doesn't prepare young people for a world fraught with ill-defined problems open to many approaches and answers.[5] Neither do such circumscribed exercises stimulate real thinking.

Yet old habits die hard. Too many classrooms are still dominated by inquisition-style questioning and by highly prescriptive assignments. That's partly because it's all too easy to crank out questions and assignments that drag students along on our own mind trips and ever-so-hard-to-design questions and tasks that send them off on their own.

The Coalition of Essential Schools has taken on that challenge. In the process, they have done nothing less than restructure high school courses around an inquiry model in which students do the inquiring and teachers "act as intellectual librarians, constantly making it possible for students to be challenged anew."[6] The questions around which courses are organized are termed essential questions—an apt term indeed, since these questions must by definition go to the heart of a particular discipline, have no one set of obvious "right" answers, and engage students in higher-level thinking. In following the work of the Coalition over the last several years, we've been struck by the right-headedness of this approach and by its practicality in imbuing classrooms with an atmosphere for real thinking and learning. Can't you make some pretty good guesses about the atmosphere in a U.S. History class directed toward the essential question, "Whose country is this, anyway?" Consider the continuity and coherence that is bound to result as that question shapes materials and activities guiding student research throughout the semester. As another case in point, consider the biology classroom in which students address this "entry-point" question for a botany unit: "Do stems of germinating seedlings always grow upward and roots downward? Devise an experiment to determine the answer."[7]

We know from our own observations that similar approaches work in the lower grades. We think of the art teacher who initiated a year-long exploration titled "Art Through the Ages" by asking her kindergarteners, "What tools did the first cave-dwellers use to make art? What did they draw?" We think also of the science and social studies teachers whose middle schoolers spent weeks tackling the problem of waste disposal. Though they began with their own homes and their own campus, they proceeded to ask a larger question: "Without spoiling or endangering the environment, how can we manage waste in ways that allow us to maintain our standard of living?" Building classroom tasks around such questions can raise the roof on thinking and charge the classroom atmosphere with high expectations.

The latter is no small point. In creating a climate for thinking, there's no getting around our own expectations: Rarely do we get more than we expect. To confirm this point for herself, elementary music teacher John Ella Fowler[8] decided to challenge the children in her piano ensemble. She did so by asking them to work on a piece of music that was somewhat beyond their current skill level with the objective of playing it on a program scheduled many weeks later. She didn't mention that the piece was particularly difficult, but set about helping them get started. Over the ensuing days, John Ella noticed that her students helped each other more than usual, that they listened to themselves more critically and tried to figure out for themselves what was working and not working. She also noticed that they began to devise methods of "fixing" problems: they played slower, played softer, and counted in rhythm. Far sooner than she would have guessed, John Ella reports, these elementary students "became interested in making music, not just in getting it right." They were justifiably proud of the addition to their repertoire and eager to master another difficult piece.

This teacher would second the straightforward advice offered by writing teacher Peter Elbow: "We should see our students as smart and capable.... We should look beyond their mistakes or ignorance to the intelligence that lies behind it."[9]

In classrooms where we expect enough to raise the roof on thinking, let's acknowledge that students will make mistakes. The higher the intellectual ante, the higher the risk. That brings us to another key point on creating an environment for thinking—the point that the teacher must build trust and make it safe to take risks, even to fail.

Does that mean throw out grades? Not at all, as you'll see when we turn our attention to evaluation. Does it mean rewarding approximations, near-misses, and reaches that exceed grasps? You bet.

But creating an atmosphere to support risk-taking seems to us more than a matter of rewards. Experience keeps telling us that it's also a matter of the way we as teachers respond to students on a minute-to-minute basis. It's the way we prolong silence after a question so that students will have time to think, even if we have to curl our toes and bite our lips to keep quiet. It's the way we listen to students and keep them going with tell-me-more and why-do-you-think-that questions. It's the language we use—words like *might, if,* and *could be*—to extend possibilities and hold off fixity.

All the while, as Elbow reminds us, we need to show students that we are on their side.[10] We have come to believe that one of the best ways to do so and to maintain a supportive environment that encourages risk-taking is to think of ourselves as coaches.

Coaches invest thenselves in those they coach. Furthermore, they know their limits as transmission devices. Lectures on the forward pass, the half-gainer, and the slam dunk just won't cut it. Coaches have to show as well as tell.

But coaching is more than modeling. To Theodore Sizer, in fact, coaching is more than a metaphor for teaching. We like the way he presses this point by drawing from the success story of a particular young student he had coached on her writing:

> There was agreement on and understanding between teacher
> and student about the academic task that the paper represented.
> The student was as keen to succeed at it as she was frightened

by it. However, it was not wholly out of her reach. Most important, she had time during her school day to connect with me, I
had time to connect with her, and there was a free place, with a
blackboard, for the consultation. Few teachers and few students,
alas, have such luxuries. Coaching absolutely requires them.[11]

Such conditions may indeed be luxuries, but doesn't a climate for thinking
require that we come as close as possible to recreating the personal time,
space, and connections that make coaching so powerful—that make it resemble so strikingly the "scaffolding" Vygotsky saw as moving young
thinkers to "intellectual higher ground"?[12]

One final point about a climate for thinking: We don't think that students should be the only ones to take chances. As teacher/coaches, we must
push ourselves beyond sure-fire correctness. That may mean following the
lead of student questions into territory not covered on the lesson plan, writing with students and sharing our own papers for response, or just saying "I
don't know" without choking. By watching us take chances, students just
might learn what physicist Peter Carruthers discovered as a young man
when he reflected on how off-balance he felt when doing his best work.
Eventually, says Carruthers, "I realized that if I understood too clearly what I
was doing, where I was going, then I probably wasn't working on anything
very interesting.... Work that really counts pushes us to the brink of confu-
sion."[13] That last statement, displayed in six-inch block letters, would make a
good poster for any classroom, wouldn't it?

Exploration

Teaching is an uneven occupation; it has its good days and its bad
days. Picture in your mind one of your good days. Remember a particular day
and a particular class. Remember a time when everything went just right,
when the class was animated and thinking was palpable. What were you
teaching? What did you do? What didn't you do? In your journal, remember that
day and record as many specific things that happened as you can.

What made that good day happen? Was it you or the kids? The material?
Could it have had something to do with atmosphere? Try to reconstruct the
how and why of that day things went so well. (If you haven't yet taught, remember such a class in which you were a student. Respond to the questions
about what the teacher did.)

Now try the flip side of the good days/bad days reality of teaching.
Think of a time when nothing seemed to go right in a particular class—a day
that definitely belongs in the bad column. In your journal, think through the
reverse side of the questions prompting recollections of your good day.

Whose "fault" was it that things didn't work—or is "fault" a useful word except perhaps on the tennis court? On that bad day, how would you describe the atmosphere in the classroom? What might you learn from that day you'd just as soon forget?

A COMMUNITY OF THINKERS

Here's another caption to consider for posters in thinking classrooms: "It is good to rub and polish our brain against that of others." Maybe Montaigne wouldn't mind our changing his word *good* to *imperative* for students headed toward a twenty-first century fraught with problems too complex for solo solutions.

To underscore this reality in our minds, we might turn to the unlikely world of big business, where communities of thinkers already do much of the mental work. In turning to Rosabeth Moss Kantor for advice on how to bring about change in schools, we've already touched on this point in chapter 1. You'll recall that one of Kantor's three *FPI*'s for contemporary business is *friendliness,* a willingness to work collaboratively rather than to go it alone. For models of such collaborative work, we might look into those quality circles of the much-celebrated Japanese auto industry and the ad hoc project teams of innovative American corporations.[14] Then we might check into other such teams—sometimes called think tanks, task forces, skunk works, and blitzkrieg groups—to get at least a glimpse of the problems they're tackling in science, technology, medicine, and government. The lesson doesn't take long to learn: Collaborative thinking is today's reality as well as tomorrow's hope.

That's one reason we believe classrooms should be places for young people to rub their minds together. Robert Sternberg offers another. He argues convincingly that even everyday problem solving most often occurs in groups. It's not just sweeping problems like saving the environment and finding a cure for cancer that stymie individual thinkers. It's also problems of everyday living—problems with time, money, family, friends, school, or work. Because problems typically involve more than one person, unilateral solutions just don't seem to work. Though Sternberg is all for teaching students to think for themselves, to be independent problem solvers, you can see why he considers the job half-done until they also learn to think with others, to be group problem solvers.[15]

Neither kind of thinking can be learned in a vacuum. That's why peer interaction is right up there with classroom climate as a factor critical to intellectual development. Since James Moffett has been telling us that for at least twenty years,[16] it should come as no surprise that thinking flourishes within a classroom structure that encourages students to learn from each other, not just from teachers and textbooks. Within a collaborative classroom, young people support and extend one another's thinking. They discover the social value of being able to ask good questions, look at all sides of an issue, and make careful judgments. In the process, they are socialized into a disposition to behave in more thoughtful ways. We like the way Sadler and Whimbey sum up this condition for intellectual growth: "The task of improving cognitive skills should be a group experience, not a solitary adventure."[17]

If that's news at all, we think it's good news. Our own students have never liked solitary adventure much anyway, especially at school. That's where they go to be with their friends as well as to learn. As working adults, most of us can identify with this need. Indeed, our experience tells us that thinking and learning need not occur in isolation. The next exploration invites you to consult your own experience with collaborative thinking.

Exploration

Take a moment to scan the two options below and choose one as the subject of a journal entry.

OPTION I

Recall times that you have worked with at least one other person on some undertaking. Which of these collaborations do you remember as being most challenging, stimulating, or rewarding? Take a few minutes to write about that particular experience as a collaborator. How did you and your partner(s) decide to work together? What special strengths did each of you bring to the undertaking? In what ways did the collaboration seem most stimulating and most productive? At what points did each of you spark new ideas from the other(s)? Did you seem to accomplish more working together than any one person might have accomplished working alone?

OPTION II

Recall classroom experiences in which you have engaged students in working together. Try especially to remember times that students seemed to teach each other—to think better together than any one would have thought individually. What was the task? How did you get them started? How did students seem to stimulate and support each other? What did students seem to learn from working together? From your perspective, what were the results?

Use your journal to think through one of these recollections. Then take a moment to think beyond the one experience you just wrote about. As you pause to take stock of your own experience as a collaborator and as a facilitator of collaboration, how do those experiences add up? At this moment, what do you see as the value of collaborative thinking in the classroom— either the classroom you now have or one you hope to have in the future?

In your own experience with collaborative thinking, you've undoubtedly had to deal with feelings of competition—feelings that are inimical to the kind of cooperation and mutual support that allow people to think together in synergistic ways. Teachers tell us that children arrive at school with an inclination to compete rather than collaborate. Linda Range's second-graders certainly did. In one early effort to nurture their ability to think together, Linda divided her young charges into five groups and gave each the challenge of creating its own aquarium. Soon, every group was hiding its project from other groups. As Linda reports, "Nobody wanted anybody from another group to know what they were doing. They were hiding their aquariums, and if somebody caught a glimpse of their treasures, the children would get really nervous. They didn't want their secrets let out of the bag."[18]

It's not easy to counter this culturally ingrained tendency to compete rather than cooperate. Yet teachers like Linda Range and Judith Friedberg find ways to do so.[19] As a teacher-technologist, Judith is concerned about the potential of computers to isolate people; she certainly doesn't want her fourth-graders to commune only with keyboards and ignore one another. Interactive simulations like "Cross-Country Texas" provide a favorite vehicle for fostering collaborative thinking. Before beginning this simulation—the object of which is to get a truckload of produce across Texas before it spoils—Judith organizes her children into teams that must make navigational decisions based on weather, road conditions, driver health and safety considerations, and changes in delivery schedule and pickup point. Armed with copies of maps and other printed information, teams must solve problems and reach critical decisions based on unexpected developments that unfold during the simulation. Only consensus decisions may be entered on the computer keyboard. No one succeeds unless everyone does: Although the simulation allows a number of alternative paths to the truck's destination, all teams must make good decisions if the truck is to arrive with its load in marketable condition.

As teachers of language, we know firsthand the importance of cultivating collaborative thinking. We know that reading a book is a lot like going to a movie: Half the fun is sharing that experience with someone else. If you have any doubts, just listen to the buzz in classrooms where reading is unabashedly social: "Hey, listen to this ...." "I wonder why ...." "That reminds me of ...." Tune in closely and we think you'll agree that talking over shared readings with a partner or peer group does more than scratch the human itch to share. It provides a sounding board for assumptions and interpretations; it lets students think out loud about their own responses to a work. As readers compare interpretations, we notice that they return again and again to the text. They question, analyze, and make judgments. What happens looks and sounds a lot like that much-vaunted "critical thinking."

So it is with classroom communities of writers. As teachers of language, we've flirted for years with Moffett's notion that discourse starts with drama ("what's happening"), that written monologue is born of oral dialogue.[20] The last few years, we've begun to acknowledge with Kenneth Bruffee that "writing is not an inherently private act but a displaced social act we perform in private for sake of convenience."[21] In more and more classrooms, we are pleased to see writing is returning to its social roots.

So it is with work in some other classrooms. We're encouraged by accounts of students' working in pairs on experiments in science labs, on problem solving in mathematics classes, and research projects in social studies. Visit such classrooms and you'll hear all kinds of exploratory talk: show-and-tell, brainstorming, debate, and just plain conversation. You will also find students trying out ideas on each other, responding critically to those ideas, and consulting on work in progress.

We're encouraged by classrooms that foster such collaborative thinking, but saying so makes us a little edgy. Too much such self-congratulatory talk could lull us into complacency when we still have a long way to go in forging classroom communities of thinkers.

We already know that it will take more than arranging chairs in circles rather than rows. We even admit that there's nothing magic about interaction for interaction's sake and nothing easy about orchestrating activities that foster thinking. Designing the kinds of tasks we'll be talking about throughout this book takes us to the edge of our competence; there's so much we don't yet know.

Is the effort worth it? Jerome Bruner certainly thinks so. During his life-long study of the mind, he has extended the theme of discovery learning sounded in early articles: "My model of the child in those days," he now writes, "was very much in the tradition of the solo child mastering the world by representing it to himself in his own terms. In the intervening years I have come increasingly to recognize that most learning in most settings is a communal activity, a sharing of culture. It is not just that the child must make his knowledge his own, but that he must make it his own in a community of those who share his sense of belonging."[22]

We can only nod agreement and add what you already know: Language is the coin of culture—especially that classroom culture Bruner considers so crucial. That point brings us to a third factor critical to intellectual development.

IMMERSION IN LANGUAGE

A language-rich classroom is easy to spot. Books abound—even if there's no money for classroom sets and the teacher must bring them in on a grocery cart from the school library or scrounge coverless discards from local shopkeepers. Seldom are those books neatly arranged in rows on shelves; they mingle with magazines and pieces of student writing to form ever-shifting stacks. Walls serve as galleries for proud display of student papers—drawings as well as writings. Words are, quite literally, everywhere.

As lovers of words ourselves, we intuitively like the idea of immersing students in them. Certainly English teachers have no monopoly on that impulse. We know science, art, social studies, computer, and even math teachers whose rooms look a lot like the one just described. Furthermore, at least some of those teachers are finding ways to do what Ann Berthoff has long urged: to work with language not as a mere tool but as an instrument for seeing in many different ways—with both microscope and telescope, both x-ray and radar.[23] At least intuitively, these teachers realize that working with language as an instrument of thought can help students put new information together in their own ways—to make sense of the subject at hand and in the process learn that meaning doesn't just happen but must be made by the mind. In working with language as an instrument of thought, these teachers are also learning a great deal about individual students' ways of thinking and working.

Before taking a closer look at the role of language in the thinking classroom, pause for a moment to reflect on your own work with language.

Exploration

If you're already teaching, call to mind a picture of your classroom, complete with students. (If you aren't yet teaching, visualize some classroom you know well, perhaps one in which you are now a student.) Take a mental inventory of that room. How many books do you see? Where? What kind? What other printed materials, such as magazines, pamphlets, even posters, do you see? What do you see on the chalkboard and bulletin boards? Who put it there? What student work do you see?

Take a mental tour of the room, focusing on students. On a typical day, what are they doing? What are they writing? How much? Who is talking to whom? About what?

With all this in mind, consider what you might learn from the things students say, the things they write, even the things they choose to read. Try to recall instances in which written work, drawings, journal entries, projects, or talk have yielded insights about the way particular students think and work.

What might you want to do more of (or less of) to make language a more powerful "microscope and telescope, x-ray and radar" in your classroom?

It took us a while to learn that a necessary first step in all of this is giving students back their language. Sad to say, that's especially hard these days for teachers, who often have so little power that they are reluctant to share that crumb by giving students speaking rights. Yet students can only make meaning with their own language, by working and playing with the words in their own heads.

That's a big reason Judith Friedberg builds writing as well as talk into her computer classes. In the "Cross-Country Texas" simulation described earlier, for example, Judith has each student keep a diary:

> As you go on your journey, keep a travel diary. Select one or more of the following to write about, or create your own idea:
>
> - Tell about your life on the road as a truck driver.
> - Imagine what it must have been like to make the long trip with only horses and/or wagons as transportation. Write about it.
> - Describe the sights or experiences you want to tell your family about when you return from your trip.
> - Create a drawing inspired by the colors and shapes you see as you make your journey.

That last option warrants special notice. Like so many good teachers we know, Judith realizes the power of visual as well as verbal language. Both help students make sense of an experience and express meanings they make themselves. Judith also realizes how much she learns by following the mental footprints students leave in their diaries. By following the tracks of different thinkers over time, she can learn a great deal about what they do well and what they need to do better. Perhaps even more importantly, she can help students trace their own progress. She extends the latter by having students list in their own words what they think was required to work successfully as a team and what they think they learned from that particular simulation. Whether talking to each other or writing—on-line or off—these students are immersed in an environment that is as rich in language as it is in technology.

So are Grace Beam's middle school science students. See if her assignment initiating a unit on cells doesn't call to mind Ann Berthoff's notion of using language as an instrument of thought.

> Below is a quotation from "The Sea Within Us" by Irvin Block:

We actually live not in air but in our own juice. Our outer layer of skin, the bag that separates us from the external environment, is dead scale. Behind that barrier, inside the bag, our metabolizing cells—what is truly alive in us—exist awash in their private ocean. From that ocean they take the nutrients they need and flush into it their waste to be carried off with the tide, just as cells have done for hundreds of millions of years.

Diffusion is the force that underlies life. It helps explain why cells do what they do.

Draw a picture of what this means to you.[24]

The drawings elicited by this assignment reflect a great deal of thought. To depict that "sea within us," Grace's students had to understand what cells are and do and what happens during diffusion. By comparing and discussing their drawings, students were able to test and extend their understandings. Drawings and discussions provided springboards for inquiry into such questions as how diffusion and osmosis help to sustain life—for example, how the body must regulate amounts of water and salt in the blood. Small groups took on such questions as how shad are able to go back and forth between fresh and salt water, why low-salt diets may help in controlling high blood pressure, and why celery and carrot sticks are put in ice water to make them crisp. This inquiry no doubt involved lots of reading, library research, talk, and writing.

As students thought their ways through this unit on the cell, their drawings and writings and discussions gave Grace at least an occasional window into their minds. She was especially intrigued by a drawing that seemed to be for a social studies or language arts class and was explained by the student this way: "Prejudice is like the cell membrane. It lets some things in and keeps some things out." In developing her students' ability to think scientifically, Grace considers books, magazines, journals, reports, drawings, and talk indispensable. Language is one of the most important instruments in her science laboratory.

Teachers like Judith and Grace both confirm and extend what we teachers of language should have known all along. They remind us that students must think first in their own language. That's why reading teachers often ease into a story with word-shaking, an aptly named association game in which students brainstorm lists of words or phrases triggered in their minds by a theme word from the story. It's also why writing teachers push jot-listing and freewriting as means of unpacking memories, information, ideas, and questions worth exploring on paper. It's why literature teachers do more than march students through an anthology to view literature from a respectful distance—why good teachers see that students relate stories and poems to personal experience, engage in lots of book talk, keep reading journals, and make pieces their own by responding in writing as well as other media.

In the delicate ecosystem of the thinking classroom, we as teachers must value the language of our students. We must hold their words carefully in our hands, realizing that words come wrapped in feelings. As students gain confidence and facility in using their own language as an instrument of thought, that instrument can be turned outward and extended by the language of others. In a language-rich classroom, we've been delighted to discover, words beget words. Talk begets reading, which begets writing, which begets talk, and so on. The result is what we like to call thinking through language.

ACTIVE EXPERIENCE

In Houston, Carol and her colleagues have a disparaging term for courses that teach students about a subject without ever letting them get too close to it. The curriculum folks in Houston wouldn't dignify such a course by calling it *Calculus;* they'd call it *Calculus Appreciation.* Unfortunately, there's also a lot of English Appreciation, History Appreciation, and Science Appreciation. To us, those courses seem to do about as much good as taking swimming by correspondence.

Since we're talking about thinking, not Thinking Appreciation, it seems almost redundant to list active experience as another of those conditions critical to intellectual development. Besides that, active experience sounds a lot like "Learn by doing," an educational cliché worn so slick with use that its meaning slides right by us. Even so, before you dismiss our insistence upon active involvement as platitude, we ask that you stifle that big ho-hum and take a few minutes to consult your primary source on matters of thinking.

Exploration

Think back over your own years as a learner. From all those years, re-call the learning experience that was most special—an experience so vivid that it remains with you today. Replay that experience in your mind. When and where did it happen? Who else participated? What kinds of thinking did that learning task make you do? How much time did you spend on it? What got you started and kept you going? How did you feel at the time, and why do you think that this learning experience has stayed with you?

- Get your experience down on paper, preferably in your journal.
- Share it with a colleague, friend, or family member. Ask that person to tell you about a special learning experience. See what parallels you can draw.

We're betting that the learning experience you just recalled didn't have much to do with sitting still and absorbing information dispensed by someone else. We're betting that it got you out of your seat and moving—maybe to locales other than school. Furthermore, we're betting that it was what you did, said, discovered, and produced yourself that made the experience so powerful. If so, you have at least one piece of firsthand evidence that learning is not a spectator sport.

Certainly, learning to think is not passive. Like any other complex human behavior, it takes practice. Consider how babies learn to walk and talk. They learn by walking and talking, trial and error, practice and more practice. Parents can help, but they can't walk and talk for babies. So it is with thinking. We can help our students, but we can't do it for them. The question is how we can help by providing rich, abundant practice. Just how does such practice look in the classroom?

To us, it often looks a lot like art. Why art? In the first place, thinking, like art, involves making—as in constructing, forming, and composing; as in everyday expressions like "making sense" and "making up our minds." Furthermore, art taps what Arnheim terms intuitive perception as well as intellectual analysis.[25] It elicits the kind of total engagement for which Bruner borrows from a colleague the coinage *perfink* to encompass perception, feeling, and thinking.[26] To that, we would add doing.

How does all this translate into classroom practice of thinking? While we don't aspire to teach Art with a capital *A*, these days we are borrowing freely from experts who do. We often ask students to draw what they see, feel, or imagine. We do so for reasons argued by art teacher Betty Edwards in her immensely helpful and readable book, *Drawing from the Artist Within:* "Drawing can objectify thought—can get it out in front, where it can be seen.... Also in drawing, one can express ideas or feelings that are too complicated or imprecise to fit into the 'reducing lens' of words. Furthermore, drawings can show more relationships that are grasped immediately as a single image, where words are necessarily locked into a sequential order."[27] You'll have a chance to test this theory on your own as you work through chapter 5, which invites you to join us in exploring the arts as a context for thinking.

Meanwhile, let us illustrate with a long-term project undertaken by several middle school language arts classes in Houston. Students were provided inexpensive automatic cameras with which to complete several photographic assignments. The first week, they were to make photographs to assemble a self-portrait; in subsequent weeks, their photographs were to explore the themes of family, community culture, and personal fantasies. After sharing and discussing photographs taken on each theme, students wrote pieces on that same theme. To culminate the project, students designed and constructed thematic posters featuring the photographs and written pieces they considered their best. On a celebratory field trip, they attached their posters to a special display wall outside the city's convention center to be viewed by visitors entering an international photography exhibition. Having read many of the pieces featured on those posters and interviewed a number of the students who wrote them, Carol can attest to the quality of thinking as well as the quality of writing generated during this project.

Granted, opportunities for such special projects don't present themselves every day. Yet we know many teachers who manage to devise thought-provoking tasks that involve students in active exploration of their own inner and outer worlds, in thinking visually as well as verbally, and in building intellectual confidence as well as intellectual competence. Those teachers value active learning, but they realize that activity is not an end in itself. As Theodore Sizer says, a school task "should lead somewhere in the eyes and the mind of the student. This means that it must connect to wherever that student is rooted—his experiences—and that it must promise to take him toward an important place. It must be ultimately useful and patently interesting to him at the time it is learned and in the future."[28]

Students recognize and respond to such tasks. As William Glasser confirmed by talking at length with high school students, they find all too few: "Most of them see quality in athletics, music, and drama.... Almost none find anything of high quality in regular classes. All except a very few admit that, while they believe that they are capable of doing high-quality work in class, they have never actually done any and have no plans to do any in the future."[29]) Though not surprising, Glasser's finding that students tune out when they aren't actively involved gets at the essence of this condition for intellectual development. Students don't mind working hard; they do mind being bored by rote, low-quality tasks that fully engage neither body nor mind.

We've seen students work hard when academic subjects became as engaging as athletics, music, and drama. There are elementary mathematics classes where children learn the concept of division by splitting up collections of baseball cards in various ways and learn concepts of geometry by making tangrams or creating shapes on geoboards. There are social studies classes where students extend learning in geography by creating table-top relief maps of clay and get to know about government by holding their own mock elections. There are high school English classes where students express their responses to literature in some visual or musical medium and engage in extended research projects that take them into the community as well as into the library.

The best of such tasks leave plenty of room for choice by individual students. To make the task their own, students need to capitalize on their own strengths and interests—indeed to personalize work with their own unique signatures. As Elliott Eisner reminds us, young thinkers need opportunities to formulate their own problems and plot their own paths toward self-defined goals.[30]

What we're after is the antithesis of the depersonalized, decontextualized exercises comprising most prepackaged programs that purport to teach thinking. Such programs treat the mind as if it were a muscle: Enough mental push-ups and it's bound to get big and strong. Ten analysis exercises ... ten nonverbal logic ... ten analogies ... ten syllogisms ...

To us, that's not authentic practice. To get beyond Thinking Appreciation, students must be actively involved in purposeful tasks that engage mind, eye, and hand in sustained effort toward some goal that matters today as well as tomorrow. Furthermore, those tasks must be rooted in a context that is both engaging and meaningful—a context that holds intellectual work together so that students can make sense of it. In subsequent chapters, we'll share some working ideas for such tasks. Right now, let's just add active experience to that list of factors critical to intellectual development.

DELIBERATE PACE

Let's also add deliberate pace. By that, we mean giving students time to think—a condition for intellectual development that seems almost too obvious to mention. Yet consider how rushed the typical classroom seems. There's so much to do and so little time to do it. Because teacher and students so often rush pell-mell to get everything "covered," too many classrooms encourage impulsive rather than thoughtful behavior.

It takes time to develop thoughtful habits of mind. Since the Bloom and Broder studies more than thirty-five years ago,[31] research has consistently found that good thinkers work in deliberate, elaborative ways, while poor thinkers are characterized by hasty, one-shot approaches.[32] Besides confirming personal observations and experiences, these findings square with our constructivist view of thinking and learning—that people are not recorders of information but makers of meaning. Information can be recorded and replayed instantly. The making of meaning takes much longer. To nourish thinking, then, we must provide time for students to question what they are told, to elaborate ideas, to examine new information in relation to old, to build new knowledge structures, indeed to create their own meaning.[33]

In most schools, it's not easy to establish and maintain this condition for thinking. For starters, it means just saying no to competitions rewarding speedy, one-shot responses—everything from number sense contests to College Bowl quiz games. It also means fewer (if any) timed tests and far more waiting time after asking questions. Most importantly, it means acknowledging the futility of trying to teach a curriculum so bloated by attempts to "cover" everything that nothing gets more than a quick brush. Such glancing encounters with information don't do much for students' minds. While students need knowledge to think with, they can't think with secondhand knowledge; as already noted, they must make their own. That's our problem with the Hirsch-Finn-Ravitch notion of curriculum as transmitter of culture. Given the exponential increase in knowledge even over recent decades, how can we delude ourselves into insisting that students learn it all in twelve years? Since none of us can ever learn everything, isn't it far more sensible for schools to focus on developing minds with both the capacity and the disposition to keep on learning?

That's what we think. Even so, we aren't suggesting the abandonment of curriculum. There are indeed things that every student needs to know and be able to do. Furthermore, thinking doesn't take place in a vacuum; students need substance to think about. Since they also need time, we are suggesting that you set some priorities and stick to them—that you try doing more by doing less.

Exploration

If you are already teaching, think about the curriculum your students are expected to work through this year. If you have not yet taught, borrow a curriculum document for the subject or grade you hope to teach. In either case, pay special attention to what students are expected to learn and be able to do by the end of the year. For what content are they responsible? What particular materials, if any, are they expected to work through?

Now take a moment to consider what you know about the way minds generate knowledge by questioning, elaborating, investigating, speculating, relating, imagining, synthesizing—in short, by thinking. Consider the amount of time required for such thinking each day and the total amount of class time available during the school year. Does the year allow enough time for thoughtful work toward all expectations specified in the curriculum? What kinds of thinking and learning do you consider most important for your students? If you invested all of your class time in working toward these priorities, what might be subordinated or omitted? How would your classroom be different?

In getting our own priorities straight, we try to keep in mind Elliot Eisner's advice to make classrooms intellectual rather than merely academic.[34] Intellectual classrooms value the exercise of mind. They operate on the premise that people seldom learn to do anything worthwhile by attempting it only once. They provide time to consider possibilities as well as "facts," to weigh alternatives, to deal with subtlety and nuance, to pose as well as solve problems, to ponder ambiguity, to sustain work from rough idea to finished product.

To create such classrooms, we must first part company with the time-on-task folks. We must act on our realization that kids aren't computers, obedient machines that can be switched on and expected to process information upon command. Furthermore, we must value quality over quantity. For one teacher we know, that meant cutting back to only three composition assignments for a six-week period so that her fourth-graders could share rough drafts, do a thorough job of revising, and select their best pieces for a school publication. For another, it meant extending a map-making project to four days rather than cutting it off after the two originally allotted. For still another, it meant allowing an extra week for students to complete their research papers.

These teachers have the right idea. Without time, students can't be expected to engage in real inquiry, to do careful work, and to develop a pride in craftsmanship. Often, however, they need help in making the most of that time. Conditioned to the pedagogical equivalent of TV news flashes, many students have no idea how to slow down and dig in intellectually. They spend little time planning their work, checking it along the way, or reflecting critically on what they have accomplished. Such habits must be cultivated by thoughtful teachers who ask timely questions: How might you go at this task? How can you tell how you are doing? What standards do you have in mind for judging results? We'll have more to say shortly about the importance of such questions. For the moment, let's focus on building in the necessary time. Doing so fosters a commitment to process, a realization that ideas and concepts and products need time to ripen and that quality is improved by sustained effort.

As writing teachers, we learned rather early to insist that our students work from abundance rather than fastening on the first idea that flickers across their minds—for example, to think of ten childhood memories they might write about and then think of ten more; to observe fifteen details of a natural object and then observe fifteen more; to generate five metaphors to illuminate some abstraction and then generate five more. We know mathematics teachers who have students work the same problem as many different ways as possible and social studies teachers who have students defend both sides of the same issue. In each case, the intent is much the same: to engage students in considering multiple possibilities and in remaining open to different points of view. That's what we're after when we invite students to question assumptions, to ask for clarification, to debate pros and cons, to request justification, and to elaborate ideas in a variety of ways.

By its very nature, writing holds thoughts still so that they can be examined. That's why it's often useful as a means of stopping the action to make thinking more deliberate. When third graders are confronted by a word problem in mathematics, the teacher may get them started by saying: "Write down what you know and what you are trying to find out." When more advanced math students get stuck on a problem, the teacher may advise them to write their way through it by jotting down what they've done so far, what they think the next step might be, and how they might go about working out a solution. Science teachers typically insist that students log steps in a lab experiment and report results in writing. Literature teachers often have young readers keep response journals.

We find it especially helpful to have students keep track of their own work over time. Portfolios of notes, drafts, drawings, and other working papers—dated and sequentially arranged—provide encouraging evidence of how thinking accrues and work gets better over time. Portfolios help students learn firsthand the value of thinking that is deliberate and elaborative rather than hasty and impulsive. A retrospective look through the entire accumulation can help students gain valuable insights into their own abilities and inclinations as a thinker. This point brings us to one more condition crucial to intellectual development.

REFLECTION

During recent years, the word *reflection* has taken on a special meaning to those who study the workings of the mind. It refers to the process of thinking about thinking, an ability unique to human beings and sometimes known as *metacognition*. Whatever it's called, this umbrella process allows us to be aware of our own thinking as we work through a task and to use this awareness to guide what we do. The point of reflection is not to replace the intuitions good thinkers trust. The point is to bring those intuitions to the surface so that they can be checked, adjusted, applied, and confirmed. Thus reflection helps us become what Lauren Resnick and others call self-regulated thinkers and learners[35]

It would be hard to overstate the importance of helping young people take charge of their own minds. That's one reason we saved this all-important condition for the nurture of thinking until last. We've been struck by research suggesting that less able thinkers differ from their more successful counterparts not so much in their repertoires of mental processes and strategies as in the tendency to use those processes and strategies.[36] The problem is not so much in knowing how to think as in knowing to do it. It seems to us that reflection can be a powerful means of helping young thinkers learn to make the most of their mental repertoires.

In order to do so, students must realize that they have mental repertoires. They must see intelligence not as the luck of the draw but as a set of incremental abilities that can be developed over time. That's another reason we're willing to take on the time-consuming and complex challenge of thinking about thinking in the classroom. Consider what happens when students step back and look at their own work over time, when they notice what went well and what could be improved, when they become aware of their own inclinations and habits as thinkers. Isn't that what athletes do when they scrutinize their own movements on videotape, what musicians do when they listen critically to recordings of their own performances, what artists do when they study their own sketchbooks? Such reflection focuses on past work but is directed toward the future.

We've learned not to count on reflection's occurring spontaneously. That's why we suggested earlier that students be encouraged to think retrospectively through portfolios of past and present work. It's also why we suggest that students be asked to reflect on paper about how they worked through a particular task. That reflection may take the form of a map, timeline, flowchart, story, or journal entry. Whatever its form, getting the process on paper helps to trigger recollections about how individual students approached the task, what they found easiest and hardest, when they became most involved, what they would like to do more of, and what they might do differently next time. Often, we find it helpful for students to compare reflections—not just so that they will learn from one another, but also so that they can see how different minds work in different ways and get to know themselves as thinkers.

Such after-the-fact reflection is powerful, but it's not the only kind of reflection. There is also before-the-fact thinking about thinking—in a word, planning, which is itself a kind of metacognition. We're convinced that students are more inclined to take on challenges when they learn to get started by asking themselves reflective questions: What do I already know about this? What will I need to find out? What have I done before that might help? What piece of the task can I handle most easily? Would that be a good place to start? Where can I go for help if I get stuck? Again, we can't count on such reflections' taking place spontaneously. Until students develop the disposition to approach mental tasks reflectively, we need to build in prompts. We also need to let students hear us reflect aloud: "Let's see.… There are at least two ways I might go about this. Let me think about which would probably work best for me and how I might get started." Students also need prompts and models for reflective thinking while work is in progress: How am I doing? Is there anything that doesn't make sense and needs to be changed? Sometimes, we find it helpful to call a time-out for students to grope aloud, to explain to themselves by explaining to someone else how the work seems to be coming along.

Such conscious, careful efforts to develop reflective thinking may not take us all the way to what Donald Schön calls reflection-in-action, that dialectic process that enables people to think about what they're doing while they're doing it.[37] Even so, we're convinced that engaging in before-, during-, and after-the-fact reflection will move us—as well as our students—in that direction. With that point, let's pause to reflect on our own work and see what it suggests about what we need to do next.

Exploration

Take a few minutes to think back through the six conditions identified in this chapter as crucial to intellectual development. Recall your thoughts and feelings as you considered what we had to say about each condition: a climate for thinking, a community of thinkers, immersion in language, active experience, deliberate pace, and reflection. Then do some preliminary checking for those conditions in your own classroom—or, if you don't yet teach, in the classroom you know best.

Preferably in your journal, reflect on these questions:

- How would I characterize my classroom as an ecosystem for thinking? How would I characterize my school as a whole?
- To make conditions more conducive to intellectual growth, what are the biggest changes I need to make in my classroom? What are the biggest changes that need to be made in the school? What stands in the way?
- What am I already doing that I need to do more of? Who might work with me?
- What do I need to learn more about?

NOTES

1. Jerome Bruner, *Actual Minds, Possible Worlds.* Cambridge: Harvard University Press, 1986.
2. Janet L. Hopson, "Conversation with Marian Diamond: A Love Affair with the Brain." *Psychology Today* (November, 1984).
3. Until late 1988, James Claypool was a social studies teacher at Yates High School in Houston.
4. Arthur L. Costa, "Teacher Behaviors That Enable Student Thinking." *Developing Minds: A Resource Book for Teaching Thinking.* Alexandria: Association for Supervision and Curriculum Development, 1985.
5. Dennie Wolf, "Opening Up Assessment: Ideas from the Arts." Unpublished paper of Project Zero, Harvard University, 1988.

6. Grant Wiggins, "The Futility of Trying to Teach Everything of Importance." *Educational Leadership* (November, 1989).

7. "Asking the Essential Questions: Curriculum Development." *Horace* (June, 1989).

8. Until the fall of 1989, John Ella Fowler was a music teacher and program coordinator at Bruce Elementary School, a magnet school for fine arts in Houston.

9. Peter Elbow, "Embracing Contraries in the Teaching Process." *College English* (April, 1983).

10. Ibid.

11. Theodore R. Sizer, *Horace's Compromise: The Dilemma of the American High School*. Boston: Houghton Mifflin Company, 1984.

12. Lev Vygotsky, *Thought and Language*. Cited in Bruner, 1986.

13. William J. Broad, "Tracing the Skeins of Matter." *New York Times* Magazine (May, 1984).

14. Thomas J. Peters and Robert H. Waterman, Jr., *In Search of Excellence: Lessons from America's Best-Run Companies*. New York: Warner Books, 1982.

15. Robert J. Sternberg, "Teaching Critical Thinking, Part I: Are We Making Critical Mistakes?" *Phi Delta Kappan* (November, 1985).

16. James Moffett, *A Student-Centered Language Arts Curriculum K–13*. Boston: Houghton Mifflin, 1968.

17. William A. Sadler, Jr., and Arthur Whimbey, "A Holistic Approach to Teaching Thinking Skills." *Phi Delta Kappan* (November, 1985).

18. Linda Range is a teacher and magnet program coordinator at Scroggins Elementary School in Houston, Texas.

19. Judith Friedberg is a teacher technologist; at the time of the episode reported, she was teaching computer classes at Bonham Elementary School in Houston.

20. James Moffett, *Teaching the Universe of Discourse*. Boston: Houghton Mifflin, 1968.

21. Kenneth Bruffee, "Collaborative Learning." *College English* (Volume 43, 1981).

22. See note 1 above.

23. Ann E. Berthoff, *The Making of Meaning*. Portsmouth, N.H.: Boynton/Cook Publishers, Inc., 1981.

24. Grace Beam is a seventh-grade science teacher at Pershing Middle School in Houston.

25. Rudolf Arnheim, *New Essays on the Psychology of Art*. Berkeley: University of California Press, Ltd., 1986.

26. See note 1 above.

27. Betty Edwards, *Drawing on the Artist Within*. New York: Simon and Schuster, 1986.

28. See note 11 above.

29. William Glasser, "The Quality School." *Phi Delta Kappan* (February, 1990).

30. Elliot W. Eisner, "What's Worth Teaching?" Address at annual conference of the Association for Supervision and Curriculum Development, March 1990.

31. Benjamin Bloom and Lois Broder, *Problem-Solving Processes of College Students*. Chicago: University of Chicago Press, 1950.

32. Allan A. Glatthorn and Jonathan Baron, "The Good Thinker." *Developing Minds: A Resource Book for Teaching Thinking*. Alexandria, Va.: Association for Supervision and Curriculum Development, 1985.

33. Lauren B. Resnick and Leopold E. Klopfer, *Toward the Thinking Curriculum: Current Cognitive Research*. Alexandria,Va.: Association for Supervision and Curriculum Development, 1989.

34. See note 30 above.

35. See note 33 above.

36. See note 33 above.

37. Donald A. Schön, *Educating the Reflective Practitioner*. San Francisco: Jossey-Bass Inc., Publishers, 1982.

UNIT II
What Matters

This section focuses on a central premise in this book: It takes thinking teachers to develop thinking students. As teachers, we don't always take care of ourselves. The first chapter in this section challenges you to do so—to embark on adventures of the mind that may or may not have anything to do with your students. It invites you to take mind trips *without* your students, to attend to your own intellectual growth, to extend your own mind. That's important. Your most important and delicate resource for teaching—especially for teaching for thinking—is your own mind. The care and feeding of that resource must become one of your highest priorities.

Thinking students grow and develop as they are nurtured by concerned and thoughtful teachers. But a little teacher goes a long way. The climate which grows thinkers is a delicate one. Too much teacher stifles minds; too little teacher leaves thinkers confused and uncertain.

Stepping back and giving students center stage takes confidence. It also takes a strong belief in students. That's what you'll focus on in chapter 4—assumptions about students, about their thinking, about intelligence itself.

Again, we hope you won't just read about these issues. We hope you'll explore them for yourself and make your own agenda for nurturing growth—your own and that of your students.

3

The Thinking Teacher

Knowledge is the currency with which a teacher
deals, and yet [schools allow] the teacher's own
knowledge to become stale and devalued, as though
ideas were not the lifeblood of the occupation.
—Gene I. Mearoff

Donald Schön has said that a profession is a job for which no one can fully prepare.[1] Certainly no amount of college course work and no amount of student teaching experience can prepare a young person to survive—much less flourish—as a teacher. In the first place, actual classrooms rarely conform to those described in textbooks or used as laboratories for student teaching. Because classrooms are unique, one-of-a-kind places shaped by the interactions of students and teachers, they defy technical or rational descriptions that can be generically applied. In the real world of school, formulas and prescriptions are seldom helpful. For this reason, Schön calls classrooms "indeterminate zones of practice."[2] Those zones of uncertainty make teaching a delicate and challenging profession.

Yet teaching takes more than learning to thrive in an uncertain zone of professional practice. Even if you're a novice, you know that learning to teach is learning to live amid the clamor and crush of young people. Sometimes that means feeling more like a missionary or Peace Corps volunteer than a mentor and an instructor. Teaching is learning to live productively among diverse colleagues in a fishbowl of successes and failures. More than anything, teaching is learning to function autonomously, finding the courage and wisdom to make those thousands of moment-to-moment decisions and choices which accumulate to make the classroom a good place or a living hell for the teacher and the students who share it.

Whether you're a fledgling or a veteran in this challenging profession, you've probably discovered that no one can teach you how to make good decisions and no one can tell you how to find your teaching persona, your teaching self that melds the right amount of intellectual and emotional toughness with compassion and understanding. You alone can develop that teaching persona through action and through reflection upon those actions.

For those of you reading this book in a methods class, we're sure your heads are full of dreams of yourself as the "teacher who makes a difference." We celebrate those bright dreams because teaching is about dreams. We want this chapter to strengthen those images of yourself as mentor and coach. But as experienced teachers know all too well, teaching can use up dreams. Teaching is a disposable art: it can deplete your enthusiasm for experimentation, dull your mind, and erode your sense of self. Experienced teachers know the drain of teaching, the wearing away of energy and resolve. They know how vulnerable they are to an anemic mental life which leaves them only going through the motions of teaching. To become a thinking teacher and remain a thinking teacher requires a great deal. To teach *thoughtfully* takes physical stamina, a growing sophistication of strategies, a strong commitment to the intellectual growth of students, and frequent reflection on the development of your own mind. Too often, what gets neglected on that list is the time for reflection and renewal.

We want this chapter to sponsor a time of reflection on your own teaching, regardless of where you are in your career. We want to speak as directly as we can about what it takes to be a thinking teacher.

- Teachers must *believe* in their own minds and those of their students.
- Teachers must *act* to develop those minds.
- Teachers must constantly *reflect* on those actions.

That's what is really at the bottom of this talk about thinking teachers: teachers' beliefs, teachers' actions, and teachers' reflections.

BELIEVING IN YOUR OWN MIND

If you've taught for a while, you've no doubt felt that you used to be a better thinker than you are now. You may recollect with fondness a time during your undergraduate days when your field began to make sense and you caught a first glimpse of yourself as a knowledgeable and competent learner. Some of you will remember a time in graduate school when you challenged yourself as a learner by taking a difficult course and not only survived that course but experienced an intellectual growth spurt as well. Most of you will remember the euphoria and intellectual freedom you felt in your first successful teaching experience. For too many teachers, those times of intellectual stimulation are in the past.

We're not suggesting that for most of you reading this book the "thrill is gone" in teaching and learning, but we are acknowledging that the routines and restrictions of schooling take their biggest toll on the minds of teachers. Some of you work in schools where thinking teachers are seen as trouble-makers or where questioning the traditional ways of doing things is seen as making waves. Unfortunately, that's not a rare phenomenon. Teachers are under tremendous pressure to conform: conform to discipline regulations, conform to building and district policies, and conform to curricula and testing. Many teachers have learned to be quiet, close their doors, and try to preserve some independence of mind within the four walls of their own classrooms. Closing the door may be a good technique for survival, but closed doors can mean closed minds. Renewing yourself as a thinker means opening doors to your colleagues in a new spirit of community. It's not a "come see how well my class is going" kind of openness, but rather a "come see what I'm working on" or "come give me some thoughts on this class" invitation.

Chances are that some of you have just neglected your own intellectual development. Many of you are women who have set high standards for yourself not only as professional teachers but also as mothers and wives. Exhaustion and a life of doing for others may now find you neglecting your own mental life. Some of you are men who work extra jobs to keep the family afloat financially. You've stayed in teaching because you love it, but you find little energy for personal renewal. Some of you are bright, eager young people who have yet to tackle the mental challenges of teaching. For all of you, we're convinced that learning to believe in your own mind means renewing your intellectual self both in a community of other professionals and on your own.

Exploration

Using your journal, reflect on some of the following questions in writing. Share your responses with a trusted colleague.

- What are some dreams you have or have had for your teaching?
- Which of these dreams have you already realized?
- Which of these dreams have you given up on?
- Which dreams are you still working on?
- What new dreams are you dreaming? What problems are you eager to work on in your teaching?
- What new ideas have you recently enacted in your teaching?

BELIEVING IN THE MINDS OF YOUR STUDENTS

Teachers' beliefs about their students' minds can forge chains and manacles for those minds. That was a major point in the previous chapter: The myths and presuppositions that cause us to judge and pigeonhole students can blind us to their potential as thinkers. Teachers' beliefs about students and their mental abilities may be the toughest obstacle to overcome on the road to thoughtful teaching. In summarizing current knowledge about learning, Newman and Brown say it so powerfully: "Learning is more likely to occur if both the teacher and the student believe that they can shape their worlds and are not victims of forces beyond their control."[3] Cultural expectations and years of grouping students on the basis of artificial selection devices—sometimes called standardized tests—have poisoned some teachers' minds about the ability of students to exert control over their own learning. All of us are too quick to categorize our students, to see them as the haves and the have-nots, the washed and the unwashed, the able and the unable. Consciously or unconsciously, we disparage those who are poor and unsophisticated or lacking fluency in English or of another race. We say those kinds of kids cannot be self-motivated and self-regulated. We say those kids aren't willing to do our activities. We tend to save our best assignments or at least our most rigorous attention for the brighter kids who are more like us; the less bright, less able tend to get worksheets and predigested learning experiences (and, if we're not careful, our disdain, or worse yet, our sympathy). Too many teachers have become victims of their own expectations of students, often formed secondhand from the numbers on the courses or from nationality or native language rather than by careful observations of kids as learners.

If that sounds harsh, hard on teachers, it's not meant to be. We consider ourselves teacher advocates, not teacher-bashers. Yet we must admit that in many cases teachers are their own worst enemies. We blame everyone else for our dreary and unloved estate, but too often we have seen the enemy and it is us. The fact is that too many of today's schools do not treat all of their students as though they had minds and the potential to learn. That's despite Bloom's research, which has led him to suggest that between 90 and 95 percent of all students have the mental capacity to learn most of what we have to teach them.[4] Even more striking is Sternberg's recent research, which documents remarkable growth in the testable intelligence of young people.[5] More on that in chapter 4.

The research results are indisputable: Students learn best in classrooms where teacher expectations are high. Students become thinkers when teachers believe in their potential to think and create the kinds of contexts that nurture intellectual growth. No approach to teaching thinking can work if it undervalues or ignores the individual minds of students.

Exploration

It might be helpful just for a moment to remember a few students from your past who confounded your stereotypes, defied your expectations, and surprised you with insight. Think for a moment about some of the most unlikely learners from your past who proved themselves in spite of your early expectations of them. Remember the first time you saw them. What framed your negative expectations? Was it last year's grades? test scores? other teachers? What do you remember about the transformation of these unlikely learners? How did it happen? What did you do when it happened?

Jot down the names of some of these surprising students. Choose one and recall the details of that student's odyssey in your class.

THOUGHTFUL ACTION

Believing in students is one thing; acting thoughtfully on those beliefs is quite another matter. Our standards for ourselves must be realistic; no one can be a brilliant teacher all of the time. There's the "good days, bad days" phenomenon that all teachers experience. What makes the difference is not so much how we act on any given day as it is the range and repertoire of our actions over the life of a course or class. Programmed, automatic, and mindless teaching is characterized by a narrow range of options. The class is organized more like a factory than a colloquium. Student and teacher roles are precisely defined, and instruction clicks along like a Japanese assembly line. Those classrooms, like Holiday Inns, offer no surprises.

We don't want to suggest, however, that thinking classes are characterized by disorder or even chaos. Thinking teachers often act quite deliberately, following carefully designed plans and even making good use of those painfully articulated curriculum guides. Structured and ordered classrooms don't necessarily decrease student freedom. We vote *YES* for discipline *and* freedom. What has given structure a bad name is that too often the word has meant a framework for teaching rather than for learning. We leave it to you to make your own judgments about "effective schools" and Madeline Hunter models, but we find them to be more about teaching than about learning.

Tracye Wear is a thoughtful art teacher who defies such closed simplistic structures. More concerned with learning than with teaching, Tracye works to help her students become good thinkers as well as good artists.

Here, for example, is her plan for teaching students to draw the human face. Notice how it engages students in close observation and sustained work.

Learning to See: Face Drawing

You will begin by drawing a face and figuring out what you know about the face and the anatomy of the face. Then, in your journal, you will draw parts of a face for two weeks. Below is a schedule. We may move faster or slower in some areas, depending on you.

Day 1—hair, hairline, forehead
Day 2 and 3—eyes
Day 4 and 5—nose
Day 6 and 7—mouth and chin
Day 8—cheeks, ears, and jaw line
Day 9—profiles and hair
Day 10—complete face

Each day you will:

1. Focus on one part of the face.
2. Make a slow, concentrated visual examination, then
3. Take a closer look.
4. Discover something anatomical that you didn't see or know before.
5. Compare parts and location of parts of the face—what's larger or smaller, darker or lighter, smoother or rougher?
6. Organize your visual perceptions in your mind and put them on paper.
7. After the day's drawing, come up with some conclusions or pose some questions—on the back of the paper, write down at least four major discoveries or observations you made about the face or questions or problems you encountered.[6]

We like Tracye's plan because she's an artist and has thought about how artists work. She helps her students work like artists by attending to detail and drawing small pieces of the face; she also helps them think like artists as they discover and compare and organize and make conclusions. Tracye's plan for this series of lessons is highly structured but leaves plenty of room for individual students to find their own way.

Thinking teachers also leave room in their planning to act spontaneously as they follow students' leads. They encourage students to become active participants in decision making and adjust the pace of a lesson according to students' responses and interests. They watch and listen to students, reading those "learner keys" much as a defensive linebacker reads and adjusts to the unfolding of an offensive play. Sometimes the class session turns out to be very different from the one that had been planned or imagined. The thinking teacher is not depressed by these surprises or chagrined by the momentary straying from the lesson plan. Instead she thinks of how she might modify future plans to capitalize on student interest and follow student thinking. That's what Barbara Elmore has learned to do. Listen to this thoughtful teacher talk about how she's changing her biology class:

> Amazingly enough, these kids seem to know how they can best be taught. We have had some eye-opening discussions and decisions made on the basis of open class discussion on how the class should be run by students and teacher alike. Among the decisions we are trying with some success are plans which allow students to work at their own speed and allow some students to pursue their learning in any manner they choose as long as they solve the problem. Of course we still keep a calendar of assignments and allow those students not yet ready to "let go of the side of the pool" to continue doing nightly homework and having frequent due dates, but the kids are involved in choosing these options.[7]

These days, Barbara is proceeding cautiously and making sure that as she opens the class she also provides the amount of structure and support that each student needs. She realizes that students have to grow into the idea of taking more responsibility for their own learning.

Because of a sudden insight or momentary inspiration, thinking teachers sometimes risk acting on intuition alone to scrap a favorite lesson and take an entirely different approach. You've probably taken such risks a few times yourself. Call a time-out in your reading to work through the following exploration.

Exploration

Remember a time in your class when the lesson went so well that it surprised you, or remember a lesson that took on a life of its own. Perhaps you'll think of a Friday that found you still working through your lesson plan for Tuesday—not because you had planned badly, but because students became so involved and were doing so much that they needed the extra time. What do you remember about that lesson or series of lessons? What do you remember about the students? What made you stay with what you were doing? What signals were you reading from the students? How did you feel after that experience? Whom did you talk with about it? If you can't remember such a time as a teacher, think of a similar experience when you were a student.

You'll recall that we used metaphors in chapter 1 as a means of examining our assumptions about minds. In so doing, we pointed to the power of metaphor to help us sort out what we think and to influence what we do. We're convinced that the reforming of our own teaching can be enhanced by using new metaphors for teaching and learning. The metaphors we want to try on you are ours, but we hope they'll help you examine your own beliefs and nudge you toward your own course of action.

ENVIRONMENT ENGINEER

The climate for thinking is critical. In chapter 2, we developed in some detail those classroom conditions that we believe teachers can control and enhance. Environmental quality is an on-going affair, however, and we can't be reminded too often that the thinking teacher continually monitors the quality of the intellectual environment by watching for pollution that results from excess teacher talk, the proliferation of trivial content, a right-answer mentality, and any human insensitivity between even two members of the class. Any of these conditions, if left unattended, can preclude a climate of safety and discourage the risk taking so necessary to the growth of thinkers. The classroom must be a sanctuary where hunting and sniping are not allowed. The intellectual atmosphere itself must favor questions over answers, and the teacher must work hard to be sure that questions are open-ended, response-centered, and in most cases generated by the students themselves.

Consider how Kathleen Brooks did exactly that when she involved her fifth-graders in a unit on the Civil War—a time pretty remote from their Information Age lives. After taking a little time to explore what life was like in America of the 1860s, Kathleen assigned some unorthodox homework: Spend a whole evening living like Abraham Lincoln. (There go TV and compact disks!) The next day, she upped the ante by asking her students to get inside the dilemmas of the Civil War by thinking like Lincoln. No fill-in-the-blanks questions—just "What goes through Lincoln's head as he faces these big questions of war and peace?" Half the class then became Lincoln and the other half a nineteenth-century press corps to interview the President on why he made these historic decisions. As Kathleen reports, her biggest job at this point was to get out of the way and let the kids construct their own versions of history.[8]

The teacher must also adjust the classroom climate by taking time to "talk about it," by altering rules and structures, and by redesigning activities based upon what students say they need for comfort and security. The teacher as environmental engineer is guided by questions such as "What do these kids need to know and be able to do?" and "How is the classroom environment contributing to or hindering the fulfillment of these needs?" But teachers must be sensitive to more than just the "its" of assignments and questions; they must also attend to the "its" of students' minds. Offering them invitations to talk about how their minds work is powerful stuff. Teachers we know say they feel closer to students when they invite them to talk about their minds. And thinking is worth talking about.

Bill Piscella's engineering lab is in a magnet high school for engineering professions, a school-within-a-school in a depressed inner-city neighborhood. If you look out the windows of Bill's classroom, you'll see a typically bleak urban landscape, but inside the room you'll see a veritable gallery of satellite and space-shuttle photos. And there's a lot of paraphernalia—things to flip, spin, and otherwise play with. Listen to Bill's description of one student's moment of discovery in that classroom:

> I passed out the problem, a six-weeks take-home problem about three-dimensional equilibrium. I posed it as a problem of maintaining a satellite in stable (non-rotating) orbit. Trey started writing immediately. Later I watched him flipping a frisbee in the air. "I have the answer!" he hollered suddenly. "Rotational and translational stability are separate."
>
> "Very good," I replied. "Now let's go over to the pictures on the wall of satellites and the space shuttle. The next step is to find the best way to apply what you've discovered so far."
>
> He said, "It's much easier to find out what's wrong than to find out what's right." He started to recount what he had learned from geometry. Then I left him; he was flipping and spinning a triangle in the air.[9]

Beyond all the "shoulds" of a thinking classroom, the bottom line is still a listening teacher, a human being like Bill who attends to what students are trying to say. Careful, reflective listening is not just for counselors. Thinking teachers really tune in to student responses, including the nonverbal, to pursue lines of student reasoning—and then leave the students to flip and spin things.

Environmental control also implies exploring alternatives beyond the four walls of the classroom, bringing outside resources in, and, where possible, taking students to other settings for learning. Field trips have fallen on hard times in many school districts of late, but exploring worlds away from school still offers some of the most irresistible opportunities for young people to use their minds. Try getting away from those four walls yourself and see if you don't have more impetus to get transportation for the kids. If that doesn't work, forget transportation. Follow the lead of Patti Eysaman, who gave each of her second-graders a magnifying glass and sent them off to wriggle around in the schoolyard dirt to see what they could find in the earth—the week before standardized tests, no less![10] Or follow the lead of Kathleen Brooks and bring the outside in. You may not be able to enlist a dancer to help your kids choreograph *The Learning Tree* and put it on video as she did, but you can import your own happening.

Exploration

Check your own environmental engineering by capturing what goes on during one class period. Tape recording is a possibility. Another is to have a colleague keep a running log of who says and does what. As the class is played back to you, see how it squares with your impressions at the time. How much talking did you do? How much did the students do? How many participated? How many and what kinds of questions did you ask? Were there any clues that certain students needed more help or encouragement? Which clues did you pick up on at the time? Which did you miss? Now that you see the class from a little distance, can you think of ways you might have altered the environment? What engineering strategies do you need to work on further?

NAVIGATOR

For the teacher as navigator, lesson plans are not the same old commute day after day, year after year. Those of you who commute to work from some distance have no doubt had the experience of arriving trancelike with little memory of the familiar route. You've been on automatic pilot, acting semiconsciously as you drove. If you've taught for a while, that may be the way you get through some of your classes—teaching material you're so familiar with that your mouth works while your brain rests: cruise-control teaching. The teacher-navigator, on the other hand, sees teaching as trips to familiar destinations by many alternative routes. The road branches, side trips present themselves, rest stops and time-outs become essential. In the thinking classroom, time and pace must become negotiable. Sometimes the entire class will clip along at freeway speeds, covering ground in a fashion that does the curriculum guide proud. At other times, the class dawdles a bit, as if it were on a country road on a Sunday afternoon; as navigator you're more relaxed as well. More often than not, however, students will set individual paces for themselves, and the teacher-navigator may become less a leader and guide and more a trail boss, rounding up strays and protecting lost dogies. The teacher may get to play navigator only when students are so lost they need help in finding alternative routes. In fact, as Nelson Goodman suggests, more often than not the best thing the teacher-navigator can do is initiate inquiry and let students find their own unique routes through problems and solutions.[11] In the thinking teacher's class, getting there is more than half the fun.

Debbie Frontiera, a kindergarten teacher working as a navigator, relates this classroom incident:

> I have tape on my carpet to mark off areas for different purposes—remnants of my classroom management training. The children arrange themselves on the tape. Today I threw out my neatly-taped squares and stripes for group lessons in favor of a U shape. What a clever way to arrange the class on the day I'm teaching that letter, I think to myself. The minute Maria walks in the door, she exclaims, "Oh look! It's a rainbow!" Forget the letter 'U'; a rainbow sounds much better. So before I ever say a word, I am changing my mind again. I tell them to please sit on the new rainbow.[12]

TEACHER AS COAUTHOR

As we said earlier in this chapter, good teachers too often have chosen to work alone behind closed doors or have been forced to do so. There are no doubt powerful reasons why that happens—fear of colleague censure, the roving eyes of rigid administrators, the need for privacy. Yet being a thinking teacher means taking risks, trying new things, discovering new insights. Often, it also means licking wounds after failures. That's one reason every thinking teacher needs a collaborator, someone to share the good, the bad, and the ugly. As a case in point, Dan's friend Martha West finished her doctorate several years ago and returned to her old high school job that fall. She was eager to implement many new-found hypotheses in her temporary classroom out behind the main building. Dan pledged himself as a collaborator, and they enjoyed some time together each week as she shared student responses and her new insights about how the classes were going. Opening her classroom door and talking things through with Dan kept Martha from facing each week alone. In a very real sense, Dan began to coauthor what happened during that most rewarding year.

One of Dan's favorite long-term groups of collaborators is a bunch of wacky Southern California teachers who have been together as a group for seven or eight years. Calling themselves the "University of California at Irvine Thinking and Drinking Group," they have maintained their enthusiasm for the classroom and continued to challenge each other to grow and experiment as teachers through an intense and long-term relationship that is both recreational and intellectual. In Houston, the "Growing Thinkers" program has provided that nurturing, collaborative environment—for Carol as well as for some of the district's best teachers.

One other kind of collaboration is important to mention here. We've been emphasizing your role as leader, mentor, planner. You're the knowledgeable professional in the classroom. But what goes on in the thinking classroom is always coauthored by teacher and students. We urge you to share openly with them what you're trying to do, where you're trying to go. Engage them in discussions about what they think is of value in your class and how they would like to see learning experiences unfold. Involve them directly in planning and evaluating and reshaping what goes on in their own classroom, as Barbara Elmore did in those biology classes.

Kathryn Timme is a veteran chemistry teacher. She's good at what she does and she knows it. She, like many good teachers, was unlikely to risk altering her teaching too much. Yet Kathryn wanted to. Perhaps that's why she sought out the stimulating and supportive atmosphere of the "Growing Thinkers" group. Listen as she describes her reorganizing of an advanced chemistry class:

> My second-year chemistry class of twelve souls has been, in the last two weeks, an open forum of discussion. Keeping them abreast of my explorations into "Growing Thinkers," I have discovered a veritable treasure of enthusiastic followers.
>
> The students are seniors, international in composition: an Egyptian, two Indians, a Vietnamese boat child, a Cambodian, a Dutch girl, and an assortment of Americans from Oklahoma, Chicago, California, and Houston. They all soar right off the map of chemistry achievement.
>
> I have had the option of developing the Chemistry 2 course along traditional lines or initiating a "Topics in Chemistry" course. I began the course as a traditional survey as I have always done. After the first meeting of our "Thinkers" group, I talked to my students. They were overwhelmingly supportive of developing "Topics in Chemistry" with me. I went for it.[13]

Alone, we can quickly find ourselves aliens among colleagues who do not value and support our efforts. With a collaborator, we can find strength to go for it as Kathryn did. With our collaborators, we can smile and say to people who challenge our approaches, "We're working on it: we'll get back to you."

Exploration

Recruit a colleague and do some team planning on a lesson or unit that you find especially challenging or risky. Arrange to observe each other teaching part of that lesson and log what happens. Share your observations. Do a little comparing and contrasting. What did you learn by planning together? By watching each other teach? How might you extend the collaboration?

Here, one caution about collaboration is in order. As some of the veterans of writing projects have found, enthusiasm, new ideas, new energy, and close collaborators can sometimes further alienate you from colleagues. Remember, collaboration is not a closed system. Avoid in-crowd, out-crowd, us-and-them distinctions. Invite others in; without being condescending, tell them what you're trying to do and talk about failures as well as successes. Seek advice from as many different sources as you can. And whatever you do, invite the principal in to see firsthand how a thinking teacher works.

TENTATIVE AND TENACIOUS SCHOLAR

Perhaps the most keenly felt loss for teachers as they age in their jobs is the diminishing sense of being a scholar, a reader, a maker of new personal knowledge. The physical exhaustion and the numbing noise of the factory school tend to leave teachers without the energy or inclination to mind their own scholarship. We hope this book will trigger a renewed sense of intellectual curiosity for you and lead you to teach more from hypotheses and hunches. The thinking teacher overcomes mindlessness by breaking free of preprogrammed, routinized approaches. Sometimes that means beginning a lesson with only the vaguest notion of where it's all going. But, as the teaching and learning proceed, the teacher begins to formulate and test hypotheses. Usually this testing will take the form of an attempt to ground learning and help students make their own sense. The teacher often says, "It seems to me that this is what we're saying." By remaining tentative, the thinking teacher helps students synthesize and construct their own knowledge and then tie that new knowledge to what they already know.

As a scholar, the teacher tinkers with old strategies and old content and tries new strategies and new content. Thinking teachers are never quite satisfied. Dan once overheard Ann Berthoff say, "You know what I like about this teaching business is that you never get it quite right. We won't get bored doing this, because we can keep tinkering with our strategies until they carry us out the door."[14] Maybe Ann would forgive us here if we use her phrase as a call for being more playful about our school lives. We need to lighten up, to confront our predicaments with humor, to cool our jets a bit. Scholars are both serious and playful people who find renewal through laughter and healthy poking of fun at their own ideas.

Of course, becoming a scholar-teacher will involve making some hard choices and breaking some old habits. Most teachers say they don't have time to read and think; they have papers to grade and other lives to lead. The scholar-teacher has to make time for a life of the mind. There must be a window of time each week when the scholar-teacher pulls back from the clamor of the classroom and, like an ascetic, retreats to a weekend monastery without the obligatory bag of ungraded papers. Some things are more important than others; for the thinking teacher, feeding the mind is a top priority.

That's why we keep urging you to carve out time for yourself. It takes time to become self-conscious, to reflect, to monitor, to become aware of our own minds. We like Schön's notion that reflection is a conversation with problems, a conversation that makes use of examples, images, understandings, and actions. If we examine our teaching carefully and in the particular, the situation talks back to us, suggesting answers and possible courses of action.[15] Scholar-teachers aren't made overnight. The transition from automatic teaching to thoughtful teaching is an incremental process that begins with a commitment to introspection and self-evaluation.

Perhaps the best way to close this chapter is for Dan to indulge in a personal example of his struggle to become a thinking teacher. His initial foray into this kind of teaching came more out of exhaustion and boredom than from any higher moral decision to alter the balance of power in his classrooms. Dan was rereading Loren Eiseley's *The Immense Journey,* listening to Jackson Browne's "The Pretender" album, preparing to teach a close observation essay, and quite surprisingly found himself deeply moved by the chapter, "The Secret of Life."[16]

Dan remembered how taken he had been by that same chapter as a college freshman some twenty-six years earlier, how Eiseley's elegant walk in a "sea of rusty stems" had triggered in him a series of semi-existential questions about meaning and truth and how the world worked. Dan wondered aloud how a simple account of a short walk in a vacant field by an aging scholar could still have such impact on him. His thoughts turned to his current group of students, and he wondered if they could find in the piece anything with which to connect. He began class the next day reading from the piece and narrating his own reaction to the reading the night before. To his surprise, there was a hushed and attentive interest in his story about that first encounter with Eiseley. Dan confessed his own uncertainty about whether Eiseley would speak to them, and he asked them to poke around a bit in the piece and use their response journals to explore their own reactions.

He began the next class by asking them to read aloud from their journals. The reading began a bit tentatively with the first student, a serious English major, commenting on Eiseley's metaphors. The discussion picked up momentum, and students read of their affection for this old man and his almost hypnotic "I" voice and his seeming dedication to a quest for answers.

Dan and his students shared their questions and doubts; they talked craft and details and puzzled over a quality in the piece they couldn't quite describe. They finally decided it was an emotional, almost religious quality. They didn't have a name for that. And Dan wondered aloud if they could write a piece like that. He asked them to think about what they would need to know and what abilities they would need and what experiences they would need to try to have an Eiseley-like encounter with the natural world.

As Dan and his students began to coauthor a genuine reading-writing-thinking experience, he could feel the energy level in the class intensify, and students began to offer suggestions: "We need practice seeing." "We need to read accounts of similar experiences by other authors." "We need to work on metaphor." Together they began to sketch out how this inquiry would go. As they talked about what experiences they would need to approach Eiseley's work as insiders, Dan sketched it out on the chalkboard and a winding snakelike set of experiences emerged. He was reminded of Coleridge's notion that the motion of reading "is like the oscillations of a snake."[17] They decided to use the snake as their instructional model and then began to slither their way through a series of experiments. Since they weren't sure where they were going, they had to take frequent breaks to talk to each other about how well things were working and what they were learning. Several years later, Dan encountered the work of Donald Schön and became aware that he and his students had been working their way toward meaning making through reflection, but at the time, he just knew they had to ask a lot of questions. The experience continued some three weeks before Dan realized that they were hopelessly off schedule with the syllabus, but all were deeply involved, and some really fine pieces of writing emerged.

Since the "Growing Thinkers" program in Houston, we have a name for classroom experiences like Dan's Eiseley experience: "Jerry lessons." Kathleen Brooks gave us the name. She reports a special day in her fifth-grade class when Jerry wanted to know if clouds reflected light back and forth continuously. Using a series of five mirrors, the class explored how light is reflected, straying far from the "curriculum" to attend to genuine curiosity. Kathleen says she learned that her goal is to teach more "Jerry lessons."

So this thinking teacher stuff involves renewal of self—attending to our own intellectual growth and curiosity. It involves a commitment to rediscover teaching and learning as an insider and to explore ways of creating contexts in which our students can do exactly the same thing. It involves thinking some new thoughts about our students' minds and giving up some old habits. Harold Rosen has described that false sense of inchargeness, the power that we feel in our own classes, as only a "crumb of power."[18] Thoughtful teaching means sharing that crumb of power with students, and it requires surrendering a substantial portion of the last vestiges of instructorship. It means finding ways to put the knowledge makers in charge of the knowledge making. Perhaps that's why it has taken us decades to begin learning how to become learner-thinkers in our own classrooms.

Exploration

Reflect on your own teaching experiences for a moment or two. Use your journal if you wish to do some jotting. Which of your own habits of teaching might you consider altering? Where do you have the most opportunity or freedom to make changes? To become a thinker and learner in your own classroom, what do you need to do first? What goals do you want to set for yourself?

NOTES

1. Donald A. Schön, *Educating the Reflective Practitioner.* San Francisco: Jossey-Bass Publishers, 1987.
2. Ibid.
3. Frank Newman and Rexford Brown, "Creating Optimal Conditions for Learning." *Educational Horizons* (Summer, 1986).
4. Benjamin Bloom, *Human Characteristics and School Learning.* New York: McGraw-Hill, 1976.
5. Robert J. Sternberg, *Beyond IQ: A Triarchic Theory of Human Intelligence.* New York: Cambridge University Press, 1986.
6. Tracye Wear teaches art at Jones High School in Houston.
7. Barbara Elmore teaches biology at Jones High School in Houston.
8. Kathleen Brooks teaches fifth grade at Kolter Elementary School in Houston.
9. Bill Piscella teaches engineering courses at the High School for Engineering Professions, a magnet school at Booker T. Washington High School in Houston.
10. Patti Eysaman teaches second grade at Forester Elementary School in Houston.
11. Nelson Goodman, *Of Mind and Other Matters.* Cambridge: Harvard University Press, 1986.
12. Debbie Frontiera teaches kindergarten at Pugh Elementary School in Houston.
13. Kathryn Timme teaches chemistry at Robert E. Lee High School in Houston.
14. Ann Berthoff, Breakfast conversation in Irvine, Calif., 1984.
15. See note 2 above.
16. Loren Eiseley, *The Immense Journey.* New York: Random House, 1986.

17. Quoted in Corcoran and Evans, *Readers, Texts, Teachers.* Portsmouth, N.H.: Boynton/Cook Publishers, 1987.
18. Harold Rosen, Speech to International Federation of Teachers of English Conference, in Ottawa, Spring, 1986.

4

The Thinking Student

Fortunately, it is almost impossible to stop the human brain from learning. Action research still abounds in classrooms as students investigate such problems as how to get an "A," how to get away with minimum labor, how to disrupt the teacher, how to be a good student, or how to think of other things while appearing to attend. The challenge for teachers is to harness this rampant brain power.

—Garth Boomer

In faculty lounges and the popular press, there's not much talk about the "rampant brain power" of students. In fact, let's acknowledge that many who hold forth in both places would find the title of this chapter wistful if not downright self-contradictory.

That's all the more reason for a whole chapter on the thinking student. Even those of us who work hardest at being the kind of thinking teacher described in the previous chapter need periodic booster shots to maintain immunity from some of the more virulent and pervasive presuppositions about young minds. We also need to bolster and inform our own beliefs by becoming students of those we teach. In this chapter, we'll talk about how. Before doing so, however, we need to confront those popular presuppositions and see how they constrain rather than harness brain power.

And constrain they do. Let's face it. Most students don't do their best thinking in our classrooms. Maybe they've gotten the same message at school that five-year-old Alexandra got at home—a message that caused her to claim, "I never think at home. My mom doesn't want me to."

There's no better way to bring this harsh reality home than to hear it from a student, especially one of your own. That's why the "Growing Thinkers" group in Houston began its first work session with a videotape of Cody talking about school. Actually, he didn't set out to talk about school, and he certainly wasn't talking to a group of teachers. As an art student in Houston's highly regarded High School for the Performing and Visual Arts, Cody was explaining on camera to his class the images in a recently completed autobiographical painting. Why, a classmate asked, the encircling gray spiral to represent school? That question really got Cody going. School is just like that, he replied. It's dull and monotonous. It "closes in your mind" and "limits the patterns of your thoughts." School is necessary, admitted Cody. It's even okay as long as it doesn't become the most important thing in life. When pressed by his teacher to say what should be most important, Cody puzzled for a long moment before blurting with devastating candor, "Well, I don't know, but not school."

Carol still hasn't confessed to Cody that he was the star of that first seminar on thinking or that he remains a presiding presence as the group continues its ongoing work. Meanwhile, to the twenty-four teachers in that group, this disarming young man is more than a stand-in for the masses of students in their city. No one can forget that Cody went to Houston's "best" schools, where he must have had teachers as caring and well prepared as they consider themselves. If Cody has found his thinking stifled since being "sentenced" to school at age five, what of the other 190,000+ students in the city's 230+ schools? That question hovers in the air each time the group meets. It keeps everyone honest.

Exploration

Ask two or three students you know when and where they do their best thinking. What challenges them to think? What gets in the way?

Jot down responses, especially those that have to do with school. Do these students echo Cody's conclusion that school is not a very good place to think? If it's not, why not?

Finally, ask yourself the same questions you asked those students. How does your own experience square with theirs?

In a backward sort of way, the disquieting question Cody fixed in the minds of the "Growing Thinkers" group keeps participants optimistic as well as honest. At least these teachers are convinced that the problem doesn't lie in those they teach. When it comes to students, their beliefs are distilled in that first drop at the bottom of the cup talked about in the last chapter. Students do indeed have minds—good minds. Very few have to make do with brains that folks in the automotive trade would call lemons. The problem is not one of defective students. It's one of defective schools. And the more we can learn about where schools go wrong, the better our chances for setting things right.

For starters, let's clear the air of at least two myths that get in the way of our seeing students as the thinkers they are.

THE MONOLITHIC IQ

This myth has it that overall intelligence can be measured by an hour's worth of short-answer questions—typically questions about word meanings, the interpretation of graphics, and the solution of verbal and mathematical problems—and then expressed as a single whole number. That number, a standardized score derived from the number of right answers on the test, shows how an individual's mental ability compares to that of a larger population of similar age. The assumption is that "intelligence" is a single faculty that can be brought to bear on any situation that requires thinking and learning.

Despite such gross oversimplification of mental ability, IQ tests have a good track record as predictors of academic achievement. And why shouldn't they? After all, those short-answer questions sample the abilities most important to success in school. No wonder scores have traditionally been used with such great confidence to sort students as if they were laundry. Toss the sub-80s into Special Education, the 81s–100s into Basic classes, the low-100s into the densely populated Regular program, and those who reach more rarified heights onto the top of a small heap reserved for the Gifted and Talented.

Fortunately, such sorting is becoming less blatant as the shortcomings of IQ tests become more public. Yet students continue to be victimized as they are sorted and subsorted according to estimated mental prowess and then instructed accordingly. As a somewhat dated case in point, we can't resist telling a true story that has haunted Carol for years. It happened in the elementary school her own children attended and started with an exceptional class of first-graders. As the principal proudly told her, all ninety or so students entering first grade that year had been given an IQ test as children in that school always were. Twenty-nine had scored 115 or above. That was enough for a whole class of bright to ultra-bright six-year-olds.

Since one of Carol's sons was in that class, she followed it closely for the next six years. On the Tuesday after Labor Day, these "exceptional" six-year-olds were subsorted into reading groups, again according to IQ. By February, those in the top group were borrowing second-grade basals while those in the bottom group were plodding laboriously through the first reader and stacks of "reinforcement" worksheets. Month by month and year by year, the gap widened and not just in reading. Expectations for that lowest group became more and more depressed, and learning tasks became more and more rote as achievement records were communicated from one grade level to the next. Most of the children in that bottom group were dropped back into a lower-track class, but twenty-two who had started first grade in that original class of twenty-nine completed sixth grade in the same school. By then, four members of the original class had been retained.

To us, that's a classic illustration of Pygmalion in the classroom. It's also an indictment of the insidious way teachers line up students along that poisonous bell-shaped curve according to assumed mental ability. Take any segment of that general ability curve and you'll have a low end. Too many teachers adjust their highly relative expectations accordingly, and students pick right up on it. They stop believing in themselves as thinkers, and the tired-but-true saga of self-fulfilling prophecy plays itself out yet again.

Emerging theories of intelligence can help us move beyond those prevailing one-dimensional views of mental ability. An excellent starting point is Howard Gardner's *Frames of Mind,* which pluralizes the concept of intelligence. Gardner argues persuasively against the myth of single-mindedness and lays out seven "intellectual regions in which human beings have the potential for solid advancement"—less elegantly put, seven different ways people can be smart. Though Gardner acknowledges that what he calls multiple intelligences "typically work in [such] harmony that their autonomy may be invisible," he argues that each has its own core of abilities and its own developmental trajectory. It follows that different human beings develop different intellectual profiles. A person with highly developed linguistic abilities, for example, may be mediocre or worse in music or logical-mathematical reasoning. Neither does excelling in what Gardner calls "interpersonal" intelligence guarantee exceptional "spatial" or "bodily-kinesthetic," or even "*intra*personal" intelligence. Yet within each of us, the various intelligences interact, and the result is a unique blend of mental abilities in which the total may well be greater than the sum of its parts.[1]

Just think how different classrooms would be if teachers worked as hard to accommodate diversity of mind as many now work to accommodate alleged deficiency. Consider the possibilities of helping students know their own "frames of mind" and capitalize upon the kinds of thinking and learning they do best. We are watching with interest at least two major efforts to explore these possibilities. One is Project SPECTRUM, undertaken by Gardner and his colleague David Feldman at a Massachusetts preschool. Here, children's strengths and interests are assessed as children play naturally within a rich setting offering a variety of choices. Over the course of the year, researchers construct a "spectrum profile" of each child and an accompanying set of concrete suggestions for what might be done at home, in school, and in the community, to help that child develop and extend his or her combination of abilities.[2] The second effort—at this writing, in its third year—is a public magnet school in Indianapolis. The Key School, founded through the efforts of eight elementary school teachers, is committed to giving all seven intelligences equal emphasis. The intent of the school's highly interdisciplinary program is to identify and to capitalize upon students' intellectual strengths and in the process create new and richer models of curriculum and assessment.[3]

Such undertakings as Project SPECTRUM and the Key School should eventually help us develop better ways of finding students' strengths rather than just forcing them to wear some one-size-fits-all number called an IQ. Evidence abounds that students labeled Gifted and Talented have no monopoly on strengths. We recently learned of a study in which forty-eight children were each tested on nineteen measures of giftedness; when results were analyzed, 92 percent of the children ranked among the top five of the forty-eight on at least one of those measures.[4] Being more keenly aware of what students do well should enable us not only to build on strengths but also to help students overcome weaknesses by bridging from an intelligence that is relatively strong. Certainly, working against the grain of a learner's abilities is futile. As Gardner puts it, "If Einstein had been raised in Mozart's house, I don't think he would have turned into another Mozart."[5]

Robert Sternberg would undoubtedly agree. A Yale professor of psychology who, in his own words, always "stunk on IQ tests," Sternberg has spent years studying the nature and nurture of intelligence. His theory is different from Gardner's, but it shares some fundamental assumptions. The first is reflected in the title Sternberg chose for his book, *Beyond IQ*.[6] In that book, he lays out a three-part theory of intelligence, which he obligingly oversimplified for the popular press: "Basically what I've said is there are different ways to be smart, but ultimately what you want to do is take the components [the mental processes themselves], apply them to your experience, and use them to adapt to, select, and shape your environment. That is the Triarchic theory of intelligence."[7]

To Sternberg, then, the ability to deal with everyday experience and to shape rather than be shaped by a situation are elements of intelligence itself. It's that kind of real-world intelligence he would like to see developed in the classroom. There, also, students should be taught to capitalize on strengths and minimize weaknesses; they should learn a sort of "mental self-management."

We can't have it both ways. If there is indeed more than one way to be smart, so much for the monolithic IQ. Let's relegate it to history where it will do no further harm.

THE HUMAN INFORMATION PROCESSOR

This second myth holds that minds, like computers, can be programmed with bits of information which, if properly processed, are stored in long-term memory for retrieval upon demand. We've touched on this view of mind in previous chapters, but return to it now because it can so distort the way we see students. To us, this myth of mind-as-computer seems little more than a high-tech version of student-as-tabula-rasa. Computer circuits, like wax tablets, are essentially blank. They're also passive—neutral processors of whatever information someone chooses to "input."

It's the myth of the human information processor that accounts for much of the mismatch Frank Smith has been warning us about for years— the reality of the human brain and the conflicting reality of most classrooms. (The latter is described in the title of Smith's book, *Insult to Intelligence*.) The crux of the matter is this: Even the youngest minds are neither blank nor passive. To the contrary, children are natural thinkers and learners. They've been making meaning all their lives and come to school ready to learn anything that makes sense.[8] Unfortunately too many classroom tasks make little sense. That's because learning is so often stripped of context and reduced to artificial fragments that can be packaged commercially, then dispensed ("input") and tested ("retrieved") one small piece at a time.

Again, no one knows this better than our more savvy students. Phil, an Advanced Placement student, sums up the result: "In many classes," he writes, "I feel that I'm not really thinking but rather feeding back information already fed into my mind." He goes on to describe what thinking he does in school as programmed: *"Yes sir, no sir, 2 BEEP. Mixobidean, dorian, penatonic BEEP, BEEP. BEEP."*[9]

Maybe Melissa, a Houston second-grader taught by Linda Range,[10] will escape the myth Phil has been subjected to. So far, she must have; otherwise, she wouldn't have written, "Thinking helps you to liarne about the stuf that you do." Right now, at least, so does Lue Williams' eighth-grade Special Education student who sees thinking as "putting your mind in charge before you act."[11] John Dewey, who always insisted on viewing the mind as a verb, would like that. So would Margaret Donaldson, who argues so compellingly that "children, even quite young ones, will not let themselves be passively led. They will actively invent and discover, using what we tell them as a starting point."[12]

With that, we'd like to dismiss the myth of the human information processor, but it shows no signs of receding into the pages of educational history. In fact, it's gaining rather than losing converts. That's why we'll keep chipping away at it as we have since the early pages of this book.

GOING TO THE SOURCE

It's no coincidence that students have big speaking parts in this chapter. We're increasingly drawn to our primary sources on students as thinkers. More and more, we're listening to those student thinkers whether they say what we want to hear or not.

Yet we must acknowledge that it isn't easy to tune in on students. It's hard enough to see them—really see them. Those of us who have taught five or six classes of thirty to thirty-five students a day know how hard it is just to hold onto 175 names and keep the faces that go with them from blurring into anonymity.

We're finding that students themselves can help in this getting-to-know-you business. With a little prompting and practice in the kind of reflection discussed earlier in this book, students can provide tracings of their own mental paths through different kinds of tasks. These tracings not only help us get to know our students as thinkers; they help those students get to know themselves.

Consider this example. Kathryn Timme involves her second-year chemistry students in a great deal of problem solving. Recently, she has tried to help these advanced students become more aware of their own ways of thinking. After one particularly challenging task, she asked each student to think back through the process followed in solving the problem and list the steps in his or her thinking.

Although all students had solved the same problem, the analyses of how they had done so were quite divergent. Ida, for example, began her analysis like this:

1. I read the problem.
2. Then I tried to remember where to find it explained in the book.
3. I studied the explanation in the book.
4. I started to work in the same way as I saw in the book.

Omprahash, an Indian student, began in an entirely different way:

1. I analyzed the information given in the problem and defined in my mind exactly what was to be found.
2. I associated facts given in the problem with things I remembered from previous experience.
3. I organized what I remembered and applied it to the new problem.

There's nothing anonymous about these two minds. Even on paper, they look as different as Ida and Omprahash must look in person. So it is with other students in the class. Not only does their teacher have new insight into the different ways they work through a chemistry problem; she has some ideas about where to start in helping them develop as thinkers.[13]

Kathryn doesn't need a cognitive psychologist to give her all those ideas. Like most of us, she's been observing thinkers all her life. She can tell a good thinker from one who's not so good. From observing good thinkers and being one herself, she knows the strengths that need to be nurtured and extended in her students. So do you.

Exploration

Take a moment to recall the very best thinker you've ever had in class. Picture that student in action in your own classroom. What approaches to mental tasks set that student apart? As you identify characteristic attributes and actions of this exceptional student, jot them down in a column headed Good Thinker.

Now recall a student that seemed to you the very opposite, someone who really struggled with the kind of thinking required in your class. Picture that student in action. Again, as you identify characteristic traits and behaviors, jot them down—this time in a second column headed Not-So-Good Thinker.

If you have colleagues who are working through this book or would be interested in trying this activity, compare your lists with theirs. Talk over recollections and find commonalities in the traits and behaviors listed in each column.

Each time we try this activity in a workshop, we're struck with the amount of agreement on what distinguishes good thinkers from those who aren't so good. The list in Table 4.1, compiled by a group of teachers and principals during a weekend retreat, is typical. Even more striking is the way such lists are confirmed by the work of theorists and researchers as well as students themselves.[14]

Though it takes an endless variety of forms, we all seem to know good thinking when we see it. That should improve our chances for helping more students do it.

We can do some useful generalizing about how minds work, as we just have, but we need to remember that there's really no such thing as a generic thinker. As Jerome Bruner reminds us, keeping that point in mind is crucial to the way we see students as well as to the way we work with them. It's indeed our mental model of the learner—of the thinking student—that

TABLE 4.1   Profiles of Thinkers

THE GOOD THINKER	THE NOT-SO-GOOD THINKER
Puts new information in own terms	Memorizes without understanding
Tolerates ambiguity	Rushes to find certainty
Looks for alternatives	Is satisfied with first attempts
Perseveres	Gives up
Is deliberate and reflective, willing to search extensively	Is hasty and impulsive; relies on "one-shot" answers
Solves problems	Is overwhelmed by problems
Makes independent decisions	Goes along with the group
Exercises initiative, self-direction	Needs frequent prodding
Takes risks; learns from errors	Is afraid of being wrong
Shows flexibility and imagination	Stays with familiar
Considers different points of view	Sees situation or problem only one way
Uses past knowledge and experience	Sees information in isolation; makes few connections
Transfers knowledge and skills to new situations	Seldom sees or makes application without being told
Can explain what's being learned, why, and how	Follows passively with little attention to purpose of task
Understands own best ways of learning and working	Knows only what appears on report card

shapes our work as teachers. We can't be reminded too often that our model must not be "fixed but various" or that "the appreciation of variety is what makes the practice of education something more than a scripted exercise in cultural rigidity."[15]

STUDENT AS STORY

We won't miss the variety Bruner talks about if we think of our students as life-stories on legs. Even a three-year-old has quite a history—more accurately, *is* quite a history—a walking, talking narrative-in-progress. In importance, that point is right up there with differing profiles of intellectual abilities. We're increasingly convinced that there's no better way to see students as thinkers than to unfold their stories and engage them in story making. Even if this idea strikes you as unlikely, we hope you'll follow it with us and see where it leads.

Let's start with a story that gets right to the heart of the matter. It's a favorite of biologist-cyberneticist Gregory Bateson and concerns a man who wants to find out about the human mind. Curiously enough—to some of us, at least—this man turned to his computer for answers. As Bateson tells it, the man asked his corporate mainframe a bottom-line question: "Do you compute that you will ever think like a human being?" The machine then set to work to analyze its own computational habits. After a long but electronically eventful pause, the machine printed out its answer: "THAT REMINDS ME OF A STORY."[16]

It doesn't take a computer to tell us that people think in stories. We know this firsthand from the narratives running through our heads each day as we recollect previous experiences, make meaning of the moment, and daydream about what might happen in the future. These narratives are more than a stringing together of events that have happened, are happening, or might happen to us. Events are just raw material. We ourselves construct the narratives that become part of our life-stories. In a very real sense, those life-stories are our lives—indeed our very identities.

That's why we believe there's no better way to see students as thinkers than to unfold their stories. Neurologist Oliver Sacks would undoubtedly agree. He points out that biologically and physiologically, we are not so different from each other. Believing that it is historically, as narratives, that each of us is unique, Sacks goes after each patient's story. That story, he's convinced, provides a window into the one-of-a-kind mind that continues to create the story from a continual stream of perceptions, feelings, thoughts, actions, and spoken narratives.[17]

We need to underscore that last means of creation. Spoken as well as written narratives are central to the way we make meaning and integrate it into our life-stories—which is to say, into ourselves. When we describe an experience in language, our narrative is more than "a straightforward copy of the events to be recounted"—to borrow a phrase from Barthes.[18] We select from an unremitting flow of events what we consider worth attending to; we arrange what we have chosen into a meaningful sequence; we interpret motives and consequence; we attach significance. In short, we make meanings. And it is the narrative itself that is the making.

Elementary teachers, especially those who work with children in the primary grades, may well wonder at this point what all the fuss is about. If you teach small children, you unfold their stories every day. You also collaborate in their story-making. Chances are it's unthinkable for you to do otherwise.

Rosalind Roberson provides a case in point. After taking her kindergarteners to the Museum of Natural Science for a special show on dinosaurs, Rosalind encouraged them to make their own dinosaur storybooks.[19] Here's the story dictated by Alexandra, whom you may remember as the five-year-old who claims never to think because her mom doesn't want her to:

The Dinosaur Went to Town

Once there was a Brontosaurus named Alexandra. One
day I went to explore the world around Houston. In Houston,
there were many high buildings. I didn't know what to think of
it.

I went to McDonald's for lunch. The people were afraid.
But I only wanted a plant.

Then I looked around the building and saw a tree. It's hard
to find a meal in the city.

The End.

Even without the surprisingly elaborate crayon drawings with which
Alexandra filled every page of her book, Rosalind has a great deal to unfold.
She's interested, of course, in what Alexandra has learned about dinosaurs—
for example, not just that they were big enough to appear menacing but also
that the brontosaurus was herbivorous. Yet she's even more interested in
what this story shows about Alexandra as a young thinker—her readiness
(despite pronoun lapses) to assume another point of view, her playful sense
of humor, and much more.

At the same time, Rosalind knows that Alexandra not only likes to
make stories but needs to. Spoken and written narratives give her a way of
bringing new experiences (like going to the museum) and new concepts
(like dinosaurs) into the flow of her life-story, into the narrative-in-progress
that is, in a very real sense, Alexandra herself.

When it comes to seeing students as stories and engaging them in story making, our colleagues in elementary school can teach the rest of us a lot.
Certainly children shouldn't be "weaned" from stories as they are from mid-
morning snacks and afternoon naps. The extent to which schools have done
so alarms British educator Harold Rosen, as it should alarm us. For good
reason, Rosen calls for us as teachers to deepen our own understanding of
the life-long educational power of narrative and to resist "menacing efforts to
install Gradgrind's progeny in the classroom with the thin gruel of drill
based on floating bits of language."[20]

Maybe Bruner can help dispel any lingering skepticism about the place
of narrative thinking in the upper grades—say through graduate school and
beyond. In his book *Actual Minds, Possible Worlds,* Bruner argues that there
are only two modes of thought: narrative and paradigmatic (logico-scientific).
These two natural ways of thinking, he insists, are not at odds. To the contrary, they are complementary; one feeds the other.[21]

Consider this live example: Katie Ekstrom's eleventh-graders seemed
to have trouble connecting with any piece of American literature that pre-
dates MTV. Certainly they showed no inclination to generalize about the past

from what they read, to sort out the Puritans from the Transcendentalists. Rather than push her students further into the mustier pages of the anthology, Katie put the books away and launched a project that culminated in the making of family heritage scrapbooks.

Veronica's scrapbook will give you the flavor of that two-week project. Bound into covers decorated with the Segura and Galvan coats of arms, the book begins with a frontispiece of maps tracing the movement of both families as they worked their way from Idaho to Texas as migrant field hands over two generations. Chapters illustrated with drawings, copies of old letters and documents, and family photographs detail what Veronica could find out about the lives and deaths of her great-grandparents and what she knows more directly about her grandparents. Other chapters chronicle the meeting of her parents at a dance in Eagle Pass, Texas; the wedding that followed a year later; the move to Houston; the opening of the family paint-and-body shop; the births of Veronica, her brother, and two sisters; and the recent move into a new home. The book concludes with a time line upon which Veronica has projected the future she would like to have for herself. All told, the scrapbook spans more than a hundred years.

You can see what the project had in it for Veronica. By collecting and connecting the fragments of her family's past, she collected herself. By constructing a family history, she gave new meaning to her own. In the process, she made new connections with the past and learned at least a little about how to interpret its stories and artifacts. Will this experience in narrative thinking guarantee an understanding of John Smith's journals and Nathaniel Hawthorne's short stories? Probably not, but it's a start. Does it give Katie new insight into Veronica and her classmates as thinking students—as life-stories on legs? You bet.[22]

Without claiming that stories are as much a staple in other subjects as they are in English, we would like to applaud the math teachers we know who have students write their own story problems. We've even heard about math stories being written to illustrate geometric and algebraic concepts. Laboratory experiments and research projects can also be cast as stories—indeed often are. In later chapters we'll suggest having students write "biographies" of various products and projects as a means of reflecting on their own mental processes. Certainly there's no shortage of possibilities for the kind of thinking we all seem to do most naturally.

Exploration

If you're now teaching a class of your own, look back over recent work collected from your students. (If not, you may need to borrow a class.) Find a piece that reflects narrative thinking. What does the piece tell you about the student behind it and the way the student thinks? What do you suppose the student got from this little experience in story-making?

Now think about what you plan to teach the next few weeks. What opportunities do you see to capitalize on the power of narrative thinking?

As we wind down this chapter on the thinking student, maybe we should give Margaret Donaldson the last word. "Human children," she says in summary, "are beings of richly varied possibilities, and they are beings with a potential for guiding their own growth in the end. They can learn to be conscious of the powers of their own minds and decide to what ends they will use them. However, they cannot do this without help—or at least it would be a long, slow business, and few would make much headway."[23]

That's why the next few chapters will explore strategies thinking teachers can use to help thinking students along the way.

NOTES

1. Howard Gardner, *Frames of Mind*. New York: Basic Books, 1984.
2. Howard Gardner, "Developing the Spectrum of Human Intelligences." *Harvard Educational Review* (May, 1987).
3. Lynn Olson, "Children 'Flourish' Here." *Education Week* (January 7, 1988).
4. Feldman and Bratton study cited by Elliot Eisner in "What's Worth Teaching?" Keynote address at annual conference of Association for Supervision and Curriculum Development, March 1990.
5. Art Levine, "Child Prodigies." *Houston Post* (1986).
6. Robert J. Sternberg, *Beyond IQ: A Triarchic Theory of Human Intelligence*. New York: Cambridge University Press, 1985.
7. Robert J. Trotter, "Beyond IQ." *Houston Chronicle* (October 6, 1986).
8. Frank Smith, *Insult to Intelligence*. New York: Arbor House, 1986.
9. In 1987, Phil was a student in Martha West's Advanced Placement English class at Parkview High School in Gwinnett County, Georgia.
10. Linda Range is a teacher and magnet program coordinator at Scroggins Elementary School in Houston.
11. Lue Williams is a social studies teacher at Sharpstown Middle School in Houston.
12. Margaret Donaldson, *Children's Minds*. New York, W.W. Norton and Company, 1978.
13. Kathryn Timme is a chemistry teacher at Robert E. Lee High School in Houston.
14. Allan A. Glatthorn and Jonathan Baron, "The Good Thinker." *Developing Minds: A Resource Book for Teaching Thinking*. Arthur Costa (ed). Alexandria: Association for Supervision and Curriculum Development, 1985.
15. Jerome Bruner, "Models of the Learner." *Educational Horizons* (Summer, 1986).
16. Gregory Bateson, *Mind and Nature: A Necessary Unity*. New York: Bantam, 1980.

17. Oliver Sacks, *The Man Who Mistook His Wife for a Hat and Other Clinical Tales.* New York: Summit Books, 1985.
18. Roland Barthes, *The Pleasure of the Text.* London: Cape, 1976.
19. Until 1989, Rosalind Roberson was a kindergarten teacher at Oak Forest Elementary School in Houston.
20. Harold Rosen, *Stories and Meanings.* Kettering, Northhamptonshire: National Association for the Teaching of English.
21. Jerome Bruner, *Actual Minds, Possible Worlds.* Cambridge: Harvard University Press, 1986.
22. In 1986, Veronica was a student in Katie Ekstrom's junior English class at Milby High School in Houston.
23. See note 13 above.

UNIT III
Particular Matters

The next four chapters get down to particulars by exploring various contexts for thinking. In each of these chapters, we invite you to enter into and interact with a world that may at first seem a little alien to you and to the students we hope you'll invite to come with you. These worlds are those of the artist, the naturalist, the inventor, and the anthropologist. Certainly these are not the only intellectual worlds worth exploring. We chose them because they represent a broad range of thinking and because they engage different frames of mind. As you work through the chapters that follow, we hope that you'll begin to feel at home in these contexts, as we're beginning to do.

The point is not to make you or your students into amateur artists, naturalists, inventors, or anthropologists—though that might not be so bad when you consider the original meaning of the word amateur, "an inexperienced lover." Most of us do our best thinking when we care about what we're doing. That's one reason what happens in school needs to matter, both to us and to our students. And in the business of developing thinking, that's where context becomes crucial.

Creating a context for thinking is a way of making the "world" hold together for a while, giving the mind time to click on and begin to make sense of things. These next four chapters represent our attempt to create contexts for thinking and to ground that thinking in particular worlds that provide a rich, stimulating environment for the making of meaning. We think of these contexts as intellectual habitats. Like all habitats, they're defined by boundaries and shaped by structures. Yet within each structure, there's plenty of room for thinkers to construct their own meaning.

As these chapters invite you to explore different contexts for your own thinking, they'll also suggest ways you can sponsor such intellectual inquiry for your students. As in previous chapters, we continue to insist that thinking students are nurtured best by thinking teachers, teachers who attend to their own intellectual development and then let the excitement of that growth spill over into their classrooms.

Because we want this experience to be more than a textbook exercise, and because we believe that personal knowledge is the basis of all other kinds of knowledge, indulge us in a little suggestion making and helpful hinting that may intensify this experience for you a bit.

- Don't rush. Don't even keep to a schedule if you don't have to. Linger over experiences that interest you. Branch out into explorations of your own. Dip into related readings. Make this your own leisurely trip through each habitat for thinking.

- Relax, give up, enter in as fully as you can. Enter each context as a participant, not a spectator. Don't hesitate to try new ways of making meaning. Experience the world of the artist, the naturalist, the inventor, and the anthropologist firsthand even if that means doing things you've never done before.

- Create your own version of these chapters through reflective jottings. Talk back to us as you read. Jot down ideas sparked by ours. Reflect on paper about your own experiences as you work through activities. Be on the lookout for news stories and TV features on thinkers in each context. Build classroom experiences around community resources.

- Take a friend along on the trip. Share experiences in each context with at least one colleague, and do lots of collaborative thinking along the way. As you try out ideas in your classroom, compare notes and confer on possibilities for your next foray into that particular context for thinking.

5

Thinking Like an Artist

Art bids us touch and taste and hear and see the world
... and shrinks from all that is of the brain only.

—W. B. Yeats

The artist creates possible worlds through the
metaphoric transformation of the ordinary and the
conventionally 'given.'

—Jerome Bruner

To some, the arts may seem a curious habitat for thinking. Aren't artists still caricatured as wild-eyed, impractical people whose creativity is just a matter of inspiration? What can teachers and students possibly learn from them? In most schools, aren't art programs still considered frills—the first to go when budget knives must be wielded? In all schools, aren't art courses still electives rather than graduation requirements? Besides, aren't artists born rather than made in school? Talent can't be taught, can it?

At the end of this chapter, we will revisit those questions. For the moment, we ask that you suspend them and pursue a contrary line of inquiry.

For more than a decade now, Houston has offered students the opportunity to pursue special interests in magnet schools. Very early, it became obvious that something special seemed to be happening in magnet schools for the arts. Test scores, a limited but ubiquitous yardstick of academic achievement, were and continue to be consistently higher than expected in magnet schools for the arts—indeed higher than in other magnet schools where students also represent a demographic cross-section of the city. Why? Why, especially, does the High School for Visual and Performing Arts continue to have the greatest proportionate number of National Merit Scholarship finalists of any school in Houston? Could this high academic achievement have something to do with the power of the arts themselves?

Could experience in the arts somehow help students learn how to learn? Could such experience nurture thinking itself?

Let's leave those questions hanging and go on to another case in point. Here, let's begin with Betty Edwards, Professor of Art at California State University, whose books such as *Drawing on the Artist Within*[1] occupy shelves in as many offices as classrooms and whose teaching now takes her to more corporations than schools. Why have companies like IBM and General Electric sought out this art teacher to conduct workshops on creativity for their executives? And here in Texas, why is it that computer magnate H. Ross Perot reportedly never hires an executive without some musical training? Again, could such phenomena have something to do with the arts themselves? Could experience in the arts somehow nurture creativity and the other kinds of productive thinking that make businesses go?

Once more, let's leave those questions hanging and turn to still another case in point—this one from the even more unlikely world of medicine inhabited by famed neurologist Oliver Sacks, whose book *The Man Who Mistook His Wife for a Hat* is filled with case studies of flawed or damaged people who have been transformed by immersion in one of the arts. What of the victims of Parkinson's disease who get stuck in one position and cannot move until some music, internal or external, seems to liberate them? What of the stroke victim who could not speak but nevertheless sang? What of the severely retarded young woman who excelled at acting because, as she put it, "I come apart, I unravel, unless there's a design." In talking about the importance of design, could this young woman have hit upon at least one empowering feature of the arts? Could Sacks be onto something big when he explains it this way?

> The power of music, narrative, and drama is of the greatest practical and theoretical importance.... What we see fundamentally is the power of music to organize.... And in drama there is still more—there is the power of role to give organization, to confer while it lasts, an entire personality. The power to perform, to play, to be, seems to be a "given" in human life, in a way which has nothing to do with intellectual differences.[2]

Before checking out such possibilities for yourself, take a moment to think about the context you are about to enter. Think first about what it is *not*—an exclusive territory open only to the gifted few whose works may be viewed by the rest of us only from a respectful distance in museums, concert halls, and theaters. The real world of the arts is not so rarefied. It's a world of getting close and personal, of opening the senses, of taking risks, of doing and undoing. Potters get their hands dirty, dancers perspire, musicians practice the same passage over and over, and actors struggle to get a line just right. In a very real sense, artists are the ultimate constructivists, and the making of meaning is messy business. It's only the finished painting that is elegantly framed, only the polished performance of a play that ends to applause.

As teachers, especially as aspiring teachers of thinking, we are primarily interested in the arts as a habitat rich in opportunities to make meaning. That's why the next section offers a series of invitations to *make* rather than merely admire art.

EXPLORING INSIDE OUT

It's no coincidence that the activities in this section feature choices. In the first place, building in choices gives us a chance to stress right up front how crucial choices are in the making of art. Since the artist quite literally makes his or her own world in every piece of art, possibilities are almost infinite. More pragmatically, we want to suggest a broad range of ways you might go about exploring the terrain of the artist, and we know that you probably don't have time right now to try them all. Finally, we like the idea of giving you plenty of room to tailor this book to your own preferences.

Exploration

Betty Edwards insists that everyone can draw. Furthermore, drawing is a good way to make thinking visible. For these reasons, drawing provides a good starting point for thinking like an artist. Choose one of the activities below to help you begin:

OPTION I

Take a moment to mull over this advice from a Chinese master: "It is not enough to consider the carp alone. But to consider the reed against which he brushes each morning, the stone under which he hides and the ripple of the water as he searches for food. The carp is an entity which has the power to affect and be affected by the world."

Equip yourself with some unlined paper and a sharp pencil.

   A. If you have a goldfish bowl or an aquarium handy at home or school, settle yourself comfortably and spend a few minutes looking closely at a particular fish and its watery environment.

   • Then, working fast, make fish-shaped marks on your paper. ("Draw" your fish or just make lines that to you equal fish.)

   • Next, make marks that look to you like the water in which the fish lives.

- Finally, make a single stroke that suggests the movement of the swimming fish.

B. If you have no aquarium handy, arrange a quick table-top still life—perhaps a few pieces of fruit (no bowl), some seashells, or a twig with acorns or pinecones. Spend a few minutes looking closely at your arrangement, perhaps from several different vantage points. Then settle into a position that offers a perspective you like.

  - Remember that how skillfully you draw is not the point; just relax and quickly make marks on your paper to stand for the objects in your arrangement.

  - Then make marks to show the space in the arrangement that is *not* the objects.

OPTION II

One way to see things in new ways and draw more freely is to draw upside down. To try out that process, you will need a line drawing done by someone else—perhaps a favorite cartoon figure or a simple drawing from an art book. You will also need some typing paper or plain bond and sharp pencil. Find a quiet place to work where no one will interrupt you.

- Turn the drawing you have chosen to "copy" upside down. Try not to right it in your head. The point is to make the subject strange—ideally, unrecognized.

- Starting anywhere you wish, start reproducing the drawing on your own paper. You may wish to work systematically from side to side or top to bottom, or you may wish to skip around. That's fine as long as you keep relationships among lines clear in your mind. Also, you may reproduce the drawing larger, smaller, or actual size.

- As you draw, clear your thoughts of anything negative, such as "I never could draw." Don't try to draw an object. Just concentrate on relationships—at what angle one line joins another, how far a particular curve is from the top of the paper, the shape of each open space.

- When you have finished, turn your own drawing and then the original right side up. Aren't you surprised how good you are?

Regardless of whether you tried Option I or Option II, spend a few minutes reflecting in your journal about what you have just done. Consider these questions:

- Did you try something for the very first time? What? How did it make you feel?

- At what point did you become most involved?

- What seemed to you easiest and most natural? What seemed hardest? Do you have any idea why?
- What kinds of thinking did you do?

During the activity you just completed, did you notice that you relied as much on your eyes as on your hands—perhaps more? That's why sculptor Barbara Hepworth liked to speak of having an "intelligent eye" to guide a "thinking hand." That's why observation lies at the core of all the arts and why the habitat of the artist is such a good place to sharpen perception.

Exploration

Now that you've loosened up your drawing hand, choose one of these options for exploring what happens when you put images on paper more than one way—when you not only look but look again and again.

OPTION I

Cut a cabbage, a green pepper, an artichoke, an onion, or a pomegranate in half horizontally. Study the exposed cross-section. Trace its patterns with your finger.
- Using a large piece of drawing paper or several pieces of typing paper taped together from the back, make a poster-size drawing of that pattern.
- On a smaller sheet of paper, draw the pattern the size of a postage stamp.

OPTION II

Find a three-dimensional object that interests you. Possibilities include a single flower, such as a chrysanthemum, an unusual rock, a piece of driftwood, even a box or bottle. Draw that object at least twice.
Possibilities:
- Draw it fast, using simple strokes to suggest line and shape.

  Then draw it more deliberately, filling in detail. You might even use dots, crosshatching, or shading for a three-dimensional effect.
- Draw it with charcoal or a soft lead pencil.

  Then draw it with pastel sticks or colored pencils or pens.
- Draw it from one perspective.

  Then draw it from another.

When you have completed the activity of your choice, do a little reflecting with pen or pencil. For starters:

- Look at the two drawings you made of a single object. How are they different? More importantly, how was the "seeing" reflected in each different?
- Do you like one drawing better than the other? Why? Which was easier to do? Which was more interesting? Why?
- What other drawings of that same object might you do? What new perspective or medium or technique might challenge you to perceive it in a totally different way?
- This time out, what different kinds of thinking did you do, or in what ways did you extend the thinking you did previously?

Are you beginning to get at least an inkling of why Piccasso undertook literally hundreds of drawings as studies before he painted *Guernica?* Why Georgia O'Keeffe painted the same closed door of her Abiquiu house repeatedly over a period of more than fifteen years? Looking and looking again is a way of life in the artist's environment.

Of course, artists do a great deal more than look. As Yeats reminds us, they touch and taste and hear as well as see the world. In "shrinking from all that is of the brain only,"[3] artists use their bodies as well as their minds. The result is total involvement. Artists fully attuned to their art bring to it an almost laser-like concentration. The next Exploration should help you at least sample such all-out involvement for yourself by trying your hand at dance, music, or drama.

Exploration

If at all feasible, recruit a friend or two to work through one or more of these activities with you. Find a private place to work, and assemble in advance any materials you may need. Relax and leave any self-consciousness at the door. Tell that critic in your head to take a time-out. Really let yourself go.

DANCE

Find yourself some floor space with no obstacles. Then think of some everyday movement—climbing stairs, running, hanging up clothes, even walking. Start that movement, gradually exaggerating it until it starts to become stylized. Move around your space, noticing the stylized pattern of movement. Build on that pattern, perhaps by repeating parts of it and setting it to some imaginary rhythm. Try slowing the pattern down or speeding it up. Make your whole body move. Imagine being on a stage, and think how your "dance" must look to an audience. Keep going for several minutes, experimenting with variations as they occur to you.

MUSIC

Cut out or draw several different shapes, all simple. Then think how each shape might *sound* and find some way of making that sound. The many possibilities include notes that you sing or make by striking some glass or metal object, hand claps and finger snaps, humming or hissing sounds. Just try to make each sound represent the shape as you "hear" it. Number or otherwise arrange your shapes and try "playing" them in sequence. Then try repeating one or more sounds to create a more interesting pattern. Experiment with volume and rhythm as you "play" your shapes several times.

DRAMA

Make up a sentence or two that could be intended and interpreted different ways in different situations—for example, "What a surprise. I never expected to see you here." Invent several scenarios in which your lines might be spoken. Visualize each scenario in detail, with you playing the character who speaks those lines. Assume each character and deliver the lines as you interpret them in that particular situation. As you do so, use gestures and facial expressions that enrich each interpretation.

Again, take a moment to sort out your thoughts and feelings as you created a small piece of dance, music, or drama. If you shared this experience with a friend, compare notes. If not, reflect solo in your journal.

- Did you try anything for the first time—at least for the first time in several years? If so, how did it feel?
- At what point—if at all—did you feel yourself letting go and trying things that seemed a little risky? At what point did you feel that you had hit upon something worth repeating or extending?
- What kinds of thinking went into creating your dance, music, or drama?

Although you have barely begun to make this context your own, we hope that you're beginning to see its possibilities as an intellectual habitat, both for yourself and your students. Certainly Carol's group of "Growing Thinkers" in Houston does. In reflecting on a variety of intellectual excursions during their year together, more than half of the charter participants rated their foray into the arts as the most powerful of all, both in terms of personal growth and in terms of influence upon their classrooms.

Later, you may wish to return to this section and try some Explorations you haven't yet tried. Better yet, you may wish to embark on some excursions of your own, preferably taking at least one friend along. Meanwhile, let's switch perspectives and see what we can learn from other thinkers in the world of the arts.

EXPLORING OUTSIDE IN

Fortunately, many artists are willing—even eager—to talk about their work. What they report about their own creative processes gives us at least a small window into the artist's mind. Talking to painters, sculptors, musicians, dancers, actors, and other artists we know can help us learn from the experts. So can reading the words of artists we would like to know.

In the activities that follow, you'll sample what a variety of creators have to say about their own ways of creating. As you work through these activities, be on the lookout for other such accounts featured in television interviews, magazine articles, and newspapers. Clip copies in your journal for comparison with those offered below and with your own experiences in the making of meaning through art.

Exploration

Consider these accounts of getting started on a piece, all from Vera John-Steiner's *Notebooks of the Mind*.[4]

From film director Frederico Fellini:

> The richest part of a preparation for a movie is the choice of faces, heads, that is the human landscape. During this period I am capable of seeing five or six thousand faces that suggest the comportment of my characters to me, their personalities, and even the cadence of the film. I would be tempted to say that this is the most serious part of my work.

From composer Aaron Copland:

> Most composers keep a notebook in which they put down germinal ideas that occur to them, thinking "Well, we'll work on that later." You can't pick the moment when you are going to have ideas. It picks you. ...
>
> You play one measure or two, the beginning of a general

idea. And then you play it over and over and over again. It is as if you are testing, where will this take me? Now is that true at all?

From choreographer Eliot Feld:

> I do one piece at a time, one gets involved in the specifics. Suddenly, when you go through a million specifics, you go away and say, "My God, there is really an art to it." It forms a whole, but you don't know how it happens.

Do a little guided reflecting on these accounts.

- What common threads do you find in how these three artists begin a new piece of work? Do you find any differences?

- Think of some piece of creative work you have done. In what ways did your experience of getting started square with that of Fellini, Copland, and Feld?

- Considering what you have experienced as well as what you have read and heard from artists, what do you consider most important during the early stages of the creative process? What kinds of thinking are most involved?

As you see, different people describe the creative process in different ways. They use different words to talk about it. Yet any talk about the beginnings of that process echoes some common themes. In one way or another, almost all artists speak of being very open and very tentative ("You can't pick the moment when you're going to have ideas."… "Where will this take me?"… "You don't know how it happens.") All work from abundance ("five or six thousand faces"…"a million specifics"). Perhaps that's why Fellini finds this beginning stage the richest in the entire creative process. Most agree that it can't be rushed, that it often requires what David Perkins,[5] Betty Edwards,[6] and others call a period of incubation.

Though we divide the process of creating into stages for convenient reference, that process is actually seamless. Gradually, almost imperceptibly, a piece of work moves beyond its beginnings. As the artist makes one choice after another, the piece begins to take shape.

Exploration

Consider these three accounts of how a work takes shape, the first two from *Notebooks of the Mind*[7] and the third from Laurie Lisle's biography of Georgia O'Keeffe.[8]

Aaron Copland again:

> It is a delicate operation to put fresh and unconventional harmonies to well-known melodies without spoiling their natural-ness. Moreover, for an orchestral score, one must expand, contract, rearrange, and superimpose the bare tunes themselves, giving them something of one's own touch.

Choreographer Anna Sokolow:

> True form comes from reducing reality to its essential shape, as Cezanne did with the apple. In the hands of the artist, form is essential, exciting. There is nothing superfluous, because the artist has stripped his work to the bare essentials. And an audience responds to this purity, this inevitability of form, which is beauty.

Artist Georgia O'Keeffe:

> Details are confusing. It is only by selection, by elimination, by emphasis that we get at the real meaning of things.

In your journal, reflect on what you have just read. These questions may help you get started:

- What common themes do you find in these accounts of what a musician, a choreographer, and a visual artist consider crucial in working out a piece of art? What different themes?
- To what in your own experience can you relate these accounts?
- What seems to you most important at this stage of the process? What kinds of thinking come most actively into play?

Again, these accounts reverberate with echoes. Selectivity lies at the heart of the creative process. Abundance gives way to the findings of form. There's a lot of arranging and rearranging, always in a way that bears the unique imprint of the artist. At this more rigorous and deliberate stage, choices are conscious but the work is delicate. Critical judgments are made, but almost always those judgments are the artist's own. Cynthia Word, a dancer, always stresses that last point:

> When I'm in the germinating process, and even way into my rehearsal process, I don't even talk about it to anyone else. I keep it. I think there's something to be said about keeping an emerging piece contained. It keeps its power when you kind of let it cook.
>
> Only around a week from the date of a performance, I will ask two or three people whom I know and trust and respect to come and look at my dance.

Though Cynthia insists that criticism be held at bay until a piece has its own strength and integrity, she values, even depends on it. Most artists do. After describing the way he met and became friends with Aaron Copland, fellow composer Leonard Bernstein says this:

> And thereafter, whenever I came to New York, I went to Aaron's. I would bring him my own music for criticism ... and he would say "This is just pure Scriabin. You've got to get that out of your head and start fresh.... This is good; these two bars are good. Take these two bars and start from there."[9]

Throughout the creative process—from the moment an idea is conceived and begins to germinate until the moment the piece is declared finished—artists seem to share one distinguishing characteristic. They are intense about their own work. Artist Judy Chicago puts it this way:

> When I look back, I wonder how I was able to make my paintings. In part, I managed to paint because I had a desire as strong as the desire for food and sex, to push through, to make an image that signified.[10]

According to David Perkins, who has studied creativity extensively, such intensity is intrinsically rather than extrinsically fueled. Artists work hard because they *want* to. They seldom need to be prodded by such external motivators as money or recognition.[11] Indeed, Mihaly Csikszentmilhalyi and others who have studied artists as models of intrinsic motivation have found that even the eventual product of such intent concentration and effort seems incidental. To artists, it's not what's done but the process of doing—of becoming totally absorbed in making art, often to the point of being lost in time—that seems to be its own reward.[12] To some degree the artist's inner capacity for intensity is present even in the novice—probably in some of your own students.

Exploration

As unobtrusively as possible, visit an art lab, orchestra practice, dance class, or drama rehearsal in which some of your students are engaged. Pay close attention to what they do and what they say. How closely do they seem to be concentrating on the task at hand? For how long? What kinds of questions do they (or don't they) ask as compared to your class? How do they seem to know what to practice or what to do next? Record key observations in your journal. You may also wish to talk to the art, music, dance, or drama teacher in charge and see what else you can learn about how one or more of your students work in this context.

Chances are good that you just got an entirely new view of at least one of your students. That point crystalizes a question that has probably been gathering in your mind as you have worked through this chapter: Since I don't teach one of the arts, what does all of this have to do with me?

That's a fair question, one that we'll address in the next section. For the moment, however, we'd like you to join us in summing up the richness of the arts as a context for developing perception, selectivity, and a whole host of other creative and critical abilities. We hope you've learned firsthand and been further convinced by secondary sources—artists themselves—that American painter Ben Shahn is right when he claims that the arts draw on "the wholeness of thinking and feeling within an individual."[13]

We hope that you're as struck as we continue to be by the power of the arts to develop certain dispositions of mind, especially a laser-like concentration and what Dennie Wolf calls "plain old stick-to-itiveness."[14] Both stem at least in part from that intrinsic motivation Perkins and Csikszentmihalyi talk about. Then there's that disposition to take risks, an absolute necessity when a new idea or some aesthetic sense pushes the artist beyond the frontiers of certainty.[15] Certainly, those are dispositions of mind well worth transporting to contexts other than the arts.

But are these dispositions of mind and the mental processes engaged and nurtured by the arts *portable?* We think so, but we'd like you to think through the big "SO WHAT?" question for yourself.

SO WHAT?

First, let's make it clear what the point is *not*. The point is not to do superficially artsy things in mathematics, science, English, social studies, et al. For example, the point is not to dance the DNA in biology class.

The challenge of helping students think like artists in other subjects is far greater. To engage the artists' processes of thinking and to develop the artists' dispositions of mind, we must dig beneath the activity level to the mental operations that activity develops. The question then becomes: How can I help students develop those powerful ways of thinking within the framework of my own subject?

Often, of course, that question leads to classroom tasks that look a lot like art. Take, for example, the episode already described in chapter 2 in which Grace Beam used a quotation from "The Sea Within Us" to introduce a science unit.[16] You'll recall that students were asked to read the passage about how diffusion supports the cells that compose our bodies and then to complete a one-line assignment: Draw a picture of what this means to you.

This drawing assignment looks a lot like art, but not gratuitously so. It engages students in thinking actively through the text and making those thoughts visible. That process involves a lot of visualizing, imagining, selecting, and forming. It requires involvement of hand as well as eye. It takes close attention to detail. Since drawings are to be shared with peers and must depict what the passage means to each student personally, the activity also involves risk—especially to seventh-graders, who hate being different.

Years ago, visiting the High School for Visual and Performing Arts, Carol was charmed but a little puzzled by another case in point—a student wordlessly *dancing* Tom Wolfe's essay "Las Vegas." Although at the time she wondered if such indulgence even by a dance student didn't border on the frivolous use of English class time, she swears to this day that she could follow that nonverbal rendition of the familiar essay without a single prompt. Now she sees what the teacher must have seen at the time. And she hadn't even read this book!

Recreating an essay in dance requires, first off, a keenly perceptive reading of that essay. Not only did this young dancer have to understand the meaning of Wolfe's words; she had to catch their tone and their cadence, then translate the whole into a wordless medium with nothing more—or less—than her own body and some carefully chosen recorded music. That's a rather challenging exercise in composition, indeed in the making of meaning.

By now, you can no doubt infer for yourself the purpose and processes underlying a few other classroom scenarios. Consider, for example, what happened when Kathryn Timme[17] had her Advanced Placement Chemistry students image a copper ion, then imagine *being* that ion as it becomes part of a chemical reaction. Consider also what happened during the longer projects in which Marla Stanley[18] had her seventh-grade math students design their own Escher-like posters and Janis Giles[19] had her six-graders invent holiday ornaments based on repetition of one geometric figure.

Though you may wish to pirate some of these ideas for Monday morning's lesson plan, they aren't really offered for that purpose. The intent is to suggest the range of possibilities for transporting the intellectual empowerment implicit in the arts to other subjects. It's also to spark ideas about how you might do so in your own classroom.

It's no coincidence that the teachers who created the lessons described above had all participated in the kind of inside-out explorations you engaged in earlier in this chapter. Several had been fortunate enough to participate also in at least one three-week summer workshop in aesthetic education. As participants in the Texas Institute for Arts in Education—modeled after New York's Lincoln Center Institute—those teachers still coauthor with teaching artists at least ten units a semester and team teach them in their own classrooms.

This background seems worth mentioning for at least two reasons. The first derives from what we've said so often throughout this book: only a thinking teacher can develop thinking students. Certainly it follows that only a teacher who's at home in the intellectual habitat of the arts can transport the kind of thinking that thrives there into other subjects. The second reason has to do within another of our major premises: collaboration enhances thinking. That's why we keep encouraging you to take a friend along on your forays into the arts. That's also why we suggest a collaborator—even though you probably don't have your very own teaching artist—as you begin to translate all this arts business into reality in your own classroom.

Exploration

Think of a unit you plan to teach soon in your subject. Think also of the mental abilities you want your students to engage and develop as they work through this unit—abilities that you have found to be developed through the arts and that you know to be important ways of thinking and learning in the subject you teach.

- Jot down those thinking processes.

- Recall your own experiences as a maker of art and perhaps some of the classroom episodes described above. Would some version of any of these activities have possibilities for developing the thinking processes you want to work on? How might those activities look within the framework of your subject? How might they be focused on the subject-area concepts and processes the unit is intended to teach? Jot down as many ideas as you can. Go for abundance.

- Recruit a colleague—ideally an art, music, drama, or dance teacher in your school—to talk over the possibilities you just listed. (Most fine arts teachers appreciate having their value acknowledged and welcome the opportunity to join the instructional mainstream.) As you test ideas on your new partner, jot down others that may be triggered. Eventually, you will want to focus on extending one or two activities. Invite your new partner to team teach—or at least observe and participate in—the lesson(s) you develop.

- Complete your lesson plans, allowing plenty of time for students to help plan the task you devise. Build those plans into the unit.

- As you teach the unit, collect student products or make notes on "performances." Also take notes on what students write and say about their own processes of making art.

- As soon as possible, sift through your notes and take another look at any student products. Use your journal to reflect on your attempt to incorporate the artist's ways of thinking into your own subject. What went well? What would you do differently next time? How well did the thinking processes you sought to develop transfer? What ideas do you have for other lessons capitalizing upon the power of the arts to develop thinking and learning in your subject?

By now, you see why we're so convinced that thinking processes can indeed be transported from the context of the arts to other subjects. What must not be lost in transit is the power of the arts to make thinking visible, audible, indeed palpable. It is this *making* we're after.

Though we want students, like artists, to make things mainly for the making, we need to remember that artists eventually perform or exhibit what they have made. In the habitat of the artist, performances and exhibitions abound. Work is celebrated as well as shared. Perhaps it is partly the resulting sense of closure and satisfaction that helps prepare an artist to embark upon still another sustained effort.

Students need that same sense of satisfaction. That's why we like to display student work and feature student performances in our own classes. These exhibitions and performances do more than let students shine for their peers. Consider these unsolicited comments by students after they had performed a self-composed dance for their classmates at Dede Middle School in Houston: "I like the feeling of being in control of myself. I've never felt this way before." "Working on this dance was really hard, and I'm glad we learned to stay with it until we got it right." "At first, I was afraid the other kids would laugh, but they really liked our dance. I didn't know I could take that big a risk and feel so good about doing it." Such satisfaction in having made something worth sharing can only contribute to that intrinsic motivation so crucial to thinking and learning.

Exploration

To focus on "exhibition" of learning, try having students keep portfolios of their own work in all subjects. Periodically, arrange for an exhibition of the work each student considers his or her best. Arrange interviews so that parents, teachers or other students can ask about how the work was done and what was learned in the process.

Before leaving this matter of exhibits and performances, let us recant—or at least qualify—something we said earlier. In stressing the arts as a context for *making,* we dismissed all too lightly the fact that they're also a context for seeing, hearing, and experiencing what others have made. It would be shortsighted indeed not to exploit the richness of museums, theaters, and concert halls in which we and our students can experience the Arts with a capital *A*.

Actually, the roles of maker and audience are complementary rather than contradictory. The more we engage in the process of making, the more we see in what others have made. Surely no one experiences a Rodin more fully than another sculptor, or a Mozart more fully than another composer. By experiencing the work of others, we extend possibilities for our own.

That's one reason local music teachers have for several years spearheaded a project culminating in a full concert by the Houston Symphony in at least two school auditoriums. This project is worth mentioning for another reason: It is interdisciplinary. Teachers of English, social studies, science, and other subjects work with the music teacher to plan lessons around the preliminary visits of symphony musicians, who not only perform but also talk informally with students. Though the project includes a "curriculum" of sorts, these teachers work much as you did during your last Exploration to focus on the creative thinking of the artist and the critical thinking of the audience, and to bring those kinds of thinking to bear on the subject they teach.

Like the many Houston teachers who've planned field trips and lessons around such special exhibitions as *I, Leonardo* and a recent festival of Hispanic art, you'll want to be on the alert for such opportunities in your community. Even if such resources aren't available where you live, public television often brings them right into your students' homes.

The community can be counted on to foster engagement in the arts because, in a very real sense, the arts help bind people into a community. Perkins's observation about creativity both underscores and extends this point: "Creativity is at once both an intensely individual act of expression and a bridge that links us to the rest of the universe."[20] Perhaps it's upon this point that we should rest our case for the infusion of thinking like an artist across the curriculum.

LOOKING BACK

As promised, let's revisit those skeptical questions we posed—then put on hold—at the beginning of this chapter. Let's start with: What can we possibly learn from artists when the popular wisdom has them pegged as such a disheveled, undisciplined lot?

By this time, we hope you'll join us in answering this question with a resounding "Plenty!" We also hope you'll join us in rejecting the spurious premise built into it. As we've seen, artists are anything *but* disorganized and undisciplined. Organizing, composing, forming are central to making, and making is what artists do. True, they remain open and tentative as they work. They extend their imaginations in the most literal sense of the word—by creating new images. The act of creating new images involves a lot of trial and error, doing and undoing, arranging and rearranging. That's where all that sustained effort, all that "stick-to-itiveness," indeed all that discipline comes in. These processes and dispositions of mind are indeed well worth learning.

If more educators understood how (even *that*) artists really *think,* the arts would move from the fringes to the center of schooling. That's about all we know to say in response to the second set of skeptical questions—those questions about why, if the arts are such a powerful context for thinking, schools consider them (in the words of Carol's Art Director friend) "nothing more than a ruffle around the academic program." There's some evidence that change is in the air, but that's a tempting tangent we won't pursue here.

What, then, about inspiration and talent? You can't teach either one, can you? Aren't only the chosen few imbued with talent and visited by inspiration?

Yes … but no. Of course, some artists are gifted with exceptional talent. And of course, artists sometimes experience those sudden, sometimes inexplicable flashes we call *inspiration.* But even the most gifted artist will tell you that the making of art involves processes far more fundamental and far less mysterious—processes like those discussed in this chapter. For the exceptionally talented, these processes can be refined; for the rest of us, they can be learned.

That's why it's worth reminding ourselves that the making or performing of any piece of art has as its first step the formulation of an interesting, sometimes difficult problem. Both formulating and working out this problem flex the imagination. That's no small point. As John Barrell points out, imagination may indeed underlie all learning since all academic subjects are founded upon the ability of human beings to call to mind—to imagine—what is not present.[21] Furthermore, from the very beginning, the process of making a piece of art requires the closest observation, attention to detail, sensitivity to pattern, and an acute sense of form. It requires discrimination, selectivity, and critical judgment.

To us, that's what it means to think like an artist. With Rudolf Arnheim, we deplore the way "the arts have been prevented in our time from fulfilling their most important function by being honored too much … from having been lifted out of the context of daily life, exiled by exultation, imprisoned in awe-inspiring treasure houses."[22] The challenge is to make this rich intellectual habitat more accessible and to borrow from it freely to develop our own thinking as we nurture that of our students.

NOTES

1. Betty Edwards, *Drawing on the Artist Within.* New York: Simon and Schuster, 1986.

2. Oliver Sacks, *The Man Who Mistook His Wife for a Hat and Other Clinical Tales.* New York: Summit Books, 1985.

3. Vera John-Steiner, *Notebooks of the Mind: Explorations of Thinking.* Albuquerque: University of New Mexico Press, 1985.

4. Ibid.

5. D. N. Perkins, *The Mind's Best Work.* Cambridge: Harvard University Press, 1981.

6. See note 1 above.

7. See note 3 above.

8. Laurie Lisle, *Portrait of an Artist: A Biography of Georgia O'Keeffe.* Albuquerque: University of New Mexico Press, 1986.

9. See note 3 above.

10. See note 3 above.

11. Stefi Weisburd, "The Spark: Personal Testimonies on Creativity." Science News, November 1987.

12. Mihaly Csikszentmihalyi and Isabella Selega Csikszentmihalyi, *Optimal Experience: Psychological Studies of Flow in Consciousness.* New York: Cambridge University Press, 1988.

13. See note 3 above.

14. Dennie Wolf, et al., *The Arts Go to School.* New York: American Council for the Arts, 1983.

15. See note 11 above.

16. Grace Beam is a science teacher at Pershing Middle School in Houston.

17. Kathryn Timme is a chemistry teacher at Robert E. Lee High School in Houston.

18. Marla Stanley is a mathematics teacher at Pershing Middle School in Houston.

19. Janis Giles is a mathematics teacher at Paul Revere Middle School in Houston.

20. See note 5 above.

21. John Barell, *Playgrounds of Our Minds.* New York: Teachers College, Columbia University, 1980.

22. Rudolf Arnheim, *Visual Thinking.* Berkeley: University of California Press, 1969.

6

Thinking Like
a Naturalist

I have always maintained that if you looked closely
enough, you could see the wind—the dim, hardly
made-out, fine debris fleeing high in the air.
                    —Stewart Edward White

In nature you lose consciousness of your own
separate existence, you blend with the landscape,
and you become part and parcel of nature.
                              —John Muir

Perhaps the title of this chapter should have been "Seeing Like a
Naturalist." Certainly naturalists spend much of their time looking, observing, and—we're convinced—making more of what they see than casual observers do. Naturalists use their sightings to interrogate the environment:
"What's going on here?" "What's happening?" Naturalists connect their observations to make sense of complicated interrelationships. They see details
of the environment through a particular frame of mind.

Earlier in this book, we noted in the literature of cognitive psychology,
especially in the work of Ulrich Neisser,[1] an emphasis upon the role of perception in the development of intellect. It's Neisser's contention that perception is the fundamental cognitive act, and that when seeing and hearing are
coupled with memory, a set of constructive processes is set in motion that
allow the thinker to make sense of new experiences in terms of previous
knowledge. Thinking and perceiving, then, are interdependent; with them
we literally make up our world. As Rudolf Arnheim offers, "Perception
would be useless without thinking; thinking without perception would have
nothing to think about."[2] Examining the way naturalists think about the
world may provide good models of thinkers who go beyond the world of vision to connect and integrate perceptions. In this chapter, we focus on such
thinkers. In exploring this territory of mind, we offer invitations for you and

your students to expand your own repertoires for seeing and to sharpen your own perception of the natural world around you.

Ask any group of teachers to evaluate their students' powers of observation, and you'll get a chorus of "They're terrible at it." Blame it on television; blame it on lack of imagination; blame it on indifference. Whatever the cause, most teachers agree that students are not careful observers. Whether you direct their attention to a poem or a microscope, a map or a gerbil, you'll likely be disappointed at what they notice.

We doubt that this failing to see is completely the students' fault. Too often when they're asked to "look" in school, they're supposed to see the things teachers have already seen or claim to have seen. (Sometimes teachers don't "see" things either.) You may remember those dreadful microscope tests in biology, when what you really saw instead of an amoeba were your own eyelashes; or that esoteric poem in the literature book, where instead of all kinds of metaphoric magic, all you saw was a poem about a duck. If students are to expand their perceiving repertoires, we must offer them real opportunities to discover. We must offer them more open-ended invitations to see for themselves. In this chapter, we hope to convince you that the natural world, because it isn't owned by schools and because it offers limitless possibilities for individual and personal seeings, provides an ideal context in which to develop students' perceptions.

Beyond offering invitations for students to see for themselves, however, we must encourage them to test those perceptions among other see-ers and to connect those perceptions to their general knowledge of how the world works. Perception is individual, but growth in perceiving comes through collaborative testing of personal perceptions and the building of frameworks and structures. I see things you don't. You organize your notices in a way I hadn't thought of. Together, we teach each other new possibilities for using perceptions to construct meanings.

Of course, all of us see far more of the world than we're aware of. Data pours into our brains through all of our senses. Much of that incoming data doesn't register at a conscious level and goes unnoticed. We can only make use of our observations if we attend to them, notice them, record them somehow. Developing our students into first-rate thinkers requires that we deal very directly with their inattention and that we design many opportunities for students to observe and to notice with more precision.

ENTERING THE NATURALIST'S WORLD

The naturalist's world is not a foreign world; it's the habitat of humanity. Even so, you may feel a bit alien in your own environment if you haven't spent much time there. Becoming "part and parcel" of the natural world, as Muir suggests, will require more than watching a few Jacques Cousteau specials on public television. But as Gerald Durrell points out, you're already well equipped for this kind of work.

> One of the great things about being a naturalist is that you are born with all your basic equipment—your eyes, your ears, and the senses of smell, taste, and touch. All these, of course, can be added to by man-made tools, but a naturalist should be capable of enjoying his/her craft naked on a desert island. Never forget that, while taking a deep interest in the world outside, you are yourself walking around inside a miracle. The human body is an extraordinary piece of adaptation and you should learn to use it in the same way as you learn to use the other adjuncts of the naturalist—the hand lens, binoculars, camera and so on.[3]

This chapter will lead you to explore the natural world using your own unique equipment. Experiencing the natural world keenly is not a gift for the few or the private property of unusually talented people. To the contrary, it draws upon abilities that reside within all of us by virtue of our humanity, abilities which can be honed to teach us about our minds as well as our world.

Don't be surprised if you feel a little awkward when you begin the explorations suggested in this chapter. At the outset, expect a few groans from your students. Naturalists, like artists, have a reputation for being a little quirky, but even the most cynical among us hang onto a little of the naturalist. Maybe some of your students are hunters; some of them are surfers or bikers; some work on farms or vacation in national parks. They may not tell you immediately, but we suspect that most of them have at one time or another remarked on an unusually beautiful sunset. Some of them have paused to watch mist rising from a small pond or the stark beauty of a bird etched against a darkening sky. Even the most insensitive of our students have felt some kinship with the earth as they sniffed the air after a long-delayed rain. We are earth's creatures, and even if we live and work in the concrete canyons of the cities, we haven't grown completely immune to the power of the natural world to reclaim us.

EXPLORING INSIDE OUT

So where do you begin the exploration? How do you get started? Before you book the bus for a field trip to the nature center, we suggest some conditioning exercises. To explore the world of the naturalist, you and your students must get in shape. You can't be "just arm-chair explorers of content—just readers of maps and takers of tests—but participants in the sport of orienteering. [You] must solve controlled and manageable versions of problems facing the experts."[4] That's where this naturalist context wants to take you, beyond vicarious experience to "orienteering." Toward that end, the following explorations are offered as ways to get the perceptual juices flowing.

Exploration

A part of seeing well is developing the receptivity for seeing, preparing your eyes to notice and your mind to receive images and to make connections. These connections help us understand what we see and make sense of things we haven't seen before. We see and make meanings based upon what we've already seen and stored in memory. This exploration is designed to help you explore images stored in your mind, some of which may be long forgotten.

IMAGING—MIND PICTURES

This is a simple exploration of your mind's ability to store and replay pictures of past experiences with nature. What's most remarkable about imaging is how much detail shows up with that image and how feelings have become wrapped around these details. The image that fills our mind's eye is the evidence of our earlier and long forgotten observing. This exploration asks you to play a few old "mind movies" in your head to see how much detail you can recall.

After reading each of the following prompts, close your eyes and relax. Let your mind travel. See what kinds of pictures your mind can make. Have your journal handy so that you can record your mind pictures after each prompt.

A Place

Remember a special place, a family place, a secret place, a lonely place, a quiet place, a place of your own. Travel there in your mind and observe as many details as you can.

A Season

Remember a season that brings particular feelings. Remember the details of that season and remember the feelings.

A Natural Thing

Remember some gift of nature, something small perhaps, something growing, or something now dead and still; a talisman you have kept, or something which appears new each season.

An Experience in Nature

Remember a time when you were frightened or a time when you were deeply moved or a time that you experienced some strong emotion because of something in nature.

Use your journal to record as many details and as many feelings as you can recall. Notice how details and feelings intermingle.

- What surprised you about your mind pictures?
- Which images were strongest and most detailed?
- Why do you think those images were so strong?
- What problems did you encounter as you imaged? Why was that?
- Would you say that the mind remembers what the eye sees or were your images more than what you actually saw?

SEEING THE FAMILIAR

Arnheim, in his book *Visual Thinking,*[5] makes an important distinction between passive reception—just seeing—and active perceiving—visual thinking.

> As I open my eyes, I find myself surrounded by a given world: the sky with its clouds, the moving waters of the lake, the windswept dunes, the window, my study, my desk, my body, all this resembles the retinal projection in one respect, namely, it is given. It exists by itself without my having done anything noticeable to produce it. But is this awareness of the world all there is to perception? Is it even its essence? By no means. That given world is only the scene on which the most characteristic aspects of perception takes place. Through that world roams the glance, directed by attention, focusing the narrow range of sharpest vision now on this, now on that spot, following the flight of a distant sea gull, scanning a tree to explore its shape. This eminently active performance is what is truly meant by visual perception.

The next exploration challenges you to practice a little visual thinking by forcing yourself to see a familiar scene in a new way.

Exploration

Position yourself in a familiar place, maybe your desk at school or your retreat at home. If you commute along a routine path to work, you might even try seeing that trip with new eyes. Shift your gaze consciously to look for the novel. Notice things you've missed through habit. If you're the imaginative type, try seeing the familiar as though you were an alien marveling and puzzling at each "new" sight.

Whatever your vantage point, try shifting your perspective to view the familiar from a different angle. (Don't try this in your car.) Go beyond the "given world." Roam, scan, focus. Practice "active" looking. See what you can discover by consciously trying to break old ways of seeing.

In your journal, list and perhaps describe some of the discoveries you made as you practiced reseeing the familiar.

USING THE MACRO AND MICRO LENSES

Tom Brown, in his marvelous book *Tom Brown's Field Guide to Nature Observation and Tracking,* teaches his students to practice what he calls "spatter vision."[6] Spatter vision (SV) is a deliberate attempt to "spread out" your field of vision. Instead of focusing your vision on particular objects, you soften your eyes and try to take in everything in a wide half-circle. The next exploration invites you to try this special way of seeing.

Exploration

You may want to take Brown's suggestion and position yourself on a hillside or in a wide field to practice SV. Notice movement; take in as much of the scene as you can without moving your head. Continue your SV practice for several minutes at a time. Take breaks to jot down your observations.

Now shift from using your wide-angle lens to your closeup lens. Select a specific object and zero in to see just that object. It may be helpful to frame the selected spot to keep your eyes from wandering. You may construct a simple frame by tearing a one-inch square hole in a sheet of paper. Look through that hole as though it were a camera lens. Notice details and notice how looking closeup differs from SV.

In your journal, reflect on what you've just seen. What new things did you discover—or rediscover—in the familiar?

SEEING LIKE AN ARTIST

Here's another of Brown's ideas for seeing: Look at a familiar scene but blot out the context in which you usually see it. Blur your eyes and forget the objects themselves. Look for shadows, shapes, textures, colors, and lighting. Try to stay away from naming and identifying specific objects. Soften your seeing and see with an impressionist's eyes. The point of this exercise, like that of the previous ones, is to get us thinking about the way we ordinarily view the world and what we miss by habitual ways of seeing. The next activity invites you to extend that thinking by *drawing* what you see. As noted in chapter 5, drawing can be particularly helpful in training the eye to focus and to notice detail. We also like drawing because it slows the act of seeing, allowing time for new insights to develop.

Exploration

ZEN DRAWING

This activity will get you out-of-doors and into the natural world. Don't be put off by its name. Even if you're a child of the sixties, you may be a little vague about the Zen of things, but don't let that bother you. We've adapted this activity from *Zen and the Art of Motorcycle Maintenance,*[7] and it's designed to help you understand and "know" an object more completely by drawing it.

You'll need your journal, of course, and several pens and pencils. Take your time and relax. Push other things out of your way. Get your mind right. Notice that this is a three-part exploration. Don't skip any of the parts.

The Search

Don't be in a big hurry. Look around for a while. Consider possibilities. Return to a familiar spot or explore new territory. Find a place where you are comfortable.

1. Find something natural, living or dead. Something small.
2. Cozy up to it. Examine it carefully.

The Seeing

3. Record details about the immediate surroundings, such as weather, light, and wind. Describe where this thing is located relative to other things.
4. Draw your objects slowly and carefully. Make your drawing large. Take your time. Get to know the object by drawing it.
5. List as many details of your object as you can notice. Note color, texture, smell, sound.

The Thinking

6. See if you can develop some metaphors for your item. What else is it like? Look at it with an imaginative eye. What else could it be?

7. Talk to your object in your journal. Tell it whatever you think it needs to know. Or tell it how you're feeling. Just a monologue. Or let it talk to you.
8. What are you wondering about as you look at your object? Record any questions you have at this point. Muse on the object.
9. Once you have completed this exploration and have returned to your usual habitat, reflect a bit on the experience. How did you feel entering the experience? Did you feel differently as you completed it? Did you notice your mind at work during the experience? What observations can you make about your feeling-thinking, thinking-feeling connections? Did the experience provide any surprises for you?

JOURNALS AND LOGS

Before you become a full-fledged apprentice naturalist, one other kind of practice is in order: log-keeping. An important part of experiencing and interacting with nature is keeping some record of the experiences so that they can be pondered and shared with others. Because we hope this journal will be something more than a factual record, we'd like you to try this approach: Use a double-entry format that looks something like this:

Observations: Details, Facts, Sightings	Thoughts, Feelings, Memories

Since keeping this kind of journal is not as easy as it appears, it might be worthwhile to get started by practicing on familiar things around your desk. Remember to use both your micro and your macro lenses. Get close to things, very close. Practice enough to get comfortable with the rather awkward problem of interrupting observations to jot. Try to find the rhythm that works best for you. Try mixing in sketches and drawings with your written observations. Practice awhile with a double-entry log. If you find that it doesn't work for you, develop your own style of note keeping.

WALKS

Naturalists are passionate about their walks. Most say they do their best thinking while on the move. We hope by now you're ready to try out your naturalist's eyes and legs. If you've done your homework, these walks should go well. One note of caution from Henry David Thoreau: "If you are ready to leave father and mother, and brother and sister, and wife and child and friends, and never see them again—if you have paid your debts, and made your will, and settled all your affairs, and are a free man, then you are ready for a walk."[8] Of course, you may not pass all of Thoreau's criteria for walking, but we thought we at least ought to warn you.

In planning your nature walks, feel free to free-lance and devise any explorations in nature that you wish. You may already have favorite spots, or you may have already spent time pouring over maps and trail guides to plan an outdoor excursion. You're in charge here, but let us suggest several different kinds of walks with a variety of specific activities, some of which you may not have considered. You won't be able to try all of these activities unless you've already retired, so select the walk that suits you best.

Exploration

WALK #1—THE SHAKEDOWN CRUISE

This walk is a good orientation walk, one on which you can try out all your seeing prowess and check to see if you have the right walking equipment. Allow about an hour for this initial excursion and treat it as a kind of shakedown cruise. Log observations about your own comfort or discomfort; observe yourself observing. Don't be surprised if you feel a bit awkward or if you feel like you're being observed as some kind of nature freak. Even experienced naturalists report such feelings.

Rather than observing randomly, try at least one of the following:

1. See something smaller than your hand. Study it. Draw it or collect it.
2. See something larger than your house. Use your spatter vision. Try to capture a panorama or an inordinately large object. Take time to let the big picture soak in. Record the details and think about how they work together.
3. Try practicing zoom vision, changing your glance from SV to close-up and back again. Focus on some specific point of interest in your side-angle vision and then zoom in and out. How do your perceptions change as you change your focus? Jot a few notes about these changing perceptions.
4. Hear something far away. Wait in solitude and listen. Strain to hear some sound that's just on the edge of your hearing.
5. Hear something very close. Sit very still and listen for the sound that's just beyond your finger tips. You may need to hold your breath and wait.
6. Explore the texture of something very rough. Close your eyes and let

your fingers edge slowly over the object. Try a Zen drawing. Or just jot down the sensations.

7. Feel something very smooth. Hold it in your hand; slide it against your cheek. Think about how it came to be smooth. Speculate about what forces wore away its edges.

8. Observe in shadow and in light. Note differences of color and shade by observing similar objects in light and shadow. How does light change your perceptions of objects?

9. After the walk is over, sit somewhere comfortable, sipping whatever you sip after such intense work, and reflect on the experience in your log. What were the highlights and lowlights? Were there any surprises? Were you disappointed in anything? With what do you need more practice? What was your mind doing as you worked through your explorations? What kinds of questions are rattling around in your head? What did you learn about naturalists and the way they use their minds?

WALK #2—SIGHTINGS

This walk is more focused and may range over less territory than the previous one. You may need to allow more time, or you may need to allocate two different blocks of time to try repeated observations. Try at least three of these sightings over several days.

1. Focus on dead things. Loren Eiseley has suggested that the riddles of nature can best be solved by examining things that are no longer alive. Collect a variety of dead objects and speculate on their demise. Use your closeup lens. Speculate about what purpose they served while alive and what purpose they serve now. Use your wide-angle lens. How are the objects related to the larger world in which you found them? What is the next stage of their continued evolution?

2. Sit or lie down somewhere. Stay there for a half hour, an hour, or as long as you wish. Tom Brown says that if you sat under a tree for a day, you'd have enough information to fill an entire book. We like his advice for sitting: "Become an inconspicuous stump, an all-seeing eye. When you are truly still, both without and within, then nature will begin to unfold its secrets."9 See what kinds of data you can collect by waiting.

3. Visit the same spot at two or three different times during the same day, or spread your observations over several days. See with your eyes, your hands, your mind. Listen to what that spot has to tell you.

4. Do an "I see." Position yourself in one spot and begin to list everything you can see. Once you have an exhaustive list, play around with different ways of organizing your list to capture different angles of the same spot—for example, I see from above as a hawk, I see from

below as a small rodent, I see as a small child, I see as a hungry deer, I see as a tired old man who has lived in this spot for a lifetime.

5. Draw off a small area of ground, perhaps three feet square, and then explore every inch of it. Try to see how things in your three-foot world are related to each other and how they relate to the world beyond. Draw or jot or describe that microcosm in any way you wish. Give it a name. Create a history for it. Define its mysteries.

6. Do a closeup study of textures. Use a frame or a homemade lens of some kind and sketch a variety of interesting and contrasting textures. Try placing a piece of paper over tree bark and rubbing the paper with charcoal or chalk or the fat side of your pencil lead.

7. Find some way to pull this experience together. Share it with another person. Develop a list of questions raised by your experience. Collect and sort some of your findings.

WALK #3— A SHERLOCK STROLL

This walk encourages you to do a little sleuthing as you go. Your attention will be directed toward any signs that other living things have passed by.

1. Puzzle over tracks. What made them? Which way was it traveling? How long ago did it pass? Why was it here? Follow the tracks.

2. Study vegetation. Look for bent or broken branches or grasses. Look for nibbled buds and stems of branches. What animal caused these disturbances?

3. Examine artifacts. Find things left by other travelers. Construct scenarios about these items. Look at fence gates, old sheds, foundations of houses long gone. Look for signs of previous human habitation and create mind mysteries about those people and how and why they constructed these items.

4. Make mysteries. Create puzzles from the clues you find and construct tentative explanations. Who were these people? Why were they here? Leave yourself with questions and unsolved riddles.

5. If you're still curious about some of your mysteries after you return home, do some research. Find out about the land and its inhabitants and its history. Talk to people at your county historical society. Check the courthouse for old maps and plats. Interview some locals about the area.

WALK #4—THE JOHN MUIR MEMORIAL HIKE

This exploration is for the serious apprentice naturalist and should be attempted only after you have become a practiced observer who is curious and serious about exploring the natural world.[10] On this walk, you'll carefully document your observations, collect specimens of flora and fauna, tag and

bag these items, and later attempt to identify and classify them. You might also wish to draw a map of your walk, indicating where you collected each specimen. Use a log or notebook to record details of locations, light, and type of soil or terrain.

You may wish to specialize. Collect bark samples or samples of tree leaves, wildflowers, or grasses. You might wish to focus on lichen, soil, rocks, or seed pods. You might wish to specialize in one species of tree and all its various manifestations—evergreens, for example, or pines. You might like to work with a particular venue—to study a pond, for example, or a creek bed or a grassy field or a small section of any natural habitat.

You might choose to make this the John James Audubon Memorial walk, in which case you'll need a field guide for birds in your area, binoculars, and a notebook. If you're uncertain about how to proceed on such a trip or where to look for the birds, consider learning by joining your local Audubon Society and practicing with people who know what they're doing.

If you're a skilled amateur photographer, you might like to try "collecting" your specimens on film. Keep a careful log of each shot, noting time of day, lighting conditions, and camera settings. You may not want to look like a camera geek in the woods, but a gadget bag with several lenses, a light meter, and a tripod will increase the quality of your collections.

If you enjoy drawing and sketching, collect your specimens in a sketch book. Try three or four sketches of the same plant, or sketch the whole plant and some of its key parts: petals, leaves, bark, blossoms, fruit, or seed pod. Note in your log other pertinent data about location and terrain. This kind of encounter with nature is obviously a very different one from some of our early suggestions, and it might seem more like homework for a botany class. Don't let it become that. Keep your spirit of discovery; engage your imagination; use your spatter vision; work on mysteries. But document these experiences with specimens.

Find some way to display and share your work, maybe with your children or your students. Reflect on the processes of doing that work and include a process map or some other step-by-step graphic which details the stages you went through to complete the project. Share insider stuff; give helpful hints; instruct others who might wish to do the same thing.

We hope that the walks we've suggested will serve as idea generators and mind openers rather than straightjackets or school assignments. We're sure you will explore this context for thinking in your own ways. Remember that the point of all this is to help you get caught up in the wonder and the magic of the natural world. Maybe then you can fully appreciate Eiseley's confession: "I never enter a wood but what I hear footsteps in the leaves tiptoeing away. I never gaze upon an animal that I do not see its reflected past

or some hidden, unguessed potential future both paradoxically written in its body. There is a dynamism about life, a centrifugal quality for which we rarely give it credit."[11] Happy walking. Expect to hear the tiptoeing in the leaves.

OUTSIDE IN

Now that you've gained some experience as a fledging naturalist and can rely on what you've learned from your own explorations, you may be ready to enter the minds of other naturalists. In fact, you've already begun to do that as you've heard some of their words resonate in earlier parts of this chapter. As you work with the following explorations, see if you concur with Arnheim when he says, "There is no basic difference between what happens when a person looks at the world directly and when he sits and thinks."[12]

Our interest in this chapter is not just in what naturalists do but how they think as they do it. We want to see if we can catch some naturalists thinking and see if their thinking is anything like the kinds of thinking you were doing as you worked in the natural world.

Exploration

Eavesdrop on the following conversation between Loren Eiseley and his mentor Frank Speck as they are strolling in the Philadelphia Zoo. Mark any lines that give you a sense of how they think.

… We came upon a wood duck paddling quietly in a little pond. These birds are most beautifully patterned. We stood watching the ducks. "Loren," Speck finally said, quite softly and uncertainly for him, "tell me honestly. Do you believe unaided natural selection produced that pattern? Do you believe it has that much significance to the bird's survival?"

… I tried to choose my words very carefully. "Frank," I said, "I have always had a doubt every time I came out of a laboratory, even every time I have had occasion to look inside a dead human being on a slab. I don't doubt that duck was once something else, just as you and I have sprung from something older and more primitive."

"It isn't that which troubles me. It's the method, the way. Sometimes it seems very clear, and I satisfy myself in modern genetic terms. Then, as perhaps with your duck, something seems to go out of focus, as though we are trying too hard, try- ing … to believe the unbelievable. I honestly don't know how to answer. I just look at things and others like them and end by mystifying myself."

... "Well," I added, as the duck paddled along slowly, displaying its intricately patterned feathers, "that's just the way I feel right now, as though the universe were too frighteningly queer to be understood by minds like ours.... I come out feeling that whatever the universe may be, its so-called simplicity is a trick, perhaps like that bird out there.... It isn't precisely that nature tricks us. We trick ourselves with our own ingenuity. I don't believe in simplicity."13

- Look at the passages you have underlined. What kinds of thinking can you identify? What surprises you most?
- What similarities can you see between these naturalists' observations and questions and your own wonderings?
- What's unique about the kinds of thinking you have identified here? How are they specific to naturalists?

Three things strike us about this passage. First, Eiseley and Speck noticed the duck, noticed his markings. Thinking begins with perception. Second, the seeing led to big questions—*why* questions about origins and evolution. We suspect that this framework of big questions is behind all of what the observing naturalists do. Theirs is a kind of quintessential curiosity that goes beyond "What kind of duck is that?" to "What kind of world is this that has ducks like that?" Finally, both observers confess a kind of frustrating inadequacy with their own knowledge and reject simple answers for difficult questions. Implied in that rejection of simplicity is a commitment to continue the search. Behind that frustration is the ultimate curiosity to know.

The passage you've just worked with was an account of Eiseley as a young student. Consider this next passage, which shows a much older, more mature Eiseley.

Exploration

Read the following passage carefully. Again, note the kinds of thinking by marking lines.

I am middle-aged now, but in the autumn I always seek for it again hopefully. On some day when leaves are red, or fallen, and just after the birds are gone, I put on my hat and an old jacket, and over the protests of my wife that I will catch cold, I start my search. I go carefully down the apartment steps and climb, instead of jump, over the wall. A bit further I reach an unkept field full of brown stalks and emptied seed pods. By the time I get to the wood I am carrying all manner of seeds hooked in my coat or piercing my socks or sticking by ingenious devices to my shoestrings. I let them ride. After all, who am I to contend against such ingenuity? It is obvious that nature, or some part of it in the shape of these seeds, has intentions beyond this field and has made plans to travel with me.

We, the seeds and I, climb another wall together and sit down to rest, while I consider the best way to search for the secret of life. The seeds remain very quiet and some slip off into the crevices of the rock. A wooly-bear caterpillar hurries across a ledge, going late to some tremendous transformation, but about this he knows as little as I.

It is not an auspicious beginning. The things alive do not know the secret, and there may be those who would doubt the wisdom of coming out among discarded husks in the dead year to pursue such questions.... Of late years, however, I have come to suspect that the mystery may just as well be solved in a carved and intricate seed case out of which the life has flown, as in the seed itself.

As I grow older ... I shall be found puzzling over the saw teeth on the desiccated leg of a dead grasshopper or standing bemused in a brown sea of rusty stems. Somewhere in this discarded machinery may lie the key to the secret.... I am sure now that life is not what it is purported to be and that nature in the canny words of a Scotch theologue, "is not as natural as it looks." I have learned this in a small suburban field, after a good many years spent in much wilder places upon far less fantastic quests.[14]

- What kinds of thinking did you mark? How is that like the thinking of the young Eiseley? How has Eiseley's thinking changed? What things is he now surer about? What questions still bother him?
- What similar experiences did your own walks produce? How were they like Eiseley's observations, questions, musings, and wonderings?

This piece again documents the careful, noticing eye of the naturalist. Eiseley sees in the particular: rusty stems and seed pods sticking by ingenious devices. Beyond seeing, though, Eiseley interacts with his observations, sees himself as being in some way related to these seeds and caterpillars, connects himself to the natural world. The reader senses awe, reverence, respect for the natural world, and uncertainty about how it works.

This uncertainty produces the inevitable questions and the steadfast resolution to reject simple answers. Small observations raise big issues.

Exploration

You've examined the mind of one naturalist, but perhaps you need more data, a larger sample upon which to conduct your mind studies. Here are three well-known naturalists thinking aloud. Read each passage several times and look for clues to their thinking processes.

In the evenings I walk down and stand in the trees, in light paused just so in the leaves, as if the change in the river here were not simply known to me but apprehended. It did not start out this way; I began with the worst sort of ignorance, the grossest of inquiries. Now I ask very little. I observe the swift movement of water through the nation of fish at my feet. I wonder privately if there are for them, as there are for me, moments of faith.

The river comes around from the southeast to the east at this point, a clean shift of direction; water deep and fast on the outside of the curve, flowing slower over the lip of a broad gravel bar on the inside, continuing into a field of shattered boulders to the west.

I kneel and slip my hands like frogs beneath the surface of the water. I feel the wearing away of the outer edge, the exposure of rootlets, the undermining. I imagine eyes in the tips of my fingers like the eyestalks of crayfish. Fish stare at my fingertips and bolt into the river's darkness. I withdraw my hands, concious of the trespass. The thought that I might be observed disturbs me.[15]

—Barry Lopez

Found here the beautiful, sensitive *Schrankia,* or sensitive brier. It is a long, prickly, leguminous vine, with dense heads of small, yellow fragrant flowers.

Vines growing on roadsides receive many a tormenting blow, simply because they give evidence of feeling. Sensitive people are served in the same way. But roadside vine soon becomes less sensitive, like people getting used to teasing—Nature, in this instance, making for the comfort of flower creatures the same benevolent arrangement as for man. Thus I found that the *Schrankia* vines growing along footpaths leading to a backwoods schoolhouse were much less sensitive than those in the adjacent unfrequented woods, having learned to pay but slight attention to the tingling strokes they get from teasing scholars.[16]

—John Muir

West of the house, Tinker Creek makes a sharp loop, so that the
creek is both in back of the house, south of me, and also on the
other side of the road, north of me. I like to go north. There the
afternoon sun hits the creek just right, deepening the reflected
blue and lighting the sides of trees on the banks. Steers from the
pasture across the creek come down to drink; I always flush a
rabbit or two there; I sit on a fallen trunk in the shade and watch
the squirrels in the sun. There are two separated wooden fences
suspended from cables that cross the creek just upstream from
my tree-trunk bench. They keep the steers from escaping up or
down the creek when they come to drink. Squirrels, the neighborhood children, and I use the downstream fence as a swaying
bridge across the creek. But the steers are there today. I sit on
the downed tree and watch the black steers slip on the creek bottom. They are all bred beef: beef heart, beef hide, beef hocks.
They're human products like rayon. They're like a field of shoes.
They have cast iron shanks and tongues like foam insoles. You
can't see through their brains as you can with other animals; they
have beef fat behind their eyes, beef stew.

... When I slide under a barbed-wire fence, cross a field, and
run over a sycamore trunk felled across the water, I'm on a little
island shaped like a tear in the middle of Tinker Creek.... I come
to this island every month of the year. I walk around it, stopping
and staring, or I straddle the sycamore log over the creek curling
my legs out of the water in winter, trying to read.... I'm drawn to
this spot. I come to it as to an oracle; I return to it as a man years
later will seek out the battle field where he lost a leg or an arm.[17]

—Annie Dillard

- What indications of thinking did you find in these passages? What
  kinds of similarities and differences did you notice as you tried to
  catch these naturalists thinking?
- In what ways do their minds seem similar to Eiseley's? In what ways
  do they seem unique?
- If you were to make some conclusions about how naturalists think,
  what would your list look like? What things still puzzle you about how
  naturalists think?

These three passages further illustrate the naturalist's eye for the particular and the search for answers that close observation seems to engender,
but they add new dimensions as well. Notice the imaginative leaps each
thinker makes: Lopez imagines eyes in the tips of his fingers; Muir connects
sensitive plants to sensitive people; Dillard sees the cattle as walking shoe

leather. All illustrate Jerome Bruner's point that thinking can take us beyond the information given.[18] Thinking involves bringing something to the given world. In each of these excerpts, an observation triggers imaginative leaps; observations of the given world spark metaphoric understandings. We've found that naturalists frequently rely on metaphor as a way to make sense of mysterious sightings.

Look back at your own double-entry journals and logs. Can you find examples of observings that triggered thoughts about other experiences? What kinds of stimuli seemed to invite imaginative and metaphoric connections? Under what conditions? In which contexts? What about smells? Sounds? Light? Artifacts? How does memory of these connections alter your emotional state?

Another remarkable quality of these passages—and indeed of the minds of naturalists—is their openness and their expectation that the natural world has things to tell them. Implicit in the minds of these thinkers is a patience, a persistence, and a sense of lifelong commitment to searching for explanations and understandings. Notice how each of these naturalists talks about repeated and continued observation.

TUNING IN TO A NATURALIST'S MIND

You've been studying the writings of naturalists and their reflected views of the natural world. Now you will listen to a naturalist thinking aloud as he responds to the things around him. On a bright March day, a group of Houston's "Growing Thinkers" accompanied naturalist George Regmund on a walk along Karankawa Trail at the Armand Bayou Nature Center. What follows are some excerpts from a transcript of George's commentary during that walk.[19]

It's spring! What a great day....

I find this fallen oak tree interesting. It demonstrates the tenacity that some living things have. The tree was pushed over by a storm we had last fall—a tornado—and it's coming out just as happy as a clam. It's a Southern Red Oak.... There's a potent life force in there.

That's a gall caused by a virus. It causes knots on the tree but doesn't really have any bad effects. (Question about whether galls aren't caused by insects.) Most are, but this one results from a viral infection.

Do y'all find that these woods are kinda junky? Some people would argue that there's a lot of junk, but all this stuff lying around out here is perfectly natural. The living things you see out here might not be the neatest things—it might be a little difficult to walk through if it weren't for the path—but in any case, all this decomposition that is happening here is extremely valuable.

There are woodpecker workings on that tree. The holes in the base of the tree are caused by the largest woodpecker in North America, which is as big as a crow. They're doing all kinds of good things, removing insect larvae that live inside that dead wood.

Here's another kind of parasite. See those little gray and green patches? That's lichen. You can look on almost any tree and see places where it looks like paint has been streaked onto it. This particular organism is really neat because it's really two organisms not found by themselves. It's fungus and an algae. The algae is a photosynthesizing plant, and fungus provides it a place to live. If the algae cells were there all by themselves, they would have a hard time. But the fungus provides a root-like place, and the algae sits there among the fibers, photosynthesizing, while the fungus extracts food. The fungus gets benefits from the algae and the algae gets benefits from the fungus.

One of the things that strikes me—having worked here at the Nature Center for a number of years—is that it seems real easy for people to kind of remove themselves and think of man and nature rather than the two together. All these things that live out here are part of us, and we're a part of that same system. Even though these plants may not seem important, they are sitting here right now making the oxygen we breathe. We're a part of all this.

Reflect for a moment on this naturalist's spontaneous monologue as he shared his habitat with a group of game apprentices. Consider the kinds of thinking and the habits of mind George's comments demonstrate. In what ways do they square with the thinking of the naturalists whose writings you've read in this chapter? How does George's thinking differ from or go beyond theirs?

SO WHAT?

As we assured you in the previous chapter, the point of sharing this context is not just to provide a list of activities to try with students in biology or physical education. The point here is to focus on some generic thinking strategies and then find ways to help students practice those in your own discipline. What does your list of ways naturalists think look like? Here's ours:

- Naturalists think with their eyes—in fact, with all their senses. In many cases, these senses are heightened by concentration and persistence, and the observing is informed by a rich understanding of what they are seeing.

- Naturalists think in the particular. They build up support for larger ideas by working with small details. They're inveterate collectors of artifacts and observations.

- Naturalists think rationally. They see particulars as related to each other and to a larger schema. They think about how things work together. Since no phenomenon exists in isolation but instead belongs to a total system, naturalists resist seeing parts. Instead, they look for wholes. Furthermore, naturalists are keenly aware of cycles—the turning of the seasons, new life from death and decay. In every way, these thinkers see the natural world as made up of interrelated systems.

- Naturalists use their observations to generate both questions and possible explanations. They delight in the puzzles and riddles of nature. They can tolerate not knowing.

- Naturalists have a respect for nature that borders on reverence. They see beauty in things others regard as ugly. They feel a sense of obligation to and responsibility for the natural world.

What does all this mean for classrooms and teachers? I guess we've already harped enough on the need to provide more opportunities for students to practice their seeing. However, we should also hoist the flag for school activities that ask students to work toward larger meanings by collecting smaller, more particular ones. Whether it's explaining a poem or the causes of instability in Central America or one of Newton's laws, students need to be encouraged to build those understandings by collecting and organizing a number of supporting observations and facts. Too often, we ask students to copy the "Big Truth" in their notebooks, or we dictate the six causes of the Revolutionary War, expecting exactly those same words to show up on the test. What students must do if they're to learn to think for themselves is conduct their own search for particulars and advance their own hypotheses, however tentatively.

By exploring the mental habitat of the naturalist, teachers discover the value of questions. For every observation a naturalist makes, a question waits to be answered. Even more importantly, the questions are big questions—many without answers, riddles and questions full of mystery. Most teachers ask a lot of questions. Unfortunately they may not ask the big questions or the questions to which they don't already have the answers. We're convinced that it's just such questions that foster intellectual development.

This might be a good time for you to tackle some big questions your-self. What are the mysteries in your subject area? What are the open-ended issues which scholars in your field debate? Could you begin your class with two or three mysteries that might direct student thinking throughout the year? Maybe you could have students follow Eiseley's lead by writing opin-ions and drafting working hypotheses early in your course. Your might then ask them to revise those opinions and hypotheses as their thinking pro-gresses. Teaching your students to love the mysteries and riddles of your discipline will stretch their thinking. So will working with big, unanswerable issues rather than just those closed questions in the textbook.

Perhaps the most valuable lesson we can learn by thinking like natu-ralists is their intellectual discipline and their ability to persevere in a search. If there's one thing students need more than anything else in order to be-come first-rate thinkers, it's this quality of sticking to a task or a line of in-quiry. Too many have been raised on short, workbooky assignments that are done quickly and often perfunctorily. Too often, they treat these assignments like factory jobs, working for the minimum wage, completing tasks routinely. We need to think about how we can develop contexts for learning that hold the world together for students long enough for them to learn the lessons of perseverance and vision and re-vision. The context of the naturalist is rich with possibilities.

From the "Growing Thinkers" program in Houston, here are a few "for examples." Patti Eysaman's second graders practiced close observation by noticing the changes in growing plants. In the process, they extended their learning in math, art, and science. Patti began by passing out seed pods and seeds for students to examine. The children described what they saw, made drawings of the artifacts, and talked about how plants grew from the pods. After planting their seeds, the children speculated on how long it would take them to sprout and how large the plants would grow. As the plants sprouted and began to grow, the children measured growth and used graphs to record and chart that growth. They kept growth logs and entered ongoing observa-tions. The assignment culminated with their drawing their own versions of the life cycle and narrating its stages.[20]

Kathryn Timme conducted a variation of this activity in an eleventh-grade chemistry class. Students charted the effect of various nutrients and different intensities of light on the growth rate of various plants. To hone ob-servational abilities, Kathryn guided her senior AP science wizards through a series of sensory studies of major teas of the world: far Eastern black and green teas and the popular herbal teas. Students thought about what taste buds can tell us and developed adjectives for tea evaluation. They then con-sulted old tea books to see what criteria others had developed for judging teas.[21]

Rosaline Roberson's kindergarten children began an elaborate activity by discovering a fallen branch beside a large tree. Rosaline first asked them to associate the branch with something else. Children's responses ranged from the imaginative giraffe and caveman tool to the more literal letter L and gun. Then, using a Venn diagram, she asked the children to look closely at both objects and discuss how they were alike and how they were different. Finally she made the big leap to mysteries and asked children what they "wondered" about as they looked at the two specimens. Children wondered, "What caused the branch to fall from the tree? What caused the holes in the branch? What did the tree look like when the branch was still attached? What was the age of the tree?" And most wonderfully childlike, "What could you carve that branch into?"[22]

Exploration

- Take some time with your journal to jot implications of this chapter for your own classes. What can teaching your students to think like naturalists offer? Which activities can you adapt for your content?

- Begin a list of possible resources and locations for the naturalist. What wonderful places are near at hand that you might visit with your students? (Don't forget museums and historical sites.) Who are some people in the community you might recruit as experts in this context for thinking?

- Which naturalists' writings have interested you? Check libraries and the naturalist section in bookstores for more of their writings.

LOOKING BACK

Pull together what you've learned from this chapter by looking back at your own logs, journals, and drawings. What kinds of thinking were you practicing as you spent time in the natural world? Consult the list you made at the beginning of the "So What?" section about the kinds of thinking that naturalists do. How many of those did you find yourself doing? Look back at your artist's log. How similar were the kinds of thinking you were doing as an artist with the kinds of thinking you were doing as a naturalist? How, for example, was observing as an artist different from observing as a naturalist? How are artists and naturalists alike? How are they different? Take some time with your journal to discuss all of this, or try a Venn diagram or some other graphic means of representing the two kinds of thinkers at work.

NOTES

1. Ulrich Neisser, *Cognition and Reality.* San Francisco.: W. H. Freeman, 1976.
2. Rudolph Arnheim, *Visual Thinking.* Berkeley: University of California Press, 1969.
3. Gerald Durrell, *The Amateur Naturalist.* New York: Alfred Knopf, 1988.
4. Holly Houston and Grant Wiggins (Eds.), *The Student As Worker.* Providence: Coalition of Essential Schools, 1987 draft.
5. See note 2 above.
6. Tom Brown, Jr., *Tom Brown's Field Guide to Nature Observation and Tracking.* New York: Berkley Books, 1983.
7. Robert Pirsig, *Zen and the Art of Motorcycle Maintenance.* New York: Bantam Books, 1975.
8. *The Portable Thoreau,* Carl Bode (Ed.). New York: Penguin Books, 1987.
9. See note 6 above.
10. See Durrell's book (note 3 above) for excellent suggestions on how to work as a naturalist.
11. *The Loose Notebooks of Loren Eiseley,* Kenneth Huer (Ed.). Boston: Little Brown and Company, 1987.
12. See note 2 above.
13. Loren Eiseley, *All the Strange Hours.* New York: Charles Scribner's Sons, 1975.
14. Loren Eiseley, *The Immense Journey.* New York: Vintage Books, 1957.
15. Barry Lopez, *River Notes.* New York: Avon Books, 1979.
16. John Muir, *A Thousand-Mile Walk to the Gulf.* Boston: Houghton Mifflin Company, 1981.
17. Annie Dillard, *A Pilgrim at Tinker Creek.* New York: Bantam Books, 1975.
18. Jerome Bruner, *Beyond the Information Given.* New York: W. W. Norton, 1973.
19. George Regmund is resident naturalist at the Armand Bayou Nature Center in Houston, Texas.
20. Patti Eysaman teaches second grade at Forester Elementary School in Houston.
21. Kathryn Timme is a chemistry teacher at Robert E. Lee High School in Houston.
22. Until recently, Rosaline Roberson taught kindergarten at Oak Forest Elementary School in Houston.

7

Thinking Like
an Inventor

An inventor should be defined as someone who
doesn't take his education too seriously.
                            —Charles Kettering

Inventors may seem a wacky lot to include in an apparently serious book that explores the intellectual territory of such thinkers as artists, naturalists, and anthropologists. In fact, Charles Kettering's irreverent comment about education may be about what you'd expect from America's most important inventor since Edison. He, like Edison and other inventors, had a healthy disrespect for formal schooling. Many creative people since then— dancers, artists, musicians, physicists, entrepreneurs—report similar dissatisfaction with their own schooling and the straightjacket of prescriptive courses and classes. Furthermore, many schools have no more tolerance for creative people than creative people have for schools. Highly inventive students have often been dismissed as followers of different drummers, who can be tolerated but certainly not encouraged.

Why do so many creative students feel uncomfortable in our schools, and why is original thinking too often seen as a dangerous commodity? Does schooling somehow retard the development of invention? These questions are seldom confronted by educators who opt for control over freedom. To them and to many members of the community at large, there's something suspect, almost unAmerican about "creative" activities in school. Even in the general culture, inventive people have not always been valued. Artists, musicians, writers, designers, architects, chefs often seem a little flaky, out of touch with reality.

Explore your own stereotypes of inventors. Say the word and what comes to mind? Dr. Frankenstein? One of Disney's outlandish professors? Strange, eccentric characters who concoct wacky machines in their basements?

Exploration

ANTICIPATING THE INVENTOR'S MIND

At this point, we'd like you to take a little time-out to think beyond such stereotypes.

- What do you remember about inventors from your school days? List the names of four or five inventors. Who seems to you the quintessential inventor on your list? What makes you think so? If you can't think of any inventors, list inventions and hypothesize about their inventors.

- Rank your own inventiveness quotient on a scale of one to ten, with ten being the most inventive. How are you like and unlike the inventors you listed? What is it you have or don't have that makes you rank yourself as you do? What hinders your inventiveness: lack of skills, knowledge, attitudes, mysterious gifts?

- Jot down a few notes about a time when you came up with a novel solution for a difficult problem. How did that happen? Where did the problem come from? Where did the solution come from? What do you consider the most important factors in this modest success? Try sketching a model of the steps you recall going through to solve the problem.

- Now speculate a bit about what inventive thinking is. How does it manifest itself in the process you just recalled? If possible, share your notes and your sketch with a partner or a group. Make comparisons about approaches to inventive problem solving.

Curiously enough, while schools have been suspicious of creativity and creative people, one of the most consistent criticisms of schools by business, science, and engineering professionals during the last five years or so has focused on the failure of American education to nurture the imagination and inventiveness of its students. Young people entering those professions seem less able to find and solve original problems than were their counterparts of the sixties. Some of our most prestigious universities have raised concerns over the lack of an inventive spirit in the students that the SAT and ACT are selecting for them. That's not too surprising, since Robert Sternberg's current research suggests only tenuous links between testable intelligence and creativity.[1] Meanwhile, the news magazines continue to feast on an endless diet of dire warnings about Japanese technical superiority, the inventiveness of German entrepreneurs, and the scientific progress of other Western European countries.

Are these concerns well founded or just part of the pendulum swing of criticism from "too free, not rigorous enough" to "too narrow, not open enough" that educators have learned to live with? We're not sure, but we look with suspicion at the legacy of the no-nonsense, back-to-basics movement and at pathological concerns about the decline of test scores that started in the middle seventies and continues to this day. The result, we believe, is a narrowed curriculum that may well have suppressed the development of original thinkers. We're convinced that it's high time to confront some tough questions: Just how important are individuality and personal initiative in our culture? Is it possible to nurture inventive minds in school? How do teachers in every discipline restructure their classrooms around inquiry rather than content?

Research now underway at Harvard and Yale by David Perkins, Howard Gardner, Robert Sternberg, and others may help us think through these questions. It may also help us find new ways of blending freedom and discipline into more potent learning experiences for students in the nineties. Meanwhile, we think teaching for inventive thinking is too important to delay. Besides, we're convinced that most of us already know more than we realize about how to make classrooms both rigorous—requiring high quality work—and open—offering students alternative ways to construct their own knowledge. This chapter seeks to extend what you already know by looking into the minds of inventors and leading you through some creative experiences of your own. On the following pages, you will hear from some flesh-and-blood backyard inventors, people who really do invent strange and wonderful gadgets. You will also listen to professional inventors such as a theoretical physicist and an IBM engineer. Though we focus on people who create new devices or processes to solve real-world problems, we interpret the word *inventor* in its broadest sense. Under this umbrella, we include novelists, scientists, designers, architects, engineers, musicians, teachers, and chefs—in fact all who think in novel and creative ways. Furthermore, we believe that inventing is not only a way of thinking but also a way of acting and being. The explorations in this chapter are offered as a means of easing you into the world of invention and encouraging you to experience this intellectual habitat for yourself.

If the prospect of inventive thinking leaves you a bit apprehensive, you're in good company. Most people don't think of themselves as original thinkers. Students are no exception; they're not particularly comfortable when given wide latitude to solve problems in their own ways. They seem similarly ill at ease when given the freedom to ask their own questions and initiate their own solutions. In such situations, you've probably seen at least one student point to a classmate and say, "She's the creative one; ask her." Or you've heard students complain that they "don't know what you want." Most of us have been socialized in the factory school to expect narrow assignments with precise specifications. It's no wonder that many of us feel uncertain of our creative abilities and apprehensive about exercising the free-dom that comes with invitations to be inventive. As teachers, we need to ask ourselves whether students really need or want to be presented with ready-made solutions to ready-made problems, or whether they're just out of prac-tice and understandably startled by real opportunities to think for them-selves. As a senior student offered in one of Dan's classes, "The hardest thing about this kind of freedom is to give myself permission to think for my-self. All of my student instincts tell me to bring my thinking into line with yours."

It's not entirely clear how creativity and inventiveness got a bad name in education, but it's a fact that when people talk about "creative" teachers and students, many kind of screw up their faces and say that word with mock appreciation. Perhaps the problem arises because being "creative" is often associated with "fun" or "fooling around." Such nonsense grates on our Puritan sensibilities. Too often, "creative" has meant interesting but seem-ingly purposeless activity. We're not interested in creativity for its own sake either, and we have some serious doubts about prepackaged programs that purport to develop it. Yet initiative and the willingness to risk original think-ing are habits of mind too important to exclude from our classrooms because of the excesses of the creativity industry.

So what can we learn by apprenticing ourselves to inventive thinkers? We've chosen to use inventing as the context for this chapter for two rea-sons. One is that our society needs more creative solutions for increasingly difficult problems. In all areas of American life—politics, social justice, quali-ty of the environment—it's clear that old solutions will not be adequate for new problems. Perhaps they never have been. Edward Schlesinger, Jr., sug-gests as much when he claims, "The entire story of civilization is based on in-ventions."[2] The second reason for exploring this context is our belief that an inventive mind is a more disciplined and productive mind. We're convinced that inventing is purposeful and that it leads not only to solutions but to more interesting problems as well. We suspect that inventive thinking is ordered by some kind of invisible logic which researchers are only beginning to find.

We hope you'll begin to uncover some of that invisible stuff as you work through this chapter. After you've done your own internship as an in-ventor, you'll consider what similar experiences might be helpful to your stu-dents. Here, many questions remain. Will expanding students' repertoire of generic problem-solving strategies help them solve particular problems, es-pecially problems specific to the various disciplines they study in school? Do problem-solving strategies have anything to do with inventive thinking, or might such strategies inhibit the making of new knowledge? Can inventive thinking actually be taught? Can quite ordinary people enact novel solutions, or is inventiveness a gift of special, uncoachable talent? How does specific knowledge function for inventive people? Do inventors need training or just opportunity? How would inventive thinking help students develop higher understandings of content? These are just some of the questions we hope you'll be pondering as you work through this chapter.

EXPLORING INSIDE OUT

So far, we've been speculating about invention; now it's time to experience firsthand what goes on inside an inventor's head. You'll begin by becoming an inventor and working through the process of creating some new device to make your life easier or more enjoyable. Your mind-set for this exploration should be a playful one. As Robert Root-Bernstein says, "One mental quality that facilitates discovery is a willingness to goof around, to play games, and to cultivate a degree of chaos aimed at revealing the unusual or the unexpected ... avoiding being overly cautious or orderly, or narrowly pragmatic."[3] You may enjoy this activity more if you enlist a partner and work collaboratively. We've suggested some time frames for each phase of the activity, but you may want to set your own pace. Find a comfortable place where you can spread out and equip yourself with some basic inventor's tools: paper for writing and drawing, pens and pencils, perhaps a ruler and compass.

Exploration

TRYING ON THE INVENTOR'S MIND

Finding a Why

- For about five minutes, brainstorm real-life problems that might be solved by a device of some kind. Think about daily complaints: What slows you down, bores you, or complicates your life? What situations do you encounter at home, at school, at play, or on the road that seem to you especially frustrating, awkward, difficult, or hazardous? Think about wishes: What would make your life more enjoyable, your leisure time more fun? What have you always wanted to do but couldn't?

- After letting your ideas flow freely, jot down problems shared by you and your partner. Check those that you agree might be solved by some kind of device. Among those checked, choose the one that interests you most and write it down as a discursive statement. Make this problem statement as clear and precise as you can.

Finding a What

- For about ten minutes, brainstorm possibilities for devices that might solve this problem. As you do so, observe the rules of brainstorming.

  Let the ideas flow and call them out fast.

  Suspend judgment—no criticism or disclaimers allowed.

  Record all ideas.

  Piggyback on each other's ideas—that is, take those ideas further or in a different direction.

  Collect as many ideas as you can; try for abundance. Go beyond the obvious. Don't hesitate to be outrageous.

- Allow five or ten minutes to go back through your brainstorming list and mark promising ideas. Consider the potential and the feasibility of each. After you narrow your list, talk through each idea. Choose the one that seems most promising of all. Write down this idea for a device to solve the problem you have identified.

- Now that you have an idea for invention, take ten to fifteen minutes to work it out in your head. How will the device be designed? What will it be made of? How will it work? As the invention takes shape in your mind, jot down details and make some sketches of this marvelous thing. (Crude drawings are just fine.)

- Now that you have a working idea and a preliminary design for your invention, take ten minutes or so to step back and look at it critically. What are the obstacles that must be overcome to make the device work? How can these obstacles be overcome? As you troubleshoot your invention, make notes or sketch design changes.

- If time permits, make a crude working model of your invention. Assume that you're now ready to introduce that invention to a potential manufacturer, apply for a patent, or even advertise it to the buying public. On a large sheet of drawing paper, make a sketch or diagram depicting your invention. You may wish to label key parts and write an accompanying explanation of how the invention works. In any case, give your invention a name and explain it to someone.

Finding a How

Spend a few minutes going back through everything you've accumulated during this project. As you revisit each stage of the project, think about how your mind worked as the invention took shape. Then consider how you might show others how your ideas evolved. One possibility is to make a flowchart or time line showing when you first got your idea, what things you tried along the way, and how you arrived at the final solution. If you prefer a verbal rather than visual display, make a diary or log that shows the different stages of your thinking.

WHAT INVENTORS DO

You've just had a little practice working as an inventor and spent a little time reflecting on that process. Let's begin to develop a working model of the inventor's mind. Where did your work as an inventor begin? Brainstorming for problems? Looking for trouble? Searching for things that need fixing? Maybe basement inventors and some think-tank scientists do that, but more often than not, people have problems presented to them by their employers or colleagues in the disciplines in which they work. More often than not, those problems are poorly defined: "Figure out how we do this," or "This doesn't work," or "We've got a mess on our hands here," or "What we need is …." Most problem solvers are presented with messes to clean up. They don't have to spend much time brainstorming for problems. They often have a warehouse of messes, and they typically find new problems as they work on others. But inventors are clearly oriented to problems. They think about large problems and the small problems contained within. They try to bring some order out of the mess and to get a clearer sense of the parameters of each problem.

What kind of thinking did you do as you practiced inventing? Did you find yourself a bit disoriented at first? Lost in the mess? Did you find your mind shuttling back and forth between big problems and small? How did you stay on track as a problem solver? How did you order and organize your work? Many inventors talk about beginning with the big, poorly defined problem and working toward the smaller details. They say they try not to worry about the small stuff, try not to get hung up on the details too early in the process. They try to formulate a clear idea of the overall problem before they begin to figure out how they might actually solve it.

Inventors talk about the time they spend worrying and wondering or just getting away and letting a problem incubate in their heads. Peter Carruthers, a theoretical physicist, says when he's puzzled or confused, he turns to the wilderness. "I feel at home in wild and remote places…. You have to have lots of quiet time to think your way out of confusions."[4] You didn't have much incubation time in that last exploration, but maybe you took some anyway. Sometimes the best problem-solving strategies are invisible; they go on inside the head and breakthroughs arrive unbidden while the thinker is relaxed or engaged in other activities. Good thinkers engage in "back burner" thinking, stalling and resting. They "watch the internal flow" of their ideas; they "listen to their gut." Inventors need time for reflection, when they move away from the problem a bit and get some distance.

But as Bryan Lawson reminds us, "Designers don't resemble Rodin. They don't just sit around thinking, chin on hand. They externalize their thoughts as part of the process itself in the form of drawings and sketches."[5] Inventors are active. They work with their hands; they build and fabricate models. To us, the most memorable account of fabricating models is the story that George Watson tells in *The Double Helix* about how he and his colleagues raced to be the first to unlock the mysteries of the DNA molecule.[6] They worked night and day welding metal discs and wires together to construct a three-dimensional model. They needed to see the molecule and manipulate possibilities in the concrete. They needed to handle ideas. That's how inventors work. They draw and tinker and try things out. They try to form ideas into concrete objects and representative hardware.

Inventors think big and small; they muddle around with problems and work on solutions in their heads. They construct models. All the while, they believe that problems can be solved. An IBM trouble-shooter who spends his time working with computers that aren't functioning properly once told Dan, "I know I can fix it; when I walk into that room I know I can get that machine running."[7] Coupled with that belief in the solvability of problems is a tenacious spirit, a bulldoglike unwillingness to let go or give up on a tough problem. Alfred North Whitehead talked of the importance of getting hold of the big ideas and "hanging onto them like grim death."[8] So there is an inventive spirit and an inventive will to consider here as well.

Before you set off on another exploration of the inventor's world, consider these questions: What role did knowledge play in your recent foray into invention? Were there questions or problems you just didn't have the knowledge to solve? Were there details on which you just didn't have enough information? How might you have found that knowledge? Think about these questions, and as you proceed, keep track of times when you just don't know enough to solve a problem. In this next exploration, the knowledge and experience you've gained as a teacher will be useful.

SOFT THINKING

Roger von Oech, a bizarre man with a wonderfully wacky book titled *A Whack on the Side of the Head,* suggests that inventors often begin a project with "soft thinking"—thinking that doesn't worry about the details, thinking that uses metaphor, thinking that relies on imagination.[9] The IBM troubleshooter says, "Look at the whole thing at once."[10] A. F. Osborne suggests the kind of brainstorming you've already practiced in the first exploration.[11] W. J. J. Gordon suggests the use of synectics, or the joining together of apparently unrelated elements into analogous relations.[12] Others suggest that data gathering is the first step in problem finding. Confused? In the next

Exploration, we try to lay out these options for you and get you to work. Remember that the various approaches suggested are just what we said: *options*. Even if you had time, you wouldn't want to use them all. As you work through the invention problem we pose for you, just choose the suggested approaches you think will work best for you. If you prefer, come up with your own.

Exploration

DESIGNING A LEARNING HABITAT

We hope that this problem will be large enough and interesting enough to keep you engaged for a while. The mess we're throwing at you is your own classroom, your *living* room, the place you spend most of your professional life. We want you to begin working on the problem of redesigning that classroom into a habitat that will provide optimum opportunities for you to teach and your students to learn. We're not sure what that means, and it's unlikely that you have much sense of it either. The problem is poorly defined right now. Maybe you don't even see it as a problem. Perhaps you like your classroom just fine the way it is. You like it neat and orderly or messy and comfortable. At first, we think it might be natural for you to think about this task only as a decorating problem or a furniture arrangement problem, but we hope the issue is much bigger than that: a habitat for learning. Forget specifics for a while. Forget about what you're going to do tomorrow. Think inventively about how things *could* be. As you try various strategies suggested below, keep track of what you try and how successful each was. A good record of your work can do more than help you keep track of your thinking; it can also document the work as your own and protect your rights to original ideas.

SOFT THINKING

Large Metaphors

Try listing some metaphors for an ideal classroom. "I like to think of my classroom as a spaceship, a beehive, a summer camp. The ideal classroom would feel like a family, a well-oiled machine, a revival meeting. I want a classroom that looks like … How is my classroom like a zoo? (I say all the time, 'It was a real zoo in there today.')" Review your list of metaphors and find the ones that have the most appeal to you. Extend those metaphors. Explain them to yourself. Carry them to absurd limits. Exhaust yourself exploring metaphors. Try another and another. See if you can find one that resonates, that represents what you think a good classroom ought to be like. Or mix metaphors; weave several together.

Try writing a fable about a classroom in a galaxy far away. Let your imagination construct an ideal classroom in an alien environment.

Try drawing the most amazing and wonderful learning environment you can imagine.

Go to sleep and dream a wonderful learning habitat.

Analogues

Try constructing a direct analogy. Think of something with which you are very familiar: tennis, cooking, mountain climbing, knitting, sailing, electricity, building decks. Try to take the knowledge you have of that activity and use it to describe how an ideal learning situation might look. (If you're not quite sure how this strategy works, call to mind one of the more famous examples of using a description of the flow of water to explain how electricity works.)

Think of environments other than school where people are brought together for specific purposes: airplanes, theaters, stadiums, courtrooms, etc. List features and hardware of those environments. Is there anything you could borrow from those settings to help you think about your own?

Try some lists of questions beginning "why can't they ..." or "what if ..." or "why don't they make ..." For example, why can't teachers and students regulate the temperature and light in their own surroundings? What if my principal said I could have thirty Macintosh computers if I could figure out how to use them every day? Why don't they make something as simple as a chalkboard that works like an overhead projector and lets students write on it at their desks?

Take the word *classroom* and list as many synonyms as you can. See if those synonyms offer ideas for a more creative look at what a learning environment might be.

ADVENTUROUS THINKING

Data Gathering

Survey your students. Ask them what a good classroom looks like, feels like. Ask them what kinds of conditions they need for learning. Ask them what comes to mind when they picture the ideal habitat for learning. Get them to draw some pictures of that place. Ask them what kind of physical arrangement they might prefer and what kind of equipment a terrific classroom needs. Try to get them to stretch beyond the obvious and dream a bit.

Survey your colleagues. Ask them to think about the ideal classroom and what it would be like. So that you tap a wide range of experience and expertise, be sure to talk to people who teach subjects and grade levels different from your own.

Look at your own lesson plans and consider the kinds of teaching you do. Make a wish list of things you've always wanted or needed in your own classroom. Go beyond that wish list to conjure up things you've never even wished for before.

Acting Out

Log a few days in your own classroom. Watch yourself teach; note how the physical environment helps and hinders your efforts and those of your students. Be a student in someone else's class. Sit through a couple of class sessions the way students do. Note problems and possible solutions.

Look at a variety of other teachers' classrooms. Note features that might be adaptable to your own environment.

Involve your students in acting out scenarios of ideal situations for learning. Experiment with arrangements in your own classroom. Involve students in your problem. Enlist their imaginations as well as your own.

Making It Personal

Think about your own best place for learning. When you really need to think or work something out, where do you go? Why? Is there anything about that location that's transportable to school?

Review your big goals as a teacher. What are your priorities? What do you value? How important is social interaction? How important is organization and order? How do those priorities help define your problem?

TIPS FOR PROBLEM FINDING

Don't be judgmental during this early thinking. Entertain any possibility regardless of its feasibility.

Avoid being overly cautious, excessively neat, or narrowly pragmatic. You want to surprise yourself here.

Go for quantity. Don't worry about errors or "dumb" ideas. Understand that failure is an important part of success. Soichiro Honda, founder of the company that makes the car many of you drive, says, "Many people dream of success. To me, success can only be achieved through repeated failure and introspection. In fact, success represents the 1 percent of your work which results only from the 99 percent that is called failure."[13]

Build in time for reflection and time to let your unconscious mind work. Remember Peter Carruthers' remark about the need for quiet time. Remember how much better chili tastes after a night in the refrigerator.

SHARPENING AND ORGANIZING THE PROBLEM

If things have gone well for you, you have collected a lot of material of varying worth. Some is immediately useful, some may need to hang around a while, and some can be shelved. Spend some time reviewing all of your ideas to this point with an eye toward sharpening the problem and organizing its dimensions. Don't let the word "organize" scare you. This is not a term paper, and neatness doesn't count. But if you can catalog what you have—first by its immediate value in helping you define the problem more clearly and second according to various dimensions to be considered—you may be able to work more effectively. Our next suggestions lead you toward a working statement of the problem to focus your task as inventor.

Sorting and Coding

You'll probably find it helpful to devise some scheme for sorting and evaluating your data. Maybe it's something as simple as "this stuff is important, this stuff may be important, and this stuff was just practice." Maybe you'll want to do a little color-coding with those wonderful highlighters. Maybe you'll just want to lay things out in piles or number them in some way.

You may already have an an idea for organizing the dimensions of the problem. If you think in terms of specific problem areas—physical space, equipment, arrangement—you'll want to code your data that way. On the other hand, you might prefer to organize your mess around the concerns of the various participants in the learning environment: students, teachers, administrators. Whatever you do here, don't let your coding close down options. And don't discard ideas because they don't seem feasible, either because the technology doesn't exist or because no one would let you do such a thing. Rather, evaluate your ideas and organize them by their potential importance in solving the central problem.

Thinking Visually

You may wish to try representing your thinking visually. One way is to make a Venn diagram like the one shown in Figure 7.1, which helps you to see interrelationships among data—both unique features of various data sets and the common ground they share.

Maybe you'll find it more useful to try some kind of cluster diagram (see

FIGURE 7.1   Example of a Venn diagram.

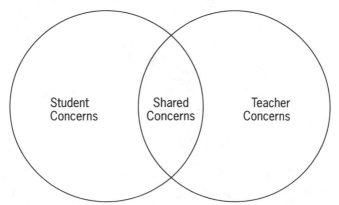

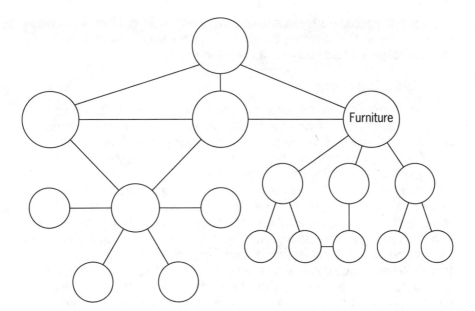

FIGURE 7.2   Example of a cluster diagram.

FIGURE 7.3   An example of a hierarchical tree diagram.

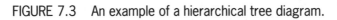

Problem Statement

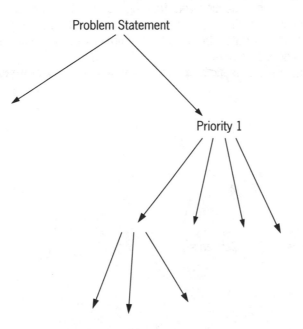

Priority 1

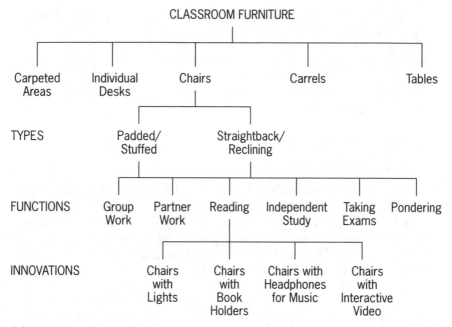

FIGURE 7.4   A tree diagram.

Figure 7.2) with lines and circles to link associated dimensions of the problem.

Still another possibility is to use a tree diagram of some kind to help you think critically about the problem. There are several versions of trees you might adapt to your data. The hierarchical tree shown in Figure 7.3 is a branching diagram[14] that sets the working problem statement at the top and then lets the problem solver move downward by connecting subsets of the problem through other branches. If you're beginning to see your problem as hierarchical—that is, one which can best be organized by priorities—this kind of visual thinking might work for you.

You may feel more comfortable using another kind of tree diagram, one which moves from general to specific. On the opening line, the problem and its component parts are stated, and then the problem solver moves downward to represent problems in increasingly specific terms. Maybe Figure 7.4, an example based on the problem of designing a chair for reading,[15] will help you see how this kind of tree diagram works.

You may want to work with something less exotic, like a matrix or a chart: categories and columns. Whichever strategies you use to focus the problem and enumerate its dimensions, remember that the goal is to come to a clear working statement of the problem.

Whenever you think you're ready to represent your problem in words, do so. Try that problem statement out on several other people. Return to your earlier data sources and try it out on them. Shop the problem statement around; explain it out loud to someone who doesn't have the slightest idea what you're talking about. Remain playful; don't get tense. Use your hunches and intuitions as well as your data. Then return to the problem statement you drafted and see if you can't sharpen it.

TRYING ON THE PROBLEM

Dreaming the Solution

Now it's time to wade into the problem and get a feel for exactly what you're up against. Prepare some preliminary drawings of the habitat you'd like to create. Initially, don't be limited by constraints of time and space. Draw some fantastic learning environments. Try out some outlandish ideas. Think of your habitat as round or suspended from the ground or on a steep hill or underwater. Try to avoid deliberately thinking about seats in rows. Do some conceptual blockbusting here. Think *tabula rasa*. Design the habitat in its most ideal dimensions. Be constrained only by your problem statement and the specific dimensions of the problem. If you think this habitat has to be in the Maine woods or a hermetically sealed bubble, so be it. If you need exotic equipment or yet-to-be invented technology, so much the better. Perhaps your earlier experience with metaphor and analogy will be helpful at this point. Revisit your earlier brainstormings. Refer to your trees and charts. Remind yourself of your primary goals. In your drawings, try to account for all aspects of the problem. Keep "can't" off your drawing board.

Try your drawings out on other teachers. Get some responses. Listen to yourself talking about what you envision. When you're ready, evaluate what you have. Circle or otherwise mark the things you like best. Label the components you feel are most essential or most workable. Note your best ideas and note areas which may become problematic as you seek to translate dreams into reality.

Inventing in the Real World

Begin to think now in terms of real space, either the real space of the classroom you now have or one you've noticed in your travels around the school that would better serve your needs. If neither space is suitable or if you currently have no classroom, decide arbitrarily how much real space you need. Using graph paper and working to scale, try a number of different layouts based upon what you've learned about the needs of those who'll use the space. Leave room for areas you don't know how to design in detail. You may also want to leave space for equipment that hasn't been invented. Work with real space, but don't be limited by anything else.

If you're good with your hands or like to build models, construct a three-dimensional model of this ideal classroom. Use any bizarre objects you wish to represent elements in your design.

TARGETING PROBLEMS

Evaluate your design for feasibility. What are the main glitches? What problems would need to be solved before you could translate your design into reality? Try listing the things you already have available and the things you might be able to scavenge.

List some of the furnishings and tools in your habitat that could be improved. Select several and list as many ways to improve them as you can. How, for instance, could a student or teacher desk be improved? Try some synonyms for desk. Think of desks in completely different contexts.

List the things in your design that are pure fantasy. Choose a couple of items from this fantasy list and "invent" them. Apply what you've learned about inventing to explain how these new devices would work and how they might be made.

Evaluate your overall design in light of your problem statement and your analysis of the habitat's dimensions. Which parts of the problem do your design and your inventions solve most effectively? Which parts of the problem does your design only partially solve? Which parts were you unable to solve at all? What problems have you left for future inventors?

REFLECTION

Now that you've completed this rather ambitious project, take some time to reflect on what you've done and how. Use your journal to respond to some of these questions:

- Think about yourself as an inventor. How well did you handle the challenge of taking on such a big mess? As you began this Exploration, what were your biggest frustrations?
- What strategies were most helpful in getting you started? Which of the problem-finding strategies worked particularly well for you? Did you return to any strategies and use them again?
- What role did images and pictures play in your inventive work? Can you remember any particularly strong or recurring images?

EXPLORING OUTSIDE IN

Now that you've tried your hand at invention, are you beginning to get an insider's view of this context for thinking? Although you'll now focus on learning from others—practicing inventors who are the real experts in this territory—don't discount your own experience. To the contrary, you'll want to keep that insider's perspective. It should sharpen your insight into the workings of inventors' minds and allow you to compare their thinking with your own.

Exploration

Listen to three inventors as they talk about how they begin their work. Watch for strategies, processes, and attitudes.

From IBM troubleshooter Gary Burns:

> When I get a call to come to a site where a computer is malfunctioning, I begin by talking to the people who are around the machine all the time. They know its personality, its temperament; those things have human qualities, you know. Then I look at it, play with it, try to get it to do things to get a sense of what's going on. I never troubleshoot by map. Indicators are all over the place, and I'll miss them if I have my head stuck in a manual. Besides, I have to analyze it my own way, learn for myself.
>
> If it's dead ... that's another problem. Then I go to bodily functions, see if I can get a pulse. I try to isolate problems in that situation by disconnecting peripherals and looking for a heartbeat. Basically I'm in a trial and error mode here. But I'm calm. I know I can fix it.[16]

From Mark Bernstein about Charles Kettering:

> "Preconception is the trap," says K. He scorned theorists, particularly the "slide rule boys" who, he said would "whip out their slide rules, make two calculations and decide something was impossible." Calculations are based on theory, the mere summary of experience, not the limit of possibility.
>
> K. believed that, although in the world the inventor must move and shake, in the lab his task often was to ask questions, listen and encourage. He believed that a problem was more than willing to be solved, provided the researcher remembered who was boss, by which he meant the problem not himself. "The only difference between a problem and a solution," he used to say, "is that people understand the solution. Solutions only involve a change in perception, since the solutions must have existed all along within the problem itself. A researcher," he argued, "is there not to master the problem but to make it give birth to its solution."[17]

From Peter Carruthers:

> I am restless. A state that is essential to the pursuit of a full creative life. There's a special tension to people who are constantly in the position of making new knowledge. You're always out of equilibrium. When I was young, I was deeply troubled by this. Finally I realized that if I understood too clearly what I was doing, where I was going, then I probably wasn't working on anything very interesting.
>
> I'm sure you've noticed how unnatural it is always to force yourself to be on the brink of confusion. At times, it's better not to push. Your unconscious ultimately has to do a lot of the work. God only knows how that happens, but it really does. You have to stuff yourself—gorge yourself on a problem—and then go and leave it.
>
> My earliest beginnings are often questions on paper, deceptively simple: Why are there so many elementary particles? Can they be grouped together, simplified? How do these tiny particles relate to gravity, to electromagnetism?"[18]

Take some time to do a little jotting in your journal about our three inventors.

- What commonalities do you notice in their thinking? What do you notice that is unique to a particular thinker? What personality characteristics can you read between the lines?
- Compare their styles of thinking to your own. Which inventor sounds most like you? In what way is your thinking different?
- What do you think are the essential qualities of the inventor who willingly tackles difficult problems?

So far, you've worked as an inventor and tuned in on some inventive minds. You've just listened to three firsthand accounts of how expert inventors approach very different problems. We hope that the result is a growing knowledge of what it means to create.

The next Exploration provides an opportunity for you to test the theories that are gathering in your mind against those generated by two of the best current researchers into creative thinking.

Exploration

Both Howard Gardner and David Perkins contend that talking about creativity in the abstract is futile. Both prefer to investigate creative people and generate theories on the basis of what those people do and how they do it.

Consider the following samples of these two researchers' theories and see how they square with your own assumptions and how they extend what you've learned for yourself.

From a speech by Howard Gardner in Houston:

> Creative individuals
> regularly
> solve problems
> or fashion products
> in a domain
> initially novel
> ultimately acceptable
> in a cultural setting.[19]

This is Gardner's definition of the creative mind. Because each word or phrase is crucial to that definition, it stands alone as if it were a line in a poem. Take some time to think about each line. "Regularly." Why regularly? Why not occasionally? "In a domain." What does that mean? See if you can expand this compressed definition into a larger, more discursive one. Try working Gardner's language into your own definition based on your recent experience as an apprentice inventor. Try thinking about Gardner's "poem" in the context of your own classroom.

From David Perkins's Six-trait Snowflake Model of Creativity:

- The first among the six traits is a strong commitment to a personal aesthetic. Creators have a high tolerance for complexity, disorganization and asymmetry. They enjoy the challenge of cutting through chaos and struggling toward a resolution and synthesis.
- The second trait is the ability to excel in finding problems. Scientists value good questions because they lead to discoveries and creative solutions, to good answers.

  Mental mobility is the third trait. It allows creative people to find new perspectives on and approaches to problems. Creative people have a strong tendency to think in opposites or contraries. They often think in metaphors and analogies and challenge assumptions as a matter of course.
- A willingness to take risks is the fourth trait. Along with risk taking come acceptance of failure as part of the creative quest and the ability to learn from such failures. By working at the edge of their competence, where the possibility of failure lurks, mental risk takers are more likely to produce creative results.

- Creative people not only scrutinize and judge their ideas or projects, they also seek criticism. Objectivity involves more than luck or talent; it means putting aside your ego, seeking advice from trusted colleagues, and testing your ideas.
- The sixth side of the snowflake is inner motivation. Creators are involved in an enterprise for its own sake, not for school grades or paychecks. Their catalysts are the enjoyment, satisfaction, and challenge of the work itself.[20]

Perkins's profile of the creative person reinforces some of the traits you've probably discovered as crucial to inventors: independence, tenacity, a propensity for hard work. Which of these traits did you see coming into play as you tried your hand at invention? Which do you see in your own teaching? Which would you like to develop in your students?

SO WHAT?

In turning our attention back to students, that last question brings us to a bottom-line issue: How might your encounters with inventive thinking as you've worked through this chapter enrich what you do in the classroom? Where might you begin to nurture inventive thinking in your students? As we've said so many times in this book, teaching for thinking must be grounded in the rich contexts of the subjects you teach. We think it would be a mistake to attempt teaching invention strategies as content. Artificial puzzles and games that ask students to solve contrived problems—like getting imaginary cannibals and imaginary missionaries across imaginary rivers—are of doubtful value. Even strategies like clustering and tree-diagraming are of little value if students don't use them as tools for thinking within an authentic context. We doubt that contrived puzzles or stock strategies contribute to useful habits of mind. Certainly teaching for inventive thinking is more than practice in brainstorming or a unit on inventors.

Begin taking stock of how well your own teaching practices nurture inventive thinking by evaluating the quality of questions that circulate in your classroom. Are they mostly your questions or textbook questions? What kinds of questions are students asking? Invention is fueled by curiosity. Without the propensity to ask good questions, there can be no discovery. How can you demonstrate to your students that questions lie at the heart of learning? That's a tough but critical issue.

Yet the inventive classroom is more than a haven for questions. It's a classroom where students' interests direct inquiry, where a teacher's instructional decisions are informed by students' desires to know, where open-ended problems encourage students to invent their own novel solutions. How can you involve your students in authoring more of their own learning experiences?

Sounds like you have a challenging invention problem of your own. Maybe hearing from some other teachers about how they're working on this problem will give you some impetus to rework your own classroom to make room for invention. The three mini case studies that follow illustrate how a second-grade teacher, a high school teacher, and a college teacher have worked at creating contexts for original thinking. Notice the kinds of strategies and attitudes on the part of the teacher which encouraged inventive thinking on the part of the students.

PAM SAILORS-BRUNE'S SECOND-GRADE CLASS

Pam Sailors-Brune is a second-grade teacher, and second-grade teachers have many things to teach: reading and arithmetic and schooling in general. But Pam believes that even the basic stuff is better taught and better learned in rich contexts that challenge students to think for themselves. As a case in point, Pam and her students had been engaged in a series of nature studies somewhat like those suggested in chapter 6. Students were noticing trees and planting seeds and keeping journals about how things grew. Each time they took nature walks, the children became quite animated about the harm discarded trash was doing to the environment. Pam gathered her students around her and asked, "So what do you think we can do about trash?" "Clean it up" was the consensus, but how? When she suggested finding out more about the problem, the children were off and running as budding inventors.

Pam's second-graders began doing a little problem finding by experimenting to see what happens to trash when it is left in the environment. They buried paper plates and napkins and styrofoam cups and plastic spoons. No doubt Pam had to resist the children's eagerness to dig up the trash the very next day and see what was happening, but they worked on related activities while waiting for their experiments to unfold. When students finally dug up their buried trash, they discovered that plastic and styrofoam objects were unchanged over time. They decided that it was important to invent alternative materials which were biodegradable but could do the same job. The result was a highly imaginative and exciting time of experimentation and invention. Meanwhile, Pam found ways to teach reading, writing, and mathematics within an important real-life context, and the students learned about original thinking by doing it.

Three things about Pam's teaching stand out for us. First, she found a way to capitalize on the children's own curiosity and interests. They were concerned about trash and wanted to do something about it. Rather than just organizing a "pick-up-the-school-grounds day," she saw the chance for an extended learning experience for her students. It no doubt meant scrapping more conventional lesson plans and heading off in an unknown direction, but Pam was willing to take that risk.

Second, she let her students pose questions and design their own experiments. Second-graders are experts at asking questions and quite adept at finding imaginative solutions. Pam could frequently turn their questions back to them by asking, "How could we find that out?" She guided their thinking, to be sure, but she let them design their own experiments to answer their questions. As experienced teachers, we know how hard it is not to co-opt kids' interests, give them a token share of the action, and teach basically the same stuff we were going to teach anyway. Negotiating the curriculum with students as full partners is a much tougher challenge.

Finally, we like Pam's teaching because she let students author the outcomes of the learning experience. We'll talk more about that point in chapter 9, but it's worth noting here that Pam's primary concern at the end of the project was not "How am I going to test my kids on this?" (Nor was it "How far have I wandered from the basal reader?") The students *demonstrated* their learning and Pam was able to collect documentation in the form of drawings and writings as well as observations of what students were able to do.[21]

BILL PISCIELLA'S ENGINEERING LABORATORY B

Bill Pisciella teaches specialized courses at Houston's magnet school for the engineering professions. The students in this specialized school-within-in-a-school are highly motivated and anticipate entering top colleges of engineering. What's unique about Bill is that he's also interested in less successful students and tutors them on Saturdays. The project we'll describe here involves five students from the High School for the Engineering Professions and two non-engineering students from the regular program in Booker T. Washington High School.

Bill loves to throw out "messes" to these students. He likes to create contexts for thinking in which students can use their developing engineering tools to find problems and invent solutions. Bill knows that at Stanford and MIT new ideas are currency, that "spectacular, innovative failures are valued more highly than tightly developed successes."[22] The mess he threw at his students this time around was "to prove the feasibility of creating a permanent colony on Mars during the first half of the twenty-first century."

Students began working in groups on various dimensions of this problem, pooling their knowledge and brainstorming just like NASA scientists and engineers. They made preliminary lists of questions and worked with metaphors, analogies, and images. They thought about science fiction literature and about NASA technology. What were all the things they must concern themselves with? How could they divide such a large, complex problem into smaller, more manageable units? What specific things would they need to invent? Sound familiar?

The semester-long research project culminated in a thirty-five-page report complete with specifications and drawings. Students wrote an introduction that compared Mars to Earth and focused on many of the problems associated with human life on Mars. Each of the students wrote a section of the report, even though all had worked as a team to brainstorm and critique each other's work. Using data from NASA Explorer documents, John wrote a detailed piece titled "Surface Conditions on Mars." Kyle summarized the transportation problems, offering three launch alternatives and specifications for various vehicles to transport people and equipment. Anna worked with the most inventive and open-ended part of the project, designing the colony itself; she included drawings for residential floor plans, site alternatives, and a most complex waste recycling system. Other students submitted reports on energy, recreation, and food production—the latter featuring a plan for hydroponic gardening. In each part of the report, students were using both specific knowledge and skills they had acquired plus highly inventive and imaginative ideas they had generated themselves. The entire report was illustrated by an intricate three-dimensional model. Bill reports that students became so absorbed in the project that he had to remind them on several occasions that this was a simulated proposal and not an actual plan which some agency was prepared to fund.

The next summer, Carol noticed Bill hanging around the computers at the administration building and asked if he were working on his Mars unit. "No way. I've already done that. If I did it again, I wouldn't learn anything and neither would the kids. Saturn's big. Next year we may work on Saturn." And that's Bill. A teacher who teaches because he learns.

But Bill also has a lot of content to teach: math and physics and design— all that engineering stuff. How does he find time for invention in his classes? Let him tell you: "The only way to know that stuff is to use it to do something interesting." Bill designs his classes so that students do something interesting. They come to know what they know because they use their knowledge to find challenging problems and invent plausible solutions.[23]

DAN KIRBY'S WRITING CLASS

Opening English and social studies classes to inventing is quite a challenge. Content—names, dates, poets, pacts—often not only controls how teachers organize these classes but also constrains student opportunities for original thinking. Written work in these classes is often formulaic stuff with specifications and procedures prescribed by the only reader of such texts: the teacher.

Dan's been restructuring his writing classes by finding new metaphors that resonate with ideas for teaching and learning. We'll talk in chapter 10 about his use of the studio metaphor. For the moment, let's just note that he uses this image to help him create an environment of experimentation and invention in crowded classrooms with students who are intially quite apprehensive and even hostile toward his subject.

Dan says that he has his best success if he stays away from traditional literature assignments and tests, and foregoes formula writing assignments like comparison/contrast and formal-argument essays. Students tend to see those activities as work they do for the teacher, and they become very good at disengaging themselves from real intellectual inquiry. Dan wants students to work on things they initiate because they're interested in them.

Memoir is a good example. Memoir is a wonderfully open and flexible form for writing, and there are many excellent examples of it around in the literature. Students in Dan's classes explore memoir by writing many short exploratory pieces and reading many short excerpts from literature. Dan doesn't assign topics for short writings; instead, he throws out ideas for exploration. Students write eight or ten short pieces—memories of family and place, of school and artifacts. They collect their short writings in a portfolio. (Portfolio is discussed in more detail in chapters 9 and 10.)

The serious work on invention begins when Dan asks his students to sort through their portfolios and select three or four particularly strong pieces and weave them together to form a memoir. The tough, creative work is in finding a scheme for weaving the short pieces into a seamless whole. No one can tell another writer how to do that, although Dan's students do rely on peers for suggestions and ideas. They have to sort through their own writings, looking for connections or themes or threads. They have to think metaphorically. They have to look for common ground in their pieces. Dan ups the ante by challenging his students to develop a scheme for a piece that tells them something new about their lives. Students find the problem difficult, but they don't quit. They frequently ask Dan what they should do, but he tells them it's their lives and their truths and only they can invent the scheme. During the course, they have done a great deal of reading of memoir, and Dan suggests that they look at how Russell Baker or Annie Dillard or Tobias Wolff did it. The students are persistent; and when they turn in their memoir as finished product, they have the satisfaction that it's a piece whose form and content they have authored.

Jeff Zevely's scheme was reflected in the title of his memoir, "Behind the White Fence." Jeff said he collected short pieces that took place or could have taken place in the poinsettia plantation behind his house. That white fence was a real barrier and a metaphoric one as well. He wasn't supposed to play over there, but he did. The fact that it was forbidden territory had something to do with the importance of events that transpired there, and Jeff still thinks about the sense of danger and independence he felt when he crossed the white fence. By constructing that memoir, Jeff didn't just do an assignment for Dan's class; he invented a life for himself, a past and a present. Jeff invented something wholly new and his own. Dan acknowledges that student schemes do not always work as well as Jeff's did, and writers are rarely completely satisfied with their final products. Even so, they all testify to the challenge and the freshness of inventing their own forms.

What Dan has done with memoir, other teachers have done with history reports on Martin Luther King (see chapter 10), science reports on the life cycle, and art projects. The important thing is that students compose a variety of short versions of something from many different angles and then select and orchestrate those short views into a larger, more comprehensive one that they alone have authored. When students scheme such a piece of writing, they're as much inventors as when they dream of colonizing Mars. After all, invention is doing your own work to solve your own problems.[24]

LOOKING BACK

Take a few minutes to think about what you teach and to whom you teach it. What particular topics in your subject always trigger student curiosity? How might you design instruction to follow that curiosity? What are some unanswered but promising questions that students might explore? How could you sponsor student-designed experiments and student-initiated questions?

In what kinds of creative applications might you engage your students as Bill did? What kinds of messes could you throw at them? What are some big problems in your content area that might be interesting and challenging? How might you develop a context that would let students apply their knowledge from your subject to novel problem-solving situations?

How might you reorganize large assignments in your class to apply Dan's idea of writing short in order to write long? How might the studio metaphor change your view of your own class? Maybe your work with the learning habitat problem has already opened a few windows on that matter.

How might you go about enacting in your school some of the things you've learned in this chapter?

Might you be able to adapt the habitat scenario you've worked on in this chapter to your own class? What kind of inventing problem could you set up for your students?

As you continue to think about creating a more inventive climate in your classroom, remember Howard Gardner's words:

> Creativity is not a matter of coincidence. Nor is it a matter of individual talent. Creativity is rather the embracing of disjunctions, of things that don't quite fit. It is the taking of risks and being stimulated by the challenge of making something for the first time. It is working near the edges of our knowledge and being exhilarated by the danger.[25]

NOTES

1. Robert J. Sternberg, *Beyond IQ: A Triarchic Theory of Human Intelligence.* New York: Cambridge University Press, 1985.
2. B. Edward Schlesinger, Jr., "An Untapped Resource of Inventors: Gifted and Talented Children." *The Elementary School Journal* (January, 1982).
3. Robert Root-Bernstein, "Setting the Stage for Discovery." *The Sciences* (May/June, 1988).
4. William J. Broad, "Tracing the Skeins of Matter." *New York Times Magazine* (May 6, 1984).
5. Bryan Lawson, *How Designers Think: The Design Process Demystified.* London: The Architectural Press, 1983.
6. George Watson, *The Double Helix.* New York: Bantam Books, 1978.
7. From an interview with Gary Burns. June 15, 1988.
8. See note 4 above.
9. Roger von Oech, *A Whack on the Side of the Head.* New York: Warner Books, 1983.
10. See note 6 above.
11. Richard E. Mayer, *Thinking, Problem Solving, Cognition.* New York: W.H. Freeman, 1983.
12. Ibid.
13. Tom Peters, *Thriving on Chaos.* New York: Alfred Knopf, 1987.
14. Adapted from Diane F. Halpern, *Thought and Knowledge: An Introduction to Critical Thinking.* Hillsdale, New Jersey: Lawrence Erlbaum Associates, 1984.
15. Ibid.
16. See note 6 above.
17. Mark Bernstein, "A Self-Starter Who Gave Us the Self-Starter." *The Smithsonian* (July, 1988).
18. See note 3 above.

19. Howard Gardner, "Fruitful Asynchrony: Key to Creativity?" Lecture at Museum of Fine Arts, Houston (May 4, 1989).

20. Neil McAleer, "On Creativity." *Omni Magazine* (April, 1989).

21. Pamela Sailors-Brune teaches at Sinclair Elementary School in Houston.

22. Doug Steward, "Teachers Aim at Turning Loose the Mind's Eye." *The Smithsonian* (September, 1985).

23. Bill Pisciella teaches engineering courses at the High School for the Engineering Professions in Houston.

24. Dan taught these writing classes while he was a Visiting Professor at the University of California at Santa Barbara, 1989.

25. See note 18 above.

8

Thinking Like
an Anthropologist

Anthropology is not the mindless collection of
the exotic, but the use of cultural richness for
self-reflection and self-growth.

—George E. Marcus and
Michael M. J. Fischer

Anthropology is an intellectual poaching license.

—Clyde Kluckhohn

As intellectual poachers, anthropologists have a lot of competition these days. Their own discipline is fast becoming a favorite poaching ground for educators, writers, literary critics—even cognitive scientists. As interlopers from neighboring professions keep streaming into their territory, anthropologists seem to be pushing the boundaries outward by rethinking their own work. If the result is not a full-scale border dispute, it's at the very least a blurring of boundaries that define the world of the anthropologist.

When you think of anthropology, what images come to mind? Margaret Mead surrounded by tawny Samoan children? What Clifford Geertz wryly stereotypes as "postcard places ... a shelved beach in Polynesia, a charred plateau in Amazonia, Adobo, Mekes, Panther Burn"?[1] You probably don't think of workaday places like hospitals, schools, factories, corporations, and courtrooms. Yet today, not only are anthropologists being hired to study such seemingly unanthropological sites; the tools of their trade are being borrowed by others—especially educators. Teachers are doing fieldwork in classrooms all over the country, and our professional journals abound with those thick anthropological descriptions called ethnographies. Why is it that we—and so many from other professions—are borrowing anthropological ways of thinking?

Might those ways of thinking be worth introducing to our students as well? Even if the young people we teach never become social scientists and never travel to faraway places with strange-sounding names, won't they need a sensitivity to the beliefs, customs, and values shared by people who belong to a particular culture? Consider also the time-honored method applied by anthropologists as they study a culture—the way they have traditionally lived among their subjects, engaged in tireless observation and collection of data, then subjected every shred of information to rigorous analysis and cross-verification before attempting to sort out what it all means. Even if anthropologists were never quite as scientific and objective as they have traditionally claimed, wouldn't some approximation of their method help students recognize and discipline their own subjectivity? Might not that kind of thinking help develop those analytical and critical abilities we hear so much about these days?

Could this kind of thinking possibly help develop creative abilities as well? Chances seem best if we listen to the radical new anthropologists who have thrown their discipline into thorough disarray. These upstarts insist that in investigating what it's like to live in a certain place at a certain time as a member of a certain culture, anthropologists do more than collect, analyze, and interpret bits of information. They follow their intuitions and make imaginative linkages. Then they compose the particulars they observe into a text telling what one person makes of that culture, thus adding one more chapter to the anthropological story of what it means to be human. Doesn't this process involve the construction of new knowledge, the making rather than the mere interpreting of meaning? And since culture is *mind-made,* isn't the bottom line actually thinking about thinking itself?

One more possibility: Anthropologists work in what Mary Louise Pratt calls *contact zones* and do a lot of what she calls *border thinking.*[2] They, more than the rest of us, work at the boundaries of races, genders, generations, social groups, and cultures. Yet they aren't the only ones who must negotiate those boundaries. As Geertz puts it, "tumbled together as [we] are in endless connection, it is increasingly difficult to get out of each other's way."[3] Might a little experience with border thinking help all of us find ways of connecting with people different from ourselves? Indeed, might it not give us new glimpses of ourselves and new insights into the predicament of our own culture?

We think so. That's why this chapter invites you to become one of those poachers in the intellectual habitat of the anthropologist—to look through anthropological lenses and make your own anthropological knowledge. Though just beginning to find our own ways around this context for thinking, we're convinced that it's worth some serious exploring.

Don't expect to cover the whole territory on a single expedition. One thing that keeps us coming back is that the boundaries are not only blurred; they keep receding. The deeper we get into this habitat for thinking, the more possibilities we see and the more questions we have. Like anthropologists themselves, we're strangers in a strange land. The remainder of this chapter invites you to join us there.

EXPLORING INSIDE OUT

Clifford Geertz offers some good advice on where to start: "If you want to understand what a science is, you should look in the first instance not at its origins or its findings, and certainly not at what its apologists say about it; you should look at what the practitioners of it do."[4] Since we're convinced that there's no such creature as an armchair anthropologist, we'd like to take that advice one step further. We urge you not merely to *look* at what the practitioners of anthropology do but to *do* what they do.

You'll need to take your journal for field notes as you set out to the site you choose for this first exploration. As in previous chapters, you'll notice that choices have been built into all activities. That's partly because potential sites for anthropological thinking differ from one locale to the next. It's also because minds differ, and because they work best—as we keep saying—when given plenty of room to chart their own paths.

Exploration

During your first foray into anthropological thinking, you'll play archaeologist. Since most towns are short on Indian mounds to excavate and most readers are probably too fastidious to hit the city dump and do a real dig, you'll concentrate on surface traces left by a particular group at a particular time. Any place rich in artifacts will do. Choose one of the following possibilities or find one of your own.

OPTION I

Go to the oldest building you can find in your area—perhaps a courthouse, home, church, school, or theater. If your community has preserved or restored some landmark such as a working farm, a blacksmith shop, a lighthouse, an unused railway station, or an old opera house or emporium, you're in luck. In any case, try for the oldest and most authentic building you can find, one that's still fully furnished so that you'll have plenty of artifacts to study.

or

Get permission to visit a workplace in which people do something you know very little about—maybe a medical lab, radio station, garage, carpentry shop, or greenhouse. Possibilities are wide open.

Journal in hand, go to the building when it's not in full use so that you can roam freely and not be distracted by people. Walk through, just seeing what you can see and getting a feel for the place. Then walk through more systematically, paying attention to every detail—furniture, equipment, tools, personal items. Examine each item closely, jotting details in your journal. Use right-hand pages only, leaving the left-hand facing pages blank for later use. As you conduct your investigation, withhold judgment, and go easy on inferences. But do lots of wondering, and jot down questions that gather in your mind. Also be open to surprises. Your job now is to collect as much data as possible. Questions and surprises may be among the most important data you collect.

OPTION 2

Go to a museum that houses at least one collection of artifacts representing a long-ago or faraway culture. Choose one such exhibition, preferably one you haven't seen before, and plan a leisurely visit.

or

Find a garage sale or a flea-market booth where miscellaneous items are for sale by the owner, preferably an owner who doesn't mind your rummaging through the merchandise.

Taking your journal with you, visit the site you've selected. Examine individual items from the collection, cataloguing them in your journal and jotting down as much descriptive detail as possible. As you do so, make special note of anything that puzzles or surprises you. Capture questions and surprises in your journal along with other data, writing only on right-hand pages.

If you took good notes, the remainder of this activity need not be done on-site. It should, however, be done while the visit is fresh in your mind. Whether you chose Option 1 or Option 2, you'll work through the same process:

Revisit your notes and take a quick inventory of artifacts found on your site. What items seem to go together in some way? Options for working through data are wide open, but you might consider some system of grouping items that seem related. Here, you might even want to dust off whatever system you used during the previous chapter to organize your invention problem—perhaps some visual device like clustering or some kind of tree diagram. As you sort items into piles, follow hunches and give your imagination full play. What patterns do you see as you shuttle between the particular and the general? Think horizontally and see what parallels or similarities you can see in items across piles. Think vertically, and see what subsets you see within piles. What kinds of items seem especially important?

Taken together, what do these artifacts seem to suggest about the people they represent? For example, what might you infer about the people who lived or worked in that old building you may have studied? If you investigated a contemporary workplace, what educated guesses can you make about what goes on there and how workers are organized? If you visited a museum, what did the artifacts in a particular exhibition suggest to you about the customs and values of the culture they represent? If you rummaged through items displayed at a garage sale, what can you infer about the family now discarding them?

On the left-hand pages you left blank in your journal, talk back to the notes on opposite pages. In writing, observe your own observations and see how they all add up in your mind. As you speculate, don't forget to take into account any odd pieces that don't quite fit any pattern. Also take into account any surprises and questions you may still be mulling over. Jot down some working explanations and the observations that support them.

Now turn back to the beginning of your journal entries and do a little reviewing. As you retrace your steps, recall the mental demands of each task. What kinds of thinking were involved in the initial walk-through of your site, in your more detailed observations of individual artifacts, in sorting and connecting collected artifacts, and in constructing some working explanations of the group represented? At what points did you work most intuitively? Most imaginatively? Most analytically and critically? What kinds of thinking did you find easiest? Most challenging? Most interesting? Turn to a clean page of your journal and reflect in writing on the way you thought through this little archaeological task.

If you have the disquieting sense that you really didn't finish what you started in the previous activity, you're absolutely right. You just sampled a process. Furthermore, in playing archaeologist, you sampled only one small corner of anthropological thinking.

Even so, the process you sampled underlies this whole territory of mind. Remember how you did a quick scan of the whole site before you began to study particulars? That kind of mental mapping is crucial to anthropologists, who always begin with an overall perspective with which they hold together the particulars.

The next activity ups the anthropological ante as it extends the processes you applied earlier. You'll continue to shuttle between the general and the particular. In the process, you'll probably find a tension—indeed a dialectic—between the local and the global. You'll also extend the kinds of collecting, connecting, and highly tentative interpreting you have already tried. In this activity, however, you'll move beyond the archaeologist's investigation of artifacts to the social anthropologist's focus on people. That means that you'll collect a greater variety and quantity of data. You'll even try the tricky business of working as a participant-observer, a role that challenges you to study a culture even as you become part of it. No matter that anthropologists are now debating whether such a balancing act is really possible. You can judge that for yourself.

Exploration

Select a commercial site specializing in some product or service you know a lot about. If you're a knitting or needlepoint buff, you might choose a needlework shop; if you live to read, a bookstore; if you know your way around food, a delicatessen specializing in gourmet items. Other possibilities range from the neighborhood laundromat or hardware store for do-it-yourselfers to a record shop, an art-supply store, or a gardening center. The important thing is to choose a place that draws people with a common interest that you share.

FIRST—

Before visiting the site, spend a few minutes thinking about what you expect to find. Considering what you know about the product or service, what objects would you expect to see, and how would you expect them to be organized? What kind of clients would you expect? Would one age group or gender predominate? Would you expect to find a particular income or educational level most prevalent? Using these questions as a starting point, do a little anticipating in your journal.

NEXT—

Now that you've inventoried your expectations and gotten your preconceptions (biases?) on the table, set them aside and visit the site, taking your journal and perhaps a small unobtrusive tape recorder with you. Allow plenty of time to look around, do some eavesdropping, and talk to people. Begin with several minutes of what ethnographers like to call "shagging around." That's really quite an apt term for the kind of ad hoc walk-through you did to get a sense of your previous site. This time, wander through the entire establishment—inside and out—for a general impression of the place and the people in it.

Start your systematic collection of data by observing cars in the parking area. Count cars of each kind, recording your findings. Then note the arrival behavior of customers—for example, whether they pause to look at window displays or hurry straight inside; whether they speak to other people and what kind of greetings they use; how they find what they want or ask for information. Note the number of customers arriving alone and the size of any groups.

Record as much demographic information as you can. Keep a running tally of customers by age group, gender, and ethnicity. You might also note clothing. Make a separate tally for employees.

Tune in on as many conversations as you can. If you don't have a tape recorder with you, write abbreviated transcriptions in your journal. Include employees as well as customers in this data collection. Be on the alert for any surprises—things that don't quite square with what you expected of the people who frequent this familiar establishment. Flag such surprises in your notes. Also, jot down questions triggered by your minute-to-minute observations.

If at all possible, talk to at least one customer who doesn't seem in too much of a hurry. Find out what brings the person there, how often, and what he or she thinks of the place. Also, talk to at least one employee for that person's impressions of the clientele. After each interview, take a few minutes to capture highlights in your journal.

FINALLY—

Following your site visit, don't wait too long to read back through your journal and flesh out notes with recollections you didn't have time to record earlier. Notice how much information you have collected—too much to try sorting out from one big pile. That's why you need to divide your data into sets before beginning to analyze it. One data set, for example, might be everything you collected about cars in the parking area. Another might be arrival behavior. Still another might be demographics. That's just an example of one obvious possibility—probably too obvious, but you get the idea. With a little thought, you can probably be much more imaginative.

Next, you'll work through each set of data, looking for connections and seeing how all those particulars add up. For example, you might take a look at your parking lot data and see what kinds of vehicles seem to predominate. Do some associating and some guessing. Based on your overall impressions of people who drive different kinds of cars, what guesses can you make about the clients who frequent this particular place of business? As you sort through each data set and make such associations and inferences, record your work.

When you finish, look at your findings in composite. Do you find any confirmation for guesses and impressions across data sets? Pay special attention to interview notes. Do your guesses and impressions square with the employee's comments about day-to-day activities and clientele? Knowing as much as you do about the product or service in which the establishment specializes, did you find anything surprising or iffy? What questions did the visit raise?

If you were writing an ethno-report—a sort of mini-ethnography of the establishment you studied, how would you profile the sampling of people and activity you found there? What particulars would you include in your eyewitness account to evoke those same impressions in the mind of a reader?

This time, you won't push your investigation further or take time to write a fully developed ethnography. It seems to us much more important to look back at the process you just followed and reflect on the kinds of thinking it entailed. Because you chose a site specializing in something you know about, you took with you the perspective of an insider. Based on your own experience with laundromats, hardware stores, bookstores, or record shops, you had some strong expectations of how the merchandise and furnishings would be arranged. You also had some expectations about the people who frequent such a place. This insider's view made you a participant as well as an observer.

This dual perspective has been considered central to the work of anthropologists since the time of Franz Boas. Known as the father of modern anthropology, this former physicist claimed that "validity must be granted to the scientific view of the outsider and the subjective view of the insider."[5] Only now is that claim being openly questioned by anthropologists themselves. Once an observer enters a culture and begins to interact with it, is scientific objectivity really possible? Is it more realistic—and more honest—to strive instead for a disciplined subjectivity? Such a view seems consistent with Geertz's observation that anthropologists practice a kind of ethnographic ventriloquism by speaking *about* a way of life even as they speak from within it.[6] These days, it's being freely acknowledged that what an anthropologist observes depends as much upon the seer as the seen, as much upon the hearer as the heard. This duality gives anthropological thinking great richness and depth. But keeping the demands of personal involvement and disciplined observation in any kind of balance is quite an intellectual feat.

The last activity gave you a little beginner's practice on this mental balancing act. It involved you in slightly more extensive tasks of collecting, analyzing, and interpreting data; you did a little cross-checking to confirm validity of that data and of your tentative interpretation. Later, you will take all this a bit further. You'll also create a text that captures what you discover and evokes it for a reader.

For this more ambitious expedition into anthropological thinking, you'll need a more ambitious subject. Rather than study a collection of strangers converging briefly because of a common interest, this time you'll study a group sustained over time and bound by shared knowledge, values, and customs. In this sense, the group that you study will comprise a miniculture.

Exploration

Take a few minutes to think about groups you know that might be considered small cultures. One especially rich possibility might be a nearby retirement home. Another might be an organization such as a Cub Scout troop or a Little League team. Still other possibilities include a country club, a fraternity or sorority, a civic or religious organization. Think especially of groups to which you don't belong but within which you can move freely as a visitor. Select one of those groups as the subject of this study.

Since you're not a member of this group, you can at least *begin* your study with a little more objectivity than you did last time out. That's important. It's also important, however, that you know as much as possible about the group before starting your on-site investigation. Time spent doing a little background work will pay big dividends. It will contribute to a working map to guide your investigation and hold your observations together.

- Begin by taking stock of what you already know about the group you plan to study. Extend that knowledge by tapping other sources. Review any written information you can find. Talk to acquaintances who know the group. In your journal, jot down what you know. Then do a little thinking about what you don't know. Is there anything about the group you find hard to understand or accept? Anything that seems especially alien? Jot down questions based on these thoughts. Then review what you've written and see how it all adds up. Keep in mind that this preliminary scan is just that—*preliminary*. It provides an informed perspective, a world view of sorts, to focus your anthropological fieldwork. Of course, only the fieldwork itself can unfold a culture.

- Adapting approaches practiced in the previous Exploration, make an initial visit to observe the group in action. If you're observing a residential site such as a retirement home or an event with lots of simultaneous activity such as a team practice or an informal club get-together, do some serious shagging around. If you're observing your group during a more formal event, you can still do some scanning to get a sense of the whole. Then begin to concentrate on particulars, including details of place. How big is it? How are any furniture and equipment arranged? What other objects do you see? Which seem to belong to individuals? Which seem to be shared by the group as a whole? Do you see any emblems, logos, or banners? What colors seem most prominent? Observe with your ears as well as your eyes and focus on people as well as place. How large is the group? What is the apparent age range? Are males and females equally represented, or does one sex seem to dominate? Do any physical characteristics seem especially common? How are people dressed? Can you identify any leaders? If so, what are they doing and saying? How do other members of the group seem to be responding? Can you identify any subgroups? Any apparent loners? Tune in on conversations. Note also when topics of conversation, interaction groups, or activities change. Does music figure at all into any of the activities, even as background? If so, what kind of music? Do participants ever sing, cheer, or speak in unison? Can you identify any repeated behaviors or recurring conversational themes? Notice how members of the group greet and say good-bye to each other. Is there any handshaking, back-slapping, hugging, or kissing? If meals or refreshments are served, notice what and how members of the group eat and drink. If you can do so without being conspicuous, take your journal or a small tape recorder to help you capture observations on this initial visit. Later, while the visit is fresh in your mind, take a few minutes to fill in details.

- As you continue to observe the group during other visits, recruit at least two inside informants. Try for members of the group who have different roles and therefore different perspectives. If you're studying a retirement home, for example, you might recruit a staff member as well as a resident. If you're studying a Little League team, pick a coach or star pitcher as well as a second- or third-stringer who usually warms the bench. Schedule at least one interview with each of your inside informants. Prepare questions to elicit as much information as possible, but during the interview leave plenty of room for the unexpected and be on the alert for promising new leads. If your informer doesn't object, tape-record the interview.

- Once your fieldwork is complete, you should have a rather extensive collection of data. The task of making sense of that data will be a little more complex and time-consuming than the work you undertook during the two previous Explorations, but the approach will be basically the same. Don't rush that interpretation, and don't hesitate to follow hunches or to allow your imagination full play. Remain open and tentative as you think back through your study. Do a lot of questioning and speculating—especially about the knowledge, values, and customs that seem to be shared within the small culture you studied. As you inch your way toward interpretations of that culture, pay special attention to negative cases. What doesn't quite fit? See if puzzling over these exceptions sparks any new insights or uncovers any previously overlooked complexities. Then do some interpreting. What sets this culture apart—indeed, what makes it a culture? Write any hypotheses you can make from your study and save them for the next activity.

- Meanwhile, take time out for a little reflection on what you've done so far. In what ways has this more ambitious investigation been more mentally demanding? How well have you handled each of these demands? Where have you had to stretch most? Where have you done your best intellectual work?

Earlier in this chapter, you were invited to take the advice of Clifford Geertz and focus your efforts on what practicing anthropologists actually do. So far, you have concentrated on fieldwork—on observing and collecting data in a natural context, then making sense of those findings. Fieldwork is indeed what anthropologists do, but it's not *all* they do. Anthropologists also write. They construct texts that evoke for others what it's like to belong to a certain group in a certain place at a certain time. Your next task is to create such a text.

Exploration

Using the field notes collected and sorted through most recently, write your own eyewitness account of the culture you studied. Begin by setting the scene and situating yourself in it. Speak in your own voice and maintain a strong presence in the story. After all, the credibility of your account depends on your having personally observed the way of life evoked by your words and those of the informants you quote from your field notes. The authority of what you have to say will be more personal than scientific. Furthermore, your presence in the text will give the reader a point of identification, a shoulder to look over as the story unfolds.

Bring the culture alive with abundant use of details that dramatize the values and customs shared by members of that particular group. Writing rapidly may help you capture the you-are-there immediacy needed to draw readers into the story of your culture. As you write, try to evoke rather than merely describe. Focus on what you found most interesting and significant.

When you complete your first draft, you might like to try it out on at least one reader. Ask that reader to share his or her dominant impressions of the group described. Ask also what passages seem most vivid and evocative. How well do these responses square with your intentions and with your reading of your own text? If at all possible, you might also take your text back to the site of your fieldwork and check it out with one of your informants or another employee of that establishment.

Before putting aside that text, take a moment to reflect on the way you went about creating it. How did you get started? What then? What kinds of thinking were involved in various stages of work? What did you find most difficult? Most satisfying? Did your thoughts ever surprise you? Now that you have put your culture on paper, do you see it any differently?

In working through these Explorations, you haven't had to venture far from home. You've learned firsthand that this context for thinking is not restricted to remote places teeming with exotic sights and sounds. Certainly, you've barely begun to sample opportunities for anthropological thinking right in your own backyard. Even so, we hope that you are beginning to find your way around the edges of this rich intellectual territory and that you'll venture into it more deeply on your own.

EXPLORING OUTSIDE IN

Now that you've done enough intellectual poaching to view the anthropologist's territory as an insider, you'll probably be more interested in what the *real* insiders have to say about how they think and work. Because the field is in flux and the dialogue so intense, this is a good time to tune in on anthropologists. Be on the alert for television interviews, newpaper stories, and magazine articles. Browse through the anthropology section of your favorite bookstores. As you do so, make notes in your journal to extend insights gleaned from the experts featured in the following activities.

Exploration

As you read each first-person account of fieldwork conducted by a young anthropologist, note the kinds of thinking involved. Note also the dispositions of mind reflected in that work. Keep a running list of each.

More than twenty years later, James Peacock recalls the study with which his work began:

> The purpose was to learn how national values were communicated to ordinary people in Indonesia. To research this question, I went to Indonesia in September 1962, accompanied by my nonanthropologist wife. I stayed one year and exposed us to two things: first, eighty-two performances of a working-class Indonesian drama known as *ludruk*; second, the lives of those

Indonesians in whose milieu *ludruk* had meaning. Contexts of "participant observation" ranged from the shantytown in which we lived to the back of the *ludruk* in which I once traveled.

The year was intense. I have had jobs requiring manual labor, intellectual effort, and social sensitivity, but fieldwork required them all, and in an alien milieu. Our human relationships were sometimes deep and significant, but, in the Javanese fashion, they were also stylized and polite.... Some [anthropologists] recount dramatic moments when the new culture grabbed and shook them, shattering their assumptions. My understandings grew more gradually.

The tangible results of the fieldwork were field notes (some six hundred pages, single-spaced, banged out on a cheap portable), tapes, photographs, articles, and books. This prosaic point reminds us that fieldwork is method as well as experience. It may have in it the potential to transform the self and teach insight. But whatever its subjective aspect, it is also a method for attempting to characterize descriptively someone else's way of life.[7]

Loring Danforth opens his book on death rituals in rural Greece with a personal reflection on recently completed fieldwork:

Anthropology inevitably involves an encounter with the Other. All too often, however, the ethnographic distance between a familiar "we" and an exotic "they" is a major obstacle to meaningful understanding, an obstacle that can only be overcome through some form of participation in the world of the Other....

Whenever I observed death rituals in rural Greece, I was acutely aware of a paradoxical sense of simultaneous distance and closeness, otherness and oneness.... To my eyes funeral laments, black mourning dress, and exhumation rites *were* exotic. Yet ... I was conscious at all times that it is not just Others who die. I was aware that my friends and relatives will die, that I will die, that death comes to all, Self and Other alike.

Over the course of my fieldwork these "exotic" rites became meaningful, even attractive alternatives to the experience of death as I had known it. As I sat by the body of a man who had died several hours earlier and listened to his wife, his sisters, and his daughters lament his death, I imagined these rites being performed and laments being sung at the death of my relatives, at my own death.... When the brother of the deceased entered the room, the women ... began to sing a lament about two brothers who were violently separated as they sat clinging to each other in the branches of a tree that was being swept away by a raging torrent. I thought of my own brother and cried. The distance between Self and Other had grown small indeed.[8]

Take a few minutes to muse on these two testimonials from the field and to compare your lists tracing operations and dispositions of mind reflected in each.

- What common ground do you find between the accounts? What differences?

- In what ways do these firsthand reports confirm your previous understanding of how anthropologists work? Do they provide any new insights or call into question any previous assumptions?

- What kinds of thinking do you find reflected in the fieldwork recounted? What dispositions of mind? Compare these ways of thinking and working with those you experienced as an apprentice anthropologist. What additional intellectual challenges do you see?

As you undoubtedly noted, both Peacock and Danforth think with their senses. That's no coincidence; observation is the anthropologist's stock in trade. Yet, as Peacock puts it, the anthropologist does more than collect particulars "as a botanist might gather plants or an archaeologist potsherds." The anthropologist's mind "is not a bucket or a basket, but a searchlight [that] seeks and highlights, notices this but not that."[9] In the accounts you just sampled, notice how each observer's purpose and perspective, a worldview of sorts, inform selectivity and focus the beam of attention. It's because they view reality through such a personal lens that field workers become part of their own anthropological cameras, and even the most scientific data collection takes on a subjective cast.

Today, such subjectivity is being freely acknowledged. More and more, the distance between Self and Other is being bridged by the kind of empathy and identification so apparent in the two passages you just read. Anthropologists participate as well as observe, feel as well as think. Ever so gradually, insights coalesce and new knowledge is made. Those patient processes involve a lot of questioning, seeking, selecting, connecting, interpreting, judging, and synthesizing. Ultimately, they involve nothing less than the creation of meanings.

The making of new cultural knowledge begins in the field, but it doesn't end there. That's why so much attention is now being focused on the construction of ethnographic texts in which cultures are evoked for readers who can know those cultures only through words. The next activity focuses on what anthropologists do at the desk rather than in the field—on the making of meaning through the making of texts.

Exploration

As you read the following comments by anthropologist-authors, again keep a running list of the mental processes and dispositions you see at work.

Mary Louise Pratt, from a book tellingly titled Writing Culture:

> Fieldwork produces a kind of authority that is anchored to a large extent in subjective, sensuous experience. One experiences the indigenous environment and lifeways for oneself, sees with one's own eyes, even plays some roles, albeit contrived ones, in the daily life of the community. But the professional text to result from such an encounter is supposed to conform to the norms of scientific discourse whose authority resides in the absolute efface-ment of the speaking and experiencing subject.... Personal narra-tive mediates this contradiction between the engagement called for in fieldwork and the self-effacement called for in formal ethno-graphic description, or at least mitigates some of its anguish, by inserting into the ethnographic text the authority of the personal experience out of which the ethnography is made. It thus recuper-ates at least a few shreds of what was exorcised in the conver-sion from the face-to-face field encounter to objectified science. That is why such narratives have not been killed by science....[10]

Clifford Geertz, in defense of "anthropology as a good read":

> The risks are worth running because running them leads to a thoroughgoing revision of our understanding of what it is to open (a bit) the consciousness of one group of people to (something of) the life-form of another, and in that way to (something of) their own. What it is (a task at which no one ever does more than not utterly fail) is to inscribe a present—to convey in words "what it is like" to be somewhere specific in the lifeline of the world.... It is above all a rendering of the actual, a vitality phrased.... The ca-pacity to persuade readers that what they are reading is an au-thentic account by someone personally acquainted with how life proceeds in some place, at some time, among some group, is the basis upon which anything else ethnography seeks to do—ana-lyze, explain, amuse, disconcert, celebrate, edify, excuse, aston-ish, and subvert—finally rests.... The textual connection of the Being Here and Being There sides of anthropology, the imagina-tive construction of a common ground between the Written At and the Written About,... is whatever power anthropology has to con-vince anyone of anything.[11]

Now pause for a few minutes to consider these comments and review your lists.

- Does either anthropologist say anything that surprises you or contradicts a previous assumption?
- In what ways do both Pratt and Geertz seem to consider anthropology an art as well as a science? How do you think this duality might complicate the anthropologist's work? Enhance it?
- Compare the two lists you just made to each other and to those you made during the previous Exploration. Focus especially on the mental processes you think are involved in the "imaginative construction" of a text. In light of your own writing experience as well as the views you just read, how is it different—and more difficult—to *inscribe* (rather than merely *transcribe*) encounters with a culture; to *evoke* (rather than merely *represent*) meaning?

This might be a good time to remind ourselves that anthropologists hold no monopoly on particular operations or attributes of mind. As you may have noticed, this context for thinking reverberates with echoes from the territories explored in previous chapters. More on that later.

This might also be a good time to caution ourselves about overgeneralizing. For convenience, we keep talking about anthropologists and other thinkers in generic terms. Don't let that mislead you; all anthropologists don't think alike any more than all artists or all naturalists or all inventors do. They share a context but, like the rest of us, have one-of-a-kind minds.

Even if it were possible to stereotype thinkers or to sort mental processes into different contexts, doing so would not be the point. The point is to expand and enrich our own thinking by grounding it in such borrowed worlds as that of the anthropologist. That's what you have sought to do so far in this chapter.

Now it's time to return to our own world and see what all this has to do with the Monday-through-Friday reality of classrooms.

SO WHAT?

Let's start by turning the anthropological lens back upon ourselves as teachers. In so doing, we will be following the lead of those who value anthropology primarily as a means of cultural critique, of reflecting self-critically on our own ways, of reexamining our taken-for-granted assumptions.[12]

Exploration

We suggest that you get started by accepting Frank Smith's challenge to become an archaeologist in your own classroom and conduct a study of artifacts—everything from how the room is furnished and arranged to the books and papers it contains. Wipe your mind clean and imagine that you're seeing that classroom for the first time. Become a stranger who knows only that the room is used to educate the young, and walk through the door. What's your first impression? How does the room feel? Move around and see what catches your eye. What do you see on the walls? What kinds of equipment do you find? What does that equipment look like it might be used for? Take stock of the furniture and how it is arranged. Try out several chairs in different parts of the room. See how they feel and what you can see from each. Then do some more walking around. What other objects, large and small, do you notice? Read anything that might be written on chalkboards, posters, bulletin boards, or the like. Spend some time browsing through any books, magazines, or papers you see.

Now, continuing to think like an archaeologist, review your observations and do a little interpreting. Assuming that you know only one thing about the site you just studied—that it's a room used to educate the young—and you have only physical evidence to go on, what would you conclude about what goes on there? What would you think was taught? What kinds of activities can you visualize in that setting? Who would you think interacted most often with whom? Most crucial of all, what would you think was really *valued* in that classroom?

As a case in point, consider the message sent by pairs of adjoining classrooms in two schools Carol knows well, one a high school and the other an elementary school many miles away. One of those high school classrooms contains six straight rows of six desk-chairs each, all facing a teacher's desk with lectern. The room next door is furnished with six scrounged tables, arranged in a U and casually flanked by varying numbers of chairs. Across town, one elementary classroom is a miniaturized version of its regimented high school counterpart: six straight rows of student desks facing the teacher's. Not so the second classroom, in which pairs of student desk-chairs have been pushed together face-to-face and the teacher's desk relegated to a back corner. Even empty, don't these classrooms telegraph clearly which belongs to a front-and-center teacher given to dispensing information and which belongs to students who collaborate and take responsibility for their own learning?

You bet they do. The students who live in these rooms know that, and so do you—even before being told that the second classroom described in each pair belongs to a teacher you've met in previous chapters. Having caught both teachers in the act of teaching, Carol can attest that what you see is what you get. The same may or may not be true of teachers in those traditionally arranged classrooms. We've all seen teachers work magic in the most conventional settings. It just seems a great deal harder when five students out of six are staring at the back of a classmate's head or at the teacher.

Telltale physical signs go far beyond room arrangement. Ask the Houston principal who played archaeologist in her own school, which prides itself on a commitment to whole-language approaches to reading and process-centered approaches to writing. Her solitary late-afternoon survey of classrooms raised some disquieting questions: Why those shelves of textbooks and sheaves of paper filled with drill and practice? Why so few trade books and so little evidence of student writing in progress? When the principal asked her faculty for help with these questions, most teachers seemed genuinely surprised. Many accepted the principal's invitation to do a little digging in their own classrooms and discuss their findings. They began to confront their own die-hard dependence on skills-driven basals and shored up one another's confidence as basals *really* began yielding ground to library books and paperbacks. They began to share student work that had been marked and graded. They shared drafts of pieces in progress. They worried together about old habits of construing errors as something to be avoided and treated punitively as opposed to something to be learned from and treated as opportunities for further learning.

These teachers still have a long way to go, but they're convinced that there's nothing like a little archaeological thinking to check theory against practice. They're grateful for their principal's late-afternoon walk-through of their empty classrooms and for the positive way she engaged them and supported them in examining their own work. Surely this experience is more than an isolated case. That's why we stick by our suggestion to take an unblinking look at artifacts in your own classroom and ask yourself what they show about the work that goes on there, about the values that shape you as a teacher, and about the values you transmit to students.

And transmit values we *all* do, even to that student who always seems to be looking out the window with studied indifference. Some students may be indifferent or otherwise difficult, but none are oblivious to the surroundings in which they do time every day. That's Frank Smith's point: "Every human child is an archaeologist and anthropologist, an unprejudiced explorer from another galaxy. Children learn from the artifacts they find in their environment and from the behavior of people around them." Let's hope that Smith isn't recalling digs in classrooms like ours when he continues, "Where do children learn ... that learning is tedious, that they are themselves dullards, that collaboration is cheating, and that nothing at school is worth doing without a score?"[13] In any case, occasional archaeological expeditions into our own classrooms can keep us honest about that insidious "hidden curriculum" we hear so much about.

So can the broader, more ambitious kinds of anthropological thinking practiced earlier in this chapter. Your classroom—like the organization, team, or retirement home you studied—is a small culture. Just imagine what you might learn by stepping back and engaging in the same kind of systematic ethnographic inquiry. Start with that openness to discovery which allows an anthropologist to generate hypotheses based on what members of a group actually do and say—not on preconceived ideas of what they are *supposed* to do or say—as they go naturally about their business. Consider also the ready-made opportunity you have to work as participant observer in your own classroom and the rich store of data available for collection as you record observations and interactions with and among students. Most importantly, imagine how much you could learn from subjecting that mass of description to critical analysis and using it to make sense of the knowledge, customs, and values that shape the culture of your classroom.

Actually *doing* all this will take time. That's why our suggestion to undertake an ethnographic inquiry is anything but casual. Even so, we're convinced that classrooms are rich subjects for anthropological thinking and that such thinking can help make us more responsive, insightful teachers.

Especially in a multicultural city like Houston, that last point is worth extending. At least that's what one group of Carol's colleagues would argue after their Saturday morning expedition to Chinatown, a tiny business enclave in which carefully preserved Asian traditions are overlaid with Texan entrepreneurship. As group members had hoped, this enclave turned out to be what Mary Louise Pratt calls a *contact zone* and challenged participants to do a lot of what she calls *border thinking*. Mr. Yo, the bank security guard who dressed like a fugitive from Austin City Limits and whose Chinese accent was combined with a drawl, came to personify for those visiting administrators the dramatic contrasts marking this intersection of cultures. (We're afraid he appeared in more than one ethnography as "Mr. Yo-Bubba.")

For this group of administrators who had insisted upon their own "Growing Thinkers" project, the Chinatown expedition stands uncontested as the highpoint of a most stimulating year. Maybe that's because the schools they work in are themselves contact zones: more than eighty languages are spoken by Houston's more than 194,000 students. Maybe it's also because many of these administrators remember the multicultural sensitivity training of the sixties and see a need to get back to unfinished business. Maybe it's even because they are themselves a multicultural group or because so many discovered or rediscovered the satisfaction of making meaning in text rather than just grinding out bureaucratic memos. In any case, this foray across cultural borders started something. Carol has heard of several semiorganized expeditions to barrios and other ethnic neighborhoods, as well as several on-campus investigations of the cultures that converge in a particular school.

Certainly, neither administrators nor teachers have a monopoly on such activities. While anthropological thinking gives us a powerful lens to turn back on ourselves as professionals, it's not for adults only. To the contrary. For starters, consider what can be done with archaeology as a context for thinking. The excavation of classroom wastebaskets, home garbage cans, even city dumps has become a local favorite among activities in this genre. Before dismissing such an admittedly messy idea, take a moment to consider trash as artifact and mull over ways you might engage your students in collecting and analyzing the data it yields—in making meaning from the residue of daily life.

That's the first thing Marla Stanley, Grace Beam, and Nancy Krpec challenged their seventh-graders to do on their field trip to the Coushatta Indian Reservation. As background for their investigation of Coushatta culture, students examined artifacts previously excavated from eighteenth-century mounds. Then, in pairs or trios, they shagged around the reservation before undertaking a more detailed and systematic investigation, which included at least one interview with a Coushatta. Observations were captured in field notes and many interviews on tape recorders. By the time students boarded the bus for the return trip to school, most had plenty of data to sift through and interpret during the next few days. As a culminating assignment, each student was asked to portray the Coushatta in a way that would evoke for others their contemporary way of life on an East Texas reservation.[14]

We like the open-endedness of that culminating assignment—a point to which we'll return in a moment. We also like the way these teachers took students beyond the confines of their classrooms to capitalize upon a rich but little-known site many miles from their school. Having both put in some years teaching seventh-graders, we know that it takes a certain daring to board buses with more than a hundred of them. We also know that it takes both careful preparation and confidence to let those students set off on their own investigations of a sprawling Indian reservation, indeed to take charge of their own learning.

Still another thing we like is the way Marla, Grace, and Nancy broke down the traditional boundaries between content areas as they planned and guided this series of learning experiences. Though Marla teaches social studies, Grace science, and Nancy language arts, they work as a team. Within the context of the Coushatta unit, they saw to it that students learned plenty about history and the natural environment, and did a lot of reading and writing. Yet none of this learning occurred in isolation, and none lacked purpose.

Back to the open-endedness of that culminating assignment. The option of portraying the Coushatta culture in a medium other than text opens up all the possibilities you sampled during your earlier exploration of artistic thinking. It also reminds us of the "Art by Anthropologists" exhibition we happened upon at Spooner Hall on the Kansas University campus a couple of years ago and especially of one artist's comment that seemed worth copying from a wall: "My goal is to wear down the old ways of seeing and to replace them (at least for the moment) with a new, learned vision and to appreciate another culture in doing so."[15]

That's a rather ambitious goal for seventh-graders, but one well worth stretching toward. We're convinced that learning in such anthropological contexts can do much to develop students' minds. Experiences that help "wear down the old ways of seeing" should certainly nurture that open-mindedness and ability to adopt other perspectives we know to be so crucial in a world Geertz describes as "tending not toward homogenization but 'mixedupness'."[16] Challenging students to construct for themselves "a new learned vision" engages and hones such key mental processes as selecting, observing, questioning, analyzing, connecting, hypothesizing, testing, and synthesizing. More importantly, it challenges them to make their own meaning and to create their own texts. Because projects in anthropology require the gathering of thick description, they help students learn to deal with complexity and ambiguity. Because such projects must be sustained over time, they cultivate habits of persistence and perseverance.

Convinced as we are that anthropology provides an especially rich context for thinking, we're *not* convinced that this context is easy to handle in the classroom. Maybe one of its advantages is that it lures us *out* of the classroom and challenges us to explore interesting new environments. Given the stickiness of arranging field trips, however, that often seems more like a disadvantage. Yet several teachers Carol knows have adapted various Explorations appearing earlier in this chapter to students of all ages. After studying Armand Bayou Nature Center as a workplace, at least two teachers engaged their students in similar on-site investigations. For fifth-graders, of course, the study was scaled down more than it was for high school sophomores. Both, however, conducted close observations of building and grounds, and both interviewed staffers as inside informants. Other field lessons have taken students to nearby Fiesta Supermarkets, as well as Mexican and Vietnamese shopping centers. Most of these trips have culminated in the writing of abbreviated ethnographic texts, many of which have been proudly collected for do-it-yourself publications.

Carol Wallingford, an elementary school librarian, tried a different approach. After a research project in anthropology, she challenged her fourth-graders to transfer this new kind of thinking to literature. As they prepared to read books representing cultures around the world, Carol asked students to think like amateur anthropologists entering a culture that's different in some ways from their own. She asked them to pay attention to detail and to make predictions or hypotheses about what characters would do and why. To set the stage, she donned a Mexican peasant dress to read aloud a folktale set in Old Mexico and paused in her reading for an occasional think-aloud.[17] Some time after reading Carol's report of this experiment, we came across Gerry Brookes's *Language Arts* article suggesting just such an approach[18] and promptly shared it with Carol as confirmation for what she'd done intuitively.

Two quick observations before you take over and explore possibilities for translating all this into reality in your own classroom. One is a return to our familiar refrain that only a thinking teacher can develop thinking students—to which we would add that only a teacher who is learning to feel at home in the intellectual habitat of the anthropologist can lead students into that habitat. That's one of the big reasons we keep lobbying for you to engage in those Explorations. We also keep lobbying for you to take a friend along. That brings us to the second observation: Collaboration enhances thinking—your own and that of your students. For that reason, we suggest that you recruit a colleague to help you translate all this anthropology into something you can use in your own classroom.

Exploration

Think of some concepts and processes you plan to teach soon. Think also of the abilities and attributes of mind you want your students to develop as they learn these concepts and practice these processes. Consider especially the abilities and attributes you've found to be developed by working within the context of anthropology.

- Recall your own experiences as an amateur anthropologist and perhaps some of the classroom applications described in this chapter. Would any version of such activities have possibilities for developing the kinds of thinking and the dispositions of mind you want your students to work on? How might such activities look within the framework of your subject? How might they be related to the concepts you wish to teach or the processes you want students to practice? Jot down as many ideas as you can.

- Test your ideas on a colleague—maybe a former anthropology major or someone else from the social sciences. As you try out ideas on this consultant, jot down others that may be triggered. After you spend some time developing one or more ideas into a full-blown lesson or unit, you might invite your new partner to team-teach (or at least observe) those lessons as they unfold in your classroom. Complete your plans, keeping in mind that you want students to become actively involved and to take as much responsibility as possible for their own learning. Be sure to build in opportunities for students to reflect on their own ways of thinking and working.

- As you implement these plans in your classroom, collect student products and make notes on various demonstrations of learning. Also collect reflections and make notes on what students say about their own processes of making meaning.

- As soon as the series of lessons is concluded, sift through your notes and take a careful look at student products. Use your journal to reflect on this attempt to engage your students in anthropological ways of thinking. What seemed to work? What might you do differently next time? What new ideas do you have for using anthropology as a context for thinking and learning in your subject?

LOOKING BACK

We hope that the last activity helped you look back over your shoulder, recall where you've been, and reflect on your experience as an intellectual poacher in the territory of the anthropologist. We also hope that it's prepared you to revisit those questions posed at the beginning of this chapter. Why the current explosion of interest in anthropology as a context for thinking, especially now that it's undergoing such an identity crisis? What's in it for us as teachers and for our students?

You'll have to answer those questions for yourself. Before doing so, let's be reminded of that key point to which we promised we'd return—the point that anthropologists have no monopoly on particular processes and habits of mind. An obvious case in point: Anthropologists are tireless observers whose work demands great persistence, but so are artists and naturalists. This might be a good time to thumb back through the three previous chapters and see how many such overlaps you can find. What kinds of thinking span all four contexts? What dispositions of mind? Within these similarities, what differences do you see?

Now, back to those questions about anthropology as a context for thinking and what that context holds for students. Our own answers to those questions took on a sharper focus just recently when we shared Dan's notes from a week-long colloquium with Clifford Geertz. Maybe a few entries will strike a responsive chord with you.[19]

"I always start with differences—contrasts," said Geertz. Isn't that where we need to start with our students, with the understanding—indeed the celebration—of human diversity? Our own forays into anthropology have sharpened our appreciation for human differences and deepened our resolve to make schools more responsive to those differences without letting up on the struggle for educational equity.

Another Geertz nugget from Dan's notes: "I like the notion of 'webs';

webs counter the 'everything fits together' view. We need disconnections as well as connections. A fully connected thing won't work. What does it mean to say these things go together?" That's quite a question—a question we've just begun to understand, much less pursue. It's one reason we'll keep returning to this context for thinking and dragging colleagues as well as students along with us.

We are also drawn to the way anthropologists embrace tentativeness and resist dogma. As Geertz puts it, "I'm concerned with destabilizing certainties." Just imagine what a little destabilization could do to open up schools and revitalize learning—especially our own. Dealing with uncertainty takes us to the edge, where we're convinced both learners and teachers do their best work. No context for thinking continues to take us closer to the edge than anthropology.

Maybe that's because this context compels us to become a stranger in a strange land, to get beyond the boundaries of accustomed ways of thinking. Geertz puts it this way: "You see your own boundaries more clearly when you have been taken outside them." That notion brings us back to the self-illuminating function of anthropological thinking, its power to make us more reflective as individuals and as teachers.

Though it's Dan's encounter with Geertz that has guided our most recent reflection on what it means to think like an anthropologist, we'd like to let Loren Eiseley have the last word. Trained as an anthropologist, this writer-naturalist-teacher best epitomizes the richness of this context for thinking: "A man comes into life with certain attitudes and is inculcated with others of his time. Then some fine day, the kaleidoscope through which we peer at life shifts suddenly and everything is reordered.... A blink at the right moment may do it, an eye applied to a crevice, or the world seen through a tear."[20] Perhaps it's the anthropologist's penchant for kaleidoscopic thinking that makes this intellectual territory so rich for us and for our students.

NOTES

1. Clifford E. Geertz, *Works and Lives: The Anthropologist as Author.* Stanford: Stanford University Press, 1988.
2. Mary Louise Pratt, Unpublished speech at Wyoming Conference on English. University of Wyoming at Laramie, June, 1988.
3. See note 1 above.
4. See note 1 above.
5. Quoted in Howard Gardner, *The Mind's New Science.* New York: Basic Books, 1985.
6. Quoted in James Clifford, *The Predicament of Culture: Twentieth-Century Ethnography, Literature, and Art.* Cambridge: Harvard University Press, 1986.

7. James L. Peacock, *The Anthropological Lens: Harsh Light/Soft Focus.* New York: Cambridge University Press, 1986.

8. Quoted in Geertz, *Works and Lives,* 1988. (See note 1 above.)

9. See note 7 above.

10. James Clifford and George E. Marcus. *Writing Culture: The Poetics and Politics of Ethnography.* Berkeley: University of California Press, 1986.

11. See note 1 above.

12. George E. Marcus and Michael M. J. Fischer. *Anthropology as Cultural Critique: An Experimental Movement in the Social Sciences.* Chicago: University Press, 1986.

13. Frank Smith, *Insult to Intelligence.* New York: Arbor House, 1986.

14. Marla Stanley, Grace Beam, and Nancy Krpec teach at Pershing Middle School in Houston.

15. Carol Hendrickson. Placard accompanying paintings in "Art by Anthropologists" exhibition in Museum of Anthropology, Kansas University, February, 1987.

16. Clifford Geertz. Unpublished remarks during colloquium at University of California at Santa Barbara, May, 1989.

17. Carol Wallingford is a librarian at Hartsfield Elementary School in Houston.

18. Gerry H. Brookes, "Exploring the World through Reading and Writing." Language Arts (March, 1988).

19. See note 16 above.

20. Loren Eiseley, *All the Strange Hours: The Evacuation of a Life.* New York: Charles Scribner's Sons, 1975.

UNIT IV
Matters of Fact

Like the chapters you've already read, those that follow bristle with questions: How can I maintain in my classroom that delicate ecosystem in which thinking flourishes? What environmental hazards in my own school and in the educational system beyond threaten that ecosystem? What about constraints of time? The skepticism of colleagues? The demands of standardized testing?

Since thinking is by nature invisible, how do I know that it's really going on—that students are thinking more and thinking better as the school year progresses? In fact, how can I be sure that I'm really doing what I *think* I'm doing to develop my own thinking and that of my students? Now that I've spent all this time thinking about thinking, what next?

Although the pages that follow point in some promising directions, they offer no one-size-fits-all answers to such questions. Instead, they challenge you to sort through the issues for yourself and chart your own course as a thinker and nurturer of thinkers. In a very real sense, this last section of the book is a beginning rather than an ending.

9

Valuing
Thinking

Late at night, listening to Mozart's Jupiter
Symphony, I worry a lot about thinking.... I worry
about our new enthusiasms for measuring thinking,
our search for easy-to-mark, forced-choice, pencil-
and-paper tests yielding single, numerical scores that
"tell all." I worry that, in the measures we choose, we
might trivialize our most wonderful human capability
by measuring simply one process and judging all
students by that single standard.... I worry that our
earnest efforts may give us the kind of music we all
deserve: terminal Salieri.

—Selma Wassermann

In this chapter, we face the music on matters of evaluation. Unless you
skipped the preceding sections of this book entirely, you have a pretty good
idea what we're not willing to face—certainly not those one-dimensional measures that trivialize thinking. We're pretty sure where you stand on this issue
too, and it's not on the side of assessment scaled to Salieris rather than
Mozarts. Readers who have stayed with us this far aren't likely to join the
chorus urging easy-to-mark, forced-choice pencil-and-paper tests that purport
to assess thinking. The kind of evaluation we're after is the very antithesis of
standardized testing—at which we'll undoubtedly take a few potshots before
this chapter concludes. Can't you just imagine standardized instruments that
yield national norms for thinking? "Amanda is thinking two months above
grade level" ... "Thinking scores for Alpha Elementary School have slipped
from the 90th percentile to the 84th." That's a tune we never want to hear.

Having just trekked with us through those contexts for thinking, you
probably didn't need that disclaimer. Now that it's on record, let's revisit
those contexts and see where they lead in our search for authentic ways to

track the intellectual development of students. If you have your own classroom and have tried some of the ideas in previous chapters, think back to
the days your students spent thinking like artists, like naturalists, like inventors, like anthropologists. Review jottings in your log and try to recall the
processes and attributes of mind you hoped your students were developing.
Wouldn't you like to know more than you do about the success of those efforts? As students thought like artists, for example, did they become more
imaginative? Did they become at least a little more persistent and willing to
stick with a task? Did working within the context of naturalists actually help
students become closer observers? As they explored the world of invention,
did they become better problem finders as well as problem solvers? Did they
become more willing to take risks? Did thinking like anthropologists really
extend students' ability to make connections without rushing to conclusions?
Does all—or any—of this effort to develop thinking really pay off?

Any attempt to evaluate thinking starts with questions like these. It's no
coincidence that the next few pages will raise a lot more. That's because evaluation is rooted in questions: What do we want to know about what students
are able to do? How can we find out? If we want to know what students are
able to do with their minds rather than merely how much information they
can retrieve, the questions multiply. How can we find out how well and in
what ways students are thinking? How can we know that they are thinking
more and thinking better as they progress in school?

The latter question brings us back to the big questions with which this
book began: What is thinking, anyway? Indeed, what is intelligence? How
can it be developed? To set a direction for this chapter, let's ask another:
How can intellectual growth be evaluated?

INTELLIGENCE REVISITED

First things first. Although there's plenty we don't know about the nature and nurture of intelligence, we know more than we've put to use in most
schools. On the most fundamental level, we know that intelligence is not genetically fixed and immutable. No one is destined to go through life with an
IQ of 92—or 120 or 140, for that matter. As Robert Sternberg has observed,
"No one is stuck with being 'less intelligent.' We are stuck with less intelligent ideas about the hopelessness of raising intellectual levels."[1]

We also know that intelligence differs less in amount than it does in
kind. Few of us would argue the question of who was "smarter"—Leonardo,
Shakespeare, or Einstein. Most of us would quickly agree that the minds that
produced the Mona Lisa, *King Lear,* and the theory of relativity defy arrangement along a bell-shaped curve. Some of us who have been influenced

by Howard Gardner's work might suppose that these acknowledged genius-es simply operated from different "frames of mind": one excelling in the spa-tial, another in the verbal, and still another in the logical-mathematical.[2] Others might view these same geniuses in terms of Robert Sternberg's tri-archic view and see various blends of analytic, creative, and practical abili-ties.[3] Still others might apply David Perkins's theory that each individual in-telligence is shaped by a unique interaction of biological endowment, experience, and reflection.[4]

Though increasingly influential in the literature, these emerging views of intelligence have yet to find a home in most American schools. The Betsys, Lees, and Ramons who bring such diversity to our classrooms may not be Leonardos, Shakespeares, and Einsteins. Of course, we don't know that yet. What we do know is that our Betsys, Lees, and Ramons are just as different. We also know that they have a long way to go before realizing their full potential for intellectual growth. That growth, we're convinced, can be stunted by the myth of the fixed, monolithic IQ. That's why we consider it so dangerous for teachers to act as if intelligence were intractable, as if it were genetically fixed and could be influenced only minimally by environment.

Even those of us who reject such intellectual determinism must admit that helping young minds develop is quite a challenge. It's hard to fathom the immense variability of the human mind. We know from experience that it's even harder to tap the multiplicity of abilities that create as many intellec-tual profiles as there are minds in any given class.

As noted in chapter 4, the way we view intelligence is crucial to the de-velopment of thinking. It's also crucial to evaluation. After all, if we are seri-ous about assessing thinking, we must be prepared to recognize its endless variability. We must also recognize its potential for growth. Only then can we find ways to gather and evaluate evidence of that growth—of each unique in-dividual's ability to behave in increasingly intelligent ways. More and more, we're convinced that intellectual growth has less to do with the honing of particular mental processes than with the building of mental habits. That conviction in no way detracts from the importance of engaging students in experiences that involve such processes as observing, synthesizing, judging, and imagining. Extending the ability to think in particular ways is indeed central to the development of thinking. Yet those abilities alone do not en-sure intelligent behavior. Acting intelligently requires more than the ability to think; it requires thought.

Thoughtfulness is a habit. Like other inclinations or dispositions of mind, it can be developed. But habits are harder to develop than skills, and they take more time. Therein may lie our greatest challenge: helping stu-dents break down thoughtless habits and build thoughtful ones. This mega-challenge includes evaluation: How can we track that growth?

Exploration

If you've been keeping the journal we so strongly recommend, turn back to entries made as you worked through chapter 4. Find the list of traits and behaviors you've observed in the best thinkers you know. You might also thumb back to page 72 and review our sample list.

Choose one attribute of good thinkers that you consider especially important to success in school and beyond—for example, perseverance, open-mindedness, or willingness to take risks. What have you already done to help students in your classes develop this particular habit of mind? What else might you do? In what ways do you model this habit? What opportunities have you given students to practice it? What other opportunities might you provide in the next few weeks? How else can you help?

Write a journal entry exploring these questions. Then turn your attention to matters of evaluation. How can you tell whether your students are progressing? How do they demonstrate the particular habit of mind you're seeking to develop? What evidence have you already collected? What else might you collect?

If you find these questions a bit daunting, don't worry. So do we. In fact, so do foremost experts in assessment. When it comes to evaluating thinking, we're all in uncertain territory.

Yet we're convinced that it's a territory we as teachers must explore—perhaps even claim—if all the current rhetoric about teaching thinking is to become reality. There's no denying that schools put their instructional money where their assessment mouths are: What's not evaluated is seldom taught. Besides, we need evaluative data to inform our work with thinking. That's why this chapter will continue to press such questions as those posed above: How do we identify different kinds of intelligence at work? How do we evaluate the quality of thinking and trace its improvement? How do we track those habits of mind that enable students to behave in increasingly intelligent ways? In short, how do we evaluate thinking?

STARTING THE SEARCH

These questions aren't new to us. They're the ones we puzzled over almost a decade ago when we took on the challenge of coauthoring *Thinking Through Language,* a thinking text for middle-schoolers.[5] What we found then holds today: There are no boilerplate methods of assessing students' growth as thinkers. As we'll discuss later in this chapter, some promising assessment models are beginning to emerge. Even so, as teachers, we remain largely on our own in following the intellectual footprints of students to detect signs of better thinking and more thoughtful behavior.

Our own fledgling attempts to evaluate thinking confirm the intuitions we've learned to trust in the classroom. Though unabashedly naive, the evaluation strategies suggested in *Thinking Through Language* distinctly prefigure those emerging models of assessment we'll sample later. For starters, we planned each of our thinking units for middle-schoolers around what we have since learned from Ted Sizer and the Coalition of Essential Schools to call "performances" or "demonstrations" of learning. We even practiced the Coalition principle of "backward" course design—that is, starting with the level of intellectual performance we wanted students to attain and then doubling back to plan a series of experiences that would help them do so. In retrospect, we realize that we could have used Grant Wiggins' help in establishing standards by which to evaluate student performance, but more on that later.[6] At least our teacherly intuition guided us to teach toward exhibits, forums, festivals, and conferences at which students could show their intellectual stuff—in more sedate terms, demonstrate the mental processes and habits they had developed.

The same kind of intuition, informed by years of working with writing journals and other tools of the teacher-as-researcher trade, led us to build in ways of collecting every possible shred of information about what students were doing and thinking as they worked on sustained projects suggested in the book. If teachers were to trace the trajectory of individual minds—to understand how different students thought through similar tasks—we knew that they would need every available clue. In suggesting ways to collect and interpret this information, we were also feeling our way toward at least two big evaluation questions now being addressed by Dennie Wolf and her Project Zero colleagues at Harvard: What can we learn about individual students' ability to sustain work over time? What can we learn about their ability to step back and reflect critically upon their own work?[7] To help teachers probe those questions, we asked students to keep journals of sorts—sketchbooks, logs, notebooks—in which they wrote daily. We also asked them to create special containers in which to collect working papers and other raw materials for projects in various contexts for thinking—an artist's portfolio, an inventor's kit, a futurist's file. Such process information figured heavily into the scheme by which we suggested that teachers arrive at an overall assessment of each student's thinking and thus determine the letter or number to be placed in that ubiquitous grade book.

We look back to *Thinking Through Language* for at least two reasons. In the first place, those early attempts to evaluate thinking set the direction for much of what would follow. In the second place, the right-headedness of those first crude efforts to evaluate thinking confirms our trust in the intuitions we all develop as teachers. We hope that you'll respect your own intuitions and be guided by them, even as you test those intuitions against the best available theory and research. That's especially important as you take on the challenge of evaluating thinking. There's still not a great deal to go on, and you'll be largely on your own in seeking answers to those big questions about how to identify different kinds of intelligence at work and how to track habits of mind that enable students to behave in increasingly intelligent ways.

CONFRONTING THE STATUS QUO

In seeking answers to these questions, we certainly can't look to assessment as now practiced in most schools. Despite the sound and fury created by all those mandated tests, the scores they yield signify little about thinking. In fact, as test-makers scramble to move in on the "thinking" market, we're more worried than ever that standardized testing will short-circuit evaluation—indeed development—of thinking. That's why we feel compelled to take a few of those potshots promised earlier. For those of us committed to making schools more thoughtful places, standardized testing is an obstacle that must be confronted head-on.

Head-on, but not blindly. Mere test bashing does little more than make us look defensive. That's why we need to do our homework about the uses, misuses, and abuses of standardized testing. It's also why we intend what follows to serve as a mini survival guide for teachers caught in the crossfire as states and school districts escalate the accountability wars.

Perhaps we need to begin by acknowledging a legitimate need for information about how well students are learning in school. Such information helps guide decision making by parents, teachers, and students themselves. It also helps citizens in a particular school community understand what they're getting for their tax dollars. Up to a point, standardized tests can be defended as a means of gathering such information.

It's no news to you that most schools passed that point years ago. Therein lies the first big problem with standardized testing—overkill. According to studies cited by the National Center for Fair and Open Testing (FairTest), public schools in this country administered more than 105 million standardized tests to approximately 39.8 million students during the 1986–1987 school year. That's an average of two and one-half tests per student per year. At this rate, by the time a student graduates from high school, he or she has been forced to take thirty standardized tests.[8] Given the continued proliferation of testing since the time of this study and the announced intent of the President to implement a national assessment, that total may now be even higher.

Considering the amount of learning time usurped, such overkill would be bad enough even if the tests were flawless and their influence benign. Unfortunately, standardized tests are anything but flawless or benign.

In the first place, they typically measure the wrong things—isolated skills erroneously termed "basic." Linda Darling-Hammond calls standardized tests "testing for the TV generation—superficial and passive." In her words, "We don't ask if students can synthesize information, solve problems, or think independently. We measure what they can recognize."[9]

Arthur Costa believes that the fundamental problem may lie in the very nature of the beast. A multiple-choice, machine-scoreable instrument that can be easily administered in a group setting can by its very nature measure only what students are able to recognize. Costa suggests that anything easily enough tested and quantified to be included on such a test may by definition be inconsequential.[10]

Regardless of how distinguished the sources, acting on hearsay is seldom good survival strategy. That's why we suggest that you do some firsthand checking into your school's testing program. The tests mandated on your campus may not be as numerous or as superficial as those prompting the concerns just expressed. On the other hand, they may be more so. In any case, you need to assess the assessment in your school and see how it forwards or obstructs your efforts to evaluate the kind of thinking you seek to develop.

Exploration

Enlist a small group of colleagues to join you in examining the testing program. Begin by listing all the tests that are required by your state, by your own school system, or by any other agency. Include criterion- as well as norm-referenced tests. In all, how many tests are administered? How much time is required for each? What's the total amount of time required for testing each year?

Next, inventory the skills and concepts assessed on each test. How significant do you consider these skills and concepts? How much overlap do you find among what is assessed on various tests? What abilities that you consider important are not assessed at all?

If copies of actual tests are available, take at least one test yourself and ask each member of your study group to take a different one. If copies aren't available, study item specifications and work through as many sample or practice items as you can find. As you do so, consider the mental demands of each item. What kind of thinking does that item require? How well does it

184 MATTERS OF FACT

measure what it purports to measure? Compare notes with other members of the group and compile a summary.

When you've completed this study, you may wish to submit an unsolicited report of your findings to your principal, your department head, or some other leader on your campus.

Before you dismiss that last suggestion as too risky even to consider, let us say a word for administrators—at least for most of the administrators Carol knows in her own city and both of us know around the country. They share teachers' perspective on mandated testing.

What Carol heard recently from a group of almost thirty Houston administrators who had studied her district's testing program provides a case in point. As dismayed as these administrators are by the 10 percent of instructional time they conservatively estimate is usurped by testing, they're more dismayed by the emptiness of the tests themselves: "We think we're measuring learning, but we're not." "We're measuring only a tiny fraction of students' abilities." "Test-makers seem to value only a narrow band of achievement." "Tests find out what students can remember, not what they can do." "How can the richness and complexity of a child's mind be reduced to a single number—the almighty score?"

Quite apart from what the tests do and do not measure, these principals expressed grave concerns about pressures to raise scores. When scores are printed on the front page of the daily paper right along with percentile ranks, that pressure is overwhelming. Principals, like teachers, know the futility of questioning norms used to compare the performance of students—though the title of Dr. John Channell's 1987 report speaks for itself: "How All Fifty States Are Above the National Average."[11] It would only make bad matters worse to acknowledge the artificial and near-universal inflation of gains so aptly dubbed the Lake Wobegon Effect.

The cost of such "gains" is incalculable. Make the stakes high enough, and test scores will go up. The curriculum becomes expendable, and so do the students who are pushed out of school both by failure and by the sheer boredom of multiple-choice teaching.

The pressures to reduce what's taught to what's tested can be overwhelming. Just ask the young teacher who recently handed Carol this question at an in-service workshop in Houston: "Why the sample unit on dinosaurs in the second-grade guide? Dinosaurs aren't on the Metropolitan Achievement Test!!!" We doubt that Carol's answer was enough to dissuade that teacher from single-mindedly hammering away at the isolated skills and bits of information she thinks her students will be expected to know when they bubble in their answer sheets one morning next April. Between now and then, her students stand to lose far more than a museum field trip to learn about dinosaurs.

Multiply this loss by thousands, and we begin to see the terrible toll being exacted by the status quo in standardized testing. It's none too soon that many states are experimenting with alternatives. A report on Connecticut's new performance-based assessment system sums up the reasons: "We believe that the time has come to develop assessments that are catalysts for the kind of learning that we value. The model currently in place—atomistic tasks, passive learning, and primarily convergent thinking—has been too well served for too many years by multiple-choice testing."[12]

A number of states—at this writing, eleven—already assess students' ability to write by evaluating a sample of actual writing. Others are venturing into performance-based assessment in science, mathematics, and social studies. New York, for example, has had more than two-hundred thousand fourth-graders conduct a short experiment and report results. California includes open-ended questions as part of its twelfth-grade mathematics test. Massachusetts has experimented with having fourth- and eighth-graders work together in pairs to solve lifelike problems using both science and mathematics.[13] Maine has included in its eighth-grade social studies test a vivid satellite photograph of the Los Angeles Basin with a wisp of smoke rising above the trees. Students were asked to find the environmental threat in the picture and to write a plan for handling that threat.

Though well-intentioned and highly encouraging, such alternatives leave us a little edgy. In the first place, they're add-ons rather than replacements for conventional multiple-choice tests. There goes more time that could be used for thinking and learning rather than testing. Furthermore, though broad and open-ended, these tasks are decontextualized and thereby stripped of meaning. They're command performances—in a word, tests.

Much more encouraging are attempts now underway to incorporate evaluation of students' "work portfolios." A proposal now on the table in Vermont calls for students, in consultation with their teachers, to prepare a portfolio of three papers reflecting their best work. Trained teachers are then to evaluate each portfolio, which may include work from English, social studies, science, or any other subject. As this pioneering work proceeds, it will be followed closely by a "conscience committee" charged with assessing the assessment and making mid-course recommendations for change.[14]

This alternative approach to assessment seems to us a giant step forward in efforts to evaluate thinking as well as learning. Besides involving teachers in developing standards and protocols for evaluating portfolios, such an approach links evaluation to ongoing classroom activities. No longer is assessment artificial and decontextualized. Rather than performing a stock task upon command, students choose the products upon which they wish to be assessed. Like their teachers, they become active participants in the evaluation of learning. In doing so, they must engage in a great deal of critical thinking about their own work and about the standards by which it will be judged. Thus the portfolio approach to assessment has the potential to extend rather than constrict thinking.

At the moment, that potential remains unrealized. Even if the portfolio approach were to offer an assessment panacea, there's no assurance that it will be widely adopted. Developing protocols and training teacher-assessors would require a huge investment. Scoring of portfolios would always be costly, since that process involves so much teacher time. Then, what if the public's appetite for test scores cannot be satisfied with scores derived from portfolios of student work? In the final analysis, the biggest obstacles to change may well be political rather than educational or economic.

Since state education agencies and national testing services are so sensitive to political pressures, we don't expect external evaluators to lead us beyond the current morass of standardized testing. Even if they do, the best we can expect is periodic assessment based on a wider sampling of more authentic learning. Though such snapshots of student achievement could be immensely helpful in gauging the success of students as well as programs and schools, they would still be snapshots—pictures of how thinking and learning look at a particular point in time. Such assessments would provide a good first step in evaluating thinking, but they would leave unanswered most of those questions posed at the beginning of this chapter.

TRACKING STUDENT THINKING

Perhaps that's just as well. Evaluating thinking is really a day-to-day responsibility of teachers and their students. It should be implicit in, rather than apart from, the ongoing business of teaching and learning. Yet *How?* remains a big question. So does *When?* Even if we knew more about how to evaluate thinking, schools don't provide much time for collecting information about how students get ideas, how they acquire and assimilate new pieces of knowledge, how they generate questions and solve problems, and how they make judgments about their work.

We're convinced that the best place to make time for collecting such information is right up front when classroom work is being planned. Starting with evaluation helps us see it not as some after-the-fact device for checking up on what students have learned but as an essential part of instruction.

For the last three years, Debbie Frontiera has found time to track the thinking of her twenty-plus kindergarteners. In a large spiral-bound notebook, which she considers indispensable equipment, Debbie keeps carefully dated anecdotal notes on each child. During learning center time—a fifteen-minute period during which children have free choice of materials and activities—she tries to focus her observations on each child at least once every few weeks. For the full fifteen minutes, these observations are guided by several questions: What materials does that child choose, and how are those materials used? Does the child use familiar materials in a new way? Does he or she seem to concentrate and stay with an idea? Does the child act on his or her own ideas or copy someone else's? Is there interaction with other children? What kind? Is the child adaptable and open to change?

Debbie also makes periodic notes on each child's drawings, focusing on degree of completeness and attention to detail. In addition, she captures "thoughtful" questions and responses during large- and small-group discussions, and logs observations of children's behavior when they do not "know" an answer. As an example of the latter, Debbie reports noting how children often sneak a look at alphabet picture cards posted on the wall when they can't remember a letter sound. During a matching exercise with cards, she also noted how a child would slip a hard one to the bottom of the stack so that it could be matched by the process of elimination.

Many teachers we know would frown upon such tactics. Not Debbie. To her, such coping strategies are indications of young problem-solvers at work: "Intelligent behavior shows up when a child knows what to do when he does not know—when he figures out where to get an answer when he doesn't have it." It's such indications of thinking that this kindergarten teacher tracks in her spiral notebook.

Though Debbie acknowledges that such tracking takes time, she sees it as central to her work with children. "The lack of kindergarteners' ability to take pencil-and-paper tests is a big advantage in evaluating thinking. It forces me to use many forms of evaluation that are more subjective but more accurate and more valuable in the long run." In Debbie's classroom, it's obvious that instructional plans are shaped by this ongoing evaluation of each kindergartener's development as a thinker. It's also obvious that daily planning leaves plenty of room for children to think in new and unexpected ways. By capturing informal evidence of this thinking and reviewing patterns that unfold over time, Debbie seeks to track as well as nurture intellectual growth throughout the school year.[15]

Though Margaret Blackstone takes a different approach, her work with second-graders is directed toward the same goals. A believer in open-ended evaluation, she frequently administers the "test" she finds most useful: She says to her children, "Show me what you have learned." Choosing their own ways to demonstrate learning makes these second-graders active participants in the evaluation process. It also fosters independent thinking and provides the teacher abundant information about the strengths, preferences, and needs of each child.

Margaret frames this day-to-day evaluation with a project designed to assess children's overall progress, especially in language. Early in the year, each child constructs an animal puppet—usually a bear. Through a series of improvised puppet shows, the children develop their animals into interesting and distinctive characters. They then spend several days writing and illustrating stories about their animal characters. Before being put away until the end of the year, each child's story is bound into a book and displayed with the puppet representing its main character. Then in late spring, Margaret has children revisit their earlier work. After a new series of activities, which include a lot of talk about books they've read together during the year, the children write and illustrate new stories about the animal characters they created the previous fall. By comparing beginning-of-year with end-of-year books, Margaret finds evidence of what children have learned along the way. She also finds evidence of different minds at work—of different strengths and different profiles of intellectual growth.[16]

In her high school art classes, Tracye Wear works hard at helping students develop their minds as well as their prowess at drawing and painting. As she begins planning a new sequence of classroom activities, she consults her list of attributes characterizing good thinkers—habits of mind like perseverance, curiosity, flexibility, and willingness to experiment. Besides modeling these characteristics herself and encouraging them in her students, Tracye structures assignments and classroom activities to ensure practice. She also builds in ways of evaluating each student's progress, both as an artist and as a thinker.

Tracye's evaluation takes into account process as well as product. A unit titled "Learning to See: Face Drawing"—which we sampled in chapter 3—provides a case in point. To culminate several weeks of learning to observe and draw the human face in a variety of ways, Tracye has each student create a self-portrait. This major drawing is submitted for evaluation along with work journals containing daily sketches and drawing exercises. On the back of each preliminary sketch, students have been asked to jot down questions, problems, and discoveries prompted by that particular task. Before handing in journals, they've also been asked to review both sketches and notes and to reflect in writing on their own ways of seeing, drawing, and thinking. Together, the self-portrait and the journal allow Tracye to assess students' progress as artists and to track their development as thinkers. Furthermore, she gives students a big piece of the action.[17]

Though Barbara Donovan teaches social studies rather than art, she takes a similar tack. In a U.S. history unit designed to develop open-mindedness as well as acquaint students with the Civil Rights Movement, Barbara begins by having students write their own individual definitions of prejudice. After several days of reading, viewing films, role-playing, research, and discussion, students are asked to rewrite their definitions of prejudice. They're also asked to retrace their own paths through the unit to see where and how their thinking has changed.[18]

Judy Friedberg, whose computer lab you heard about in chapter 2, goes beyond teaching her elementary students to interact with computers. You may recall how Judy draws upon principles of cooperative learning to teach those students to interact with one another. Keenly aware that children need to be prepared for a complex world in which most problems must be tackled by teams rather than by individuals, Judy teaches toward collaboration. In introducing the "Cross-Country Texas" simulation described in chapter 2, Judy explains that only one person will be at the computer keyboard and that this student will enter commands as directed by various teams. Before beginning the simulation, Judy also takes time to involve her students in setting standards for the kind of teamwork that will help everyone succeed in reaching a common goal. After it ends, students take a backward look to see how teams measured up to those standards and how they need to improve. Judy teaches not only collaborative thinking but also collaborative evaluation.[19]

All of these approaches to evaluation closely resemble those advocated by Grant Wiggins and others involved in the Coalition of Essential Schools. Coalition educators argue that "tests"—which they define as performances or exhibitions of learning—should lie at the center rather than at the edges of instruction. A cornerstone of the Coalition approach is the kind of "backward" course design we intuitively tried in our middle school thinking text—that is, starting with the desired intellectual performances, then doubling back to plan day-to-day experiences that would help students achieve them. Across the curriculum, Coalition schools test progress by having students perform authentic tasks that lie at the heart of a particular academic discipline. As students work at these tasks, the standards by which their performances will be judged is no secret. To the contrary, students have worked— and teachers have coached—toward those standards from the outset.[20]

For many years, that's the way we've worked as teachers of writing. It didn't take either of us long to learn that students can be expected to write good pieces only if they know what "good" means. It didn't take much longer to discover that letting students in on standards helps to demystify grading. Since an overall evaluation of each student's work must periodically be squeezed into a small box on the report card, grading is an issue we have never ducked. If grades reflect what we're really after and if students participate in their own evaluation, we have no qualms about putting down a grade—even a numerical or letter grade.

Dan's "checkpoint" scheme for evaluating writing yields a numerical score. The sample that appears in Figure 9.1 was devised for college students—in fact, for the memoir assignment described in chapter 7—but the approach it illustrates is adaptable to any level.

The criteria comprised in this checkpoint were no surprise to Dan's students. These standards had been implicit in the memoir assignment distributed weeks before. They had become increasingly explicit as students had selected short pieces from their portfolios and had woven those pieces together according to a scheme of their own devising. Reading memoirs by professional writers and responding to each other's drafts had strengthened their sense of craft. Since the standards they were working toward had become familiar and the class had developed its own verbal shorthand for talking about them, criteria on this checklist could be cryptic. When students saw a rating of five on detail and two on beginning and ending, they knew ex-

FIGURE 9.1

CHECKPOINT FOR MEMOIR

_____
Writer's Name

Your piece was rated using the following criteria. If you wish to work further on the piece in hopes of raising the score, please do so.

DETAIL
    1   2   3   4   5   X4 _____

BEGINNING AND ENDING
    1   2   3   4   5   X4 _____

CRAFT
    1   2   3   4   5   X4 _____

INSIDE/OUTSIDE STUFF
    1   2   3   4   5   X4 _____

MECHANICS AND USAGE
    1   2   3   4   5   X4 _____

OVERALL EFFECTIVENESS
    1   2   3   4   5   X4 _____

    TOTAL SCORE

COMMENTS: _____

_____

_____

_____

actly where to build on success and where to do some serious improving. Since the total score is simply the sum of ratings on weighted criteria, the grade eventually recorded for each student's memoir was no mystery.

Firsthand experience on all grade levels has convinced us that students write better when they write with an eye to evaluation. It's also convinced us that evaluation works best when students participate in the shaping of criteria by which their work is to be judged and when they become evaluators as well as evaluatees. As students become partners in the process, evaluation hones thinking as well as writing.

Even at its best, however, product evaluation tells only part of the story. That's why Dan went beyond a checkpoint rating in evaluating his college students' memoirs. He also assigned this in-class freewrite:

> Reflect on the process you have just experienced as you tried to put your memoir piece together.
>
> - What did you try to do with this piece? What were you trying to leave a reader with?
> - How well did it work? What parts of the piece work best? If you were going to continue work on the piece, what parts would you spend more time with?
> - What were the most difficult parts of this process?
> - How did you go at this project? What were your work habits?
> - What are you learning about your own processes as a writer these first few weeks in this class?
> - How well did this approach to a final piece work for you?

Reflecting on such questions helps students follow their own mental tracks and, in the process, learn more about themselves as thinkers as well as as writers. Reading those reflections allows the teacher to follow the same mental tracks and, over time, to find clues to the processes and habits of each individual mind.

In his classes, Dan doesn't stop at having students reflect on how they've gone about writing individual pieces. The next chapter will include an example of the periodic portfolio audits he uses to engage students in looking at their own work across time—to take stock of where they've been, where they are, and where they're going as writers and as thinkers. By assessing their own efforts over time and reflecting on their own work habits, students become partners in evaluation. They also provide for Dan windows into individual minds. As you'll see during the next chapter, these periodic glimpses of mind do more than make students participants in evaluation. They also help teachers monitor their own teaching and plan *with* rather than merely *for* their students.

What Dan calls portfolio audits in his writing classes can take many forms. We are especially interested in work now underway in Pittsburgh where students are involved in composing "biographies" of their projects and teachers are being trained to read those biographies. Such an approach seems to us transportable across content areas. We also wonder whether tape recordings might be similarly transportable beyond music classes. Consider Dennie Wolf's account of a musical group sitting around a tape recorder that repeatedly plays a segment of their most recent performance. The tape then switches to an earlier rendition of the same segment, and the teacher asks, "What do you hear? ... So what do you think we need to work on next week?"[21] Might it be that audiotapes of group problem-solving might provide a *class* portfolio to track progress in collaborative thinking? What about the possibility of recording individual think-alouds or reflective interviews? Such extensions of portfolio evaluation seem well worth exploring.

As you've worked to nurture young thinkers in your own classroom, you may have ventured into new territory of evaluation. You undoubtedly have some good ideas about how to track thinking in whatever subjects you teach. This might be a good time to reflect on your own efforts to evaluate thinking and to follow up on ideas sparked by what you've just read.

Exploration

Rummage through your recollections of personal efforts to place thinking at the center of your teaching. Call to mind the project or unit that you found most successful for at least some of your students. How did you know that these students were indeed thinking more and thinking better as they worked through the assigned tasks? What signs of progress did you see? In what ways did you collect information about the ways students approached these tasks? Toward what kind of standards did they work? How were these standards set? How well did final products meet these standards? What role did students have both in process and product evaluation? In retrospect, how might you extend and refine your evaluation of students' thinking and learning in this particular project or unit?

Now think ahead to projects or units still on the drawing board. What new strategies for evaluation might you build in? Take a moment to jot down promising possibilities.

The longer and harder we work at evaluating student thinking and learning, the more convinced we become that the process must be open. First of all, it must be open to students. If teachers unilaterally set all of the standards and do all of the evaluating, students will never develop the ability to recognize excellence when they see it and to make the critical judgments necessary to reach it. As Dennie Wolf points out, young people need to develop their own ways of judging—to internalize their own standards to use as guideposts in minute-to-minute decision-making about "what word to choose, whether to take a risk, how to select among alternatives."[22]

Students can't make such decisions if they work on only prefabricated, prestructured assignments. That's one reason we like to assign open-ended tasks that leave plenty of mental elbowroom. The kind of independent thinking we seek to develop—and to evaluate—is the kind students will undoubtedly need once they leave school and encounter all kinds of messy, ill-defined problems and opportunities.

The more open and authentic the tasks we assign, the less those tasks fit neatly into fifty-five-minute class periods and six-week grading cycles. That's why we also need to open up time. It often takes months for students to think their ways through a project, to move from early attempt to finished product or performance. Along the way, we need tracings of process: science notebooks logging an experiment from the dawning of an idea to final report, audiotapes recording the progress of a flute solo from sight-reading to recital, journals and drafts capturing the evolution of a research paper from prewriting to publication, notes and working files that tell the story of a mathematics project from start to finish.

Granted, we don't know yet how to examine these tracings systematically and to interpret them reliably. Yet even the novices among us can learn a great deal by examining evidence of how individual students generate ideas, pose questions, select among alternatives, solve problems, work through preliminary drafts, seek and respond to criticism, sustain effort over time, and reflect critically upon their own work. Wouldn't such insights take us a long way toward evaluating the processes and habits of mind we work so hard to develop? We think so. That's why we cringe when notes and drafts of works in progress are tossed away.

Analyzing the artifacts of thought may never be an exact science, but we're watching with great interest two assessment projects that address problems of reliability and validity head-on. One is the experimental Key School in Indianapolis, and the other is PROPEL, a collaborative venture of the Pittsburgh Schools and the staff of Project Zero at Harvard from which we've already borrowed. Focusing on music, visual arts, and imaginative writing, PROPEL seeks to devise assessment instruments that can document thinking and learning through the later elementary and high school years. Besides asking students to make "biographies" of their projects and training teachers to read them, PROPEL takes a longitudinal approach to systematic examination of "process-folios." The intent is to develop ways of building personal profiles of each student's work—of his or her ability to conceptualize and carry out a project, the seeking out and assimilation of others' ideas, the regularity and quality of portfolio entries, the capacity to think directly in a particular medium, signs of linkage from one work to another, the student's own sensitivity to his or her own development, and the ability to express personal meanings.

Those involved in PROPEL stress a point that all of us need to keep in mind: Regardless of the psychometric success or failure of attempts to evaluate progress in thinking, students and teachers find portfolio activities engaging, exciting, and useful in their own right. Classrooms come alive when students as well as teachers become involved in following intellectual tracks.[23]

That's no small point. We're convinced that students are nothing less than coauthors in this business of evaluating thinking. After all, it's their thinking. We need their help—and they need ours—in probing those really big evaluation questions posed at the beginning of this chapter, the questions that matter so much but about which the results of standardized tests tell us so little.

Maybe this is a good time to take stock of how all this adds up and where it might take you in your own efforts to track intellectual growth over time, especially those all-important habits of mind.

Exploration

Imagine for a moment that you've been asked to write an in-depth evaluation of one of your students—perhaps a progress report to parents, an assessment of qualifications for a special program, or a profile to be considered by a college admissions committee. In any case, the focus is to be upon the student's repertoire of mental abilities and his or her dispositions of mind.

Consider all the evidence you have to draw upon, formal and informal. What tells you most about that student's capacity to pose interesting questions, to find as well as solve problems? What tells you how well that student is able to sustain long-term serious work and what repertoire of abilities he or she brings to it? What tells you how well the student is able to plan and monitor his or her own work, then step back and reflect on it criticially? What indicators of intellectual growth do you find?

Among all the stacks and drawers of papers in your classroom, what would contribute most to a well-documented evaluation of one of your students if the focus were to be on thinking—that is, on processes and habits of mind? What would be virtually useless? Where might there be gaps? As you look toward future efforts to evaluate thinking, how might those gaps be filled?

The importance of working at the kind of evaluation you just attempted is summed up by Howard Gardner and David Perkins: "Across the curriculum, we ought to be studying complex, long-term learning rather than students' acquisition of particulate facts in isolation. We ought to make use of the naturally occurring developmental materials students generate—rather than separate tests. In making those assessments, we must hunt down not merely the immediately visible, but also invisible, processual dimensions of learning."[24]

Realistically, we have to hedge a bit on the admonition to use the naturalistic approaches just discussed "*rather than* separate tests." In most schools we know, tests can't be dismissed so easily. Maybe we should think instead of the alternative proposed by Rexford Brown after a two-year study of testing and its effects upon development of "higher literacies"—defined as the ability to create, construct, negotiate, and communicate meaning. Rather than calling for a moratorium on tests, Brown calls for a new concept of testing directed toward making schools more thoughtful places. Based on extensive study of schools across the country, Brown claims that the best tests of thoughtfulness are those generated by students themselves.[25]

Having dared a few times to test by requiring students to create their own questions rather than to answer ours, we nod in agreement at Brown's rationale. In learning how to ask the right questions, to sort good answers from the not-so-good and the relevant from the irrelevant, students do indeed "get learning in their bones."[26] Carol recalls especially what Advanced Placement seniors claimed to be her hardest but most interesting literature test: What three to five questions would you ask to find out whether a reader really got to the heart of this story (or essay or poem or play)? We suspect that Margaret's second-graders feel much the same about her challenge, "Show me what you have learned." We even speculate that by walking in the test-makers' shoes, students might well develop a savvy that could carry over to those standardized tests, which we don't see going away any time soon.

In any case, if day-to-day and semester-by-semester testing were redirected toward thoughtfulness, we might be coaxed into peaceful coexistence with standardized tests if they were scaled down and placed in perspective. In our minds, the challenge is not so much to exterminate tests as to keep them from dominating schools, distorting priorities, and blocking efforts to make classrooms more thoughtful places.

As we put the finishing touches on this chapter, a coalition of noted educators, professional organizations, and civil-rights groups is taking on that formidable challenge. In a public appeal addressed to the President of the United States and the nation's governors, this coalition urges policy makers not to be "seduced by the siren song of standardized testing" but to use alternative forms of assessment to measure progress toward national goals.

Citing the inadequacy of traditional multiple-choice measures, it is also urging that governors set a timetable for phasing out existing standardized tests and replacing them with alternatives. While acknowledging that such alternative forms of assessment would be expensive, the coalition notes that excellence costs money and that it would pay big dividends. The bottom line, it's claimed, would be *genuine* "accountability."[27]

We like the concept but can't help wincing at the word *accountability*. Perhaps because of its root and its association with the world of finance, this word seems to cramp the kind of evaluation we're after. In our experience, *accountability* connotes a preoccupation with test scores, norms, and percentiles; it also translates into praise or blame. That's one reason Kenneth Sirotnik insists that *accountability* must give way to *responsibility*. We agree that this crucial shift would be more than semantic if indeed symbols (like numbers and letters) would give way to meanings and short answers to long-term inquiry.[28]

We're heartened by such challenges to status quo assessment as those just cited. To that outnumbered but swelling chorus, add the voice of Gordon Cawelti, who also calls for more authentic and more trustworthy evidence of student achievement.[29] Rather than continuing to pile on one dubious standardized test after another, Cawelti asks: Why not require high school graduates to do things, to demonstrate representative behaviors exhibited by competent adults in the world beyond school? Similar to the exhibitions of mastery required in schools following the coalition's guidelines, such a "test" might require students to write a 300-word piece on a word processor, to read five previously unread novels and discuss them with a teacher, to apply mathematical knowledge to several situations that are likely to be encountered in the future. Schools could require demonstrations of whatever they believe students need to know and be able to do. This kind of performance assessment can certainly be as rigorous as it is authentic. To Cawelti, it calls to mind the earning of merit badges as evidence of successful accomplishments. Not a bad metaphor for the kind of evaluation urged in this chapter.

STEERING BY PRINCIPLES

Though this chapter urges teachers to reclaim the territory of evaluation, we've acknowledged from the outset that this territory becomes uncertain when it comes to matters of the mind. As you explore this territory for yourself, we'd like to offer a few principles that continue to steer our search for better ways to evaluate thinking. These principles aren't really new; they just gather the threads of this chapter into what we hope will be a useful synthesis.

1. *Standards are qualities, not quantities.* Here, we invoke the words of Grant Wiggins: "Thinking of 'standards' as the setting of cutoffs hides the fact that standards represent differences in kind, not degree—desirable behaviors, not the best typical behavior."[30] What we're really after is not some magic number that draws the line between "correct" and lesser responses to a set of test questions. It is, instead, a set of desirable habits—behavior that suggests that students are indeed diligent, thoughtful, engaged, persistent, and thorough, no matter what they learn.

   Translating this principle into practice isn't easy. Nothing we've advocated in this chapter is. Even so, we want to press the point: If we think only in terms of what can be quantified, we're probably going to fall into the trap of counting what doesn't count— the test-maker's game of trivial pursuit.

2. *Process counts as much as product.* If we really want to track thinking—not just where students arrive but the mental processes by which they got there—this principle is self-evident. Just think back over your own experience. What do final products tell you? What else do you need to trace the mental footprints of students as they move from Point A to Points B, C, and D? What intellectual tracings help you most in evaluating growth in habits as well as processes of mind? You undoubtedly rely a great deal on logs, journals, and other such data suggested and illustrated in this chapter. Such tracings tell you not only where students have been and what they've learned along the way but also where you as a teacher might need to go next.

   Products alone don't yield such information. That's why we depend upon tracings of process to show the thinking that went into each product. To us, the quality of that thinking figures heavily into evaluation.

3. *Meta-information is crucial.* By definition, growth occurs over time. Growth in thinking is no exception. That's why evaluation of thinking needs to be continuous and overarching, not just ad hoc. As teachers, we need to see the big picture—how students work across time and across tasks. We need to capture information about how they plan what they're to do, how they monitor their own work as they do it, and how they assess their own success after the fact. In short, we need to know as much as we can possibly learn about how individual students think and how they think about their own thinking. Such information—"meta-information"—informs our teaching. More importantly, it informs learning by helping students gain insights into the workings of their own minds.

4. *Students must coauthor their own evaluation.* We won't belabor this principle, since it echoes such an obvious theme. Rex Brown's point about the power of having students' author their own tests comes to mind. So does our own experience in having students collaborate on the development of criteria by which their work will be evaluated. The bottom line is that we as teachers have no windows into students' minds except those that students themselves provide. To that point we would add only this: Students won't always have us around; to become reflective, self-directed thinkers, they must also become their own evaluators.

5. *Teacher judgment is central.* Despite our most strenuous attempts to construct measures that are valid and reliable, evaluation is *not* an exact science. Because it depends so heavily upon inference and interpretation, we prefer to see it as critical inquiry that relies upon the professional judgment of a thoughtful teacher. If indeed the intent is to evaluate thinking—which by definition involves nuance and the weighing of alternatives rather than fixed answers—we hardly see how it can be otherwise. Certainly when it comes to tracking those all-important habits of mind—not just what we want students to do, but what we want them to become—the most powerful assessment tool of all is sustained observation by a good teacher.

    Admittedly, we all have a long way to go in learning what to make of on-the-spot observations and how to sort out qualitative materials. Even so, a good teacher can make informed judgments about students' ability to pose and solve problems, sustain work over time, and think critically about their own thinking. No multiple-choice, machine-scoreable test can do that, and we'll take authenticity over statistical reliability any day.

6. *Evaluation reflects values.* As the title of this chapter suggests, we like to think of the word *evaluation* as meaning, quite literally, finding the value in something. That definition does more than rule out the *gotcha* approach that all too often reduces evaluation to a hunt for errors. It also forces us to confront the bedrock issue of what we are teaching toward, what we consider important—in short, what we value. That's what we look for in evaluating student work.

    For those of us committed to developing thinking, the way we approach evaluation takes the measure of our own minds. It reflects what we believe to be most important for young people to learn and to become. Because the focus of our evaluation sends such a strong message to students, it can raise the roof on thinking or reduce it to what Dewey has called "superior mediocrity." The spectre of Salieri again comes to mind. Maybe this is a good time to put on some Mozart and take a little time to ponder the challenge of *valuing* thinking.

NOTES

1. Michael F. Shaughnessy, "An Interview with Robert J. Sternberg." *Human Intelligence Newletter* (Spring-Summer, 1989).
2. Howard Gardner, *Frames of Mind.* New York: Basic Books, 1983.
3. Robert J. Sternberg, *Beyond IQ: A Triarchic Theory of Human Intelligence.* New York: Cambridge University Press, 1985.
4. David N. Perkins, "Mindware: The New Science of Learnable Intelligence." Speech at Annual Conference of ASCD. March, 1989.
5. Dan Kirby and Carol Kuykendall, *Thinking Through Language.* Urbana: National Council of Teachers of English, 1985.
6. Grant Wiggins, "Teaching to the Authentic Test." *Educational Leadership* (April, 1989).
7. Dennie Palmer Wolf, "Opening Up Assessment: Ideas from the Arts." Unpublished paper, Project Zero, Harvard University, 1988.
8. D. Neill Monty and Noe J. Medina, "Standardized Testing: Harmful to Educational Health." *Phi Delta Kappan* (May, 1989).
9. Ibid.
10. Arthur L. Costa, "The School as a Home for the Mind." Speech at Annual Conference of ASCD. March, 1989.
11. See note 8 above.
12. Robert Rothman, "Connecticut: Moving Past Paper and Pencil." *Education Week* (September 13, 1989).
13. Ibid.
14. Robert Rothman, "Vermont Plans to Pioneer with 'Work Portfolios'." *Education Week* (October 26, 1988).
15. Debbie Frontiera teaches at Ashford Elementary School in Houston.
16. Margaret Blackstone teaches at Travis Elementary School in Houston.
17. Tracye Wear teaches at Jones High School in Houston.
18. Barbara Donovan is a teacher in the Bureau of Community Services of the Houston Independent School District. Most of her classes are composed of hospital-bound teenagers.
19. Until 1989, Judy Friedberg was a teacher technologist in Bonham Elementary School in Houston.
20. See note 6 above.
21. See note 7 above.
22. See note 7 above.
23. Howard Gardner, "Arts PROPEL." Project Zero paper prepared for *Studies in Art Education* (September, 1988).
24. Howard Gardner and David Perkins, *Art, Mind, and Education: Research from Project Zero.* Urbana: University of Illinois Press, 1989.
25. Rexford Brown, "Testing and Thoughtfulness." *Educational Leadership* (April, 1989).
26. Ibid.
27. Robert Rothman, "Coalition Implores Bush, Governors to Avoid Use of Standardized Tests." *Education Week* (January 31, 1990).
28. Kenneth A. Sirotnik, "Evaluation in the Ecology of Schooling: The Process of

School Renewal." *The Ecology of School Renewal, Eighty-sixth Yearbook of the National Society for the Study of Education.* Chicago: University of Chicago Press, 1987.

29. Gordon Cawelti, "Better Measures of Student Achievement Called For." *ASCD Update* (June, 1988).

30. Grant Wiggins, "'Standards' Should Mean 'Qualities,' Not 'Quantities'." *Education Week* (January 24, 1990).

10

Growing
Thinkers

Mentoring is the main way to increase intellectual
skills. What a good school provides is good role
models. That is the main thing we can give to the
next generation. It is what I try to give my students,
and my children as well. Sometimes I succeed.

—Robert Sternberg

You're a growing thinker, and you want to be about the business of
growing thinkers; you're going to find ways to bring these commitments
alive in your classroom. You're not going to be pushed around by the curriculum or by habit. Great. You're resolved and enthusiastic, but how do you
go about getting all this in place in your classes? Where do you go from
here? What things do you worry about first? Second? What things do you decide not to worry about? How do you keep your edge, your mental sharp-
ness, and your resolve to grow and change? And how do you go about enlist-
ing colleagues and students in this process? The unfortunate truth of living
in schools is that teachers are not always encouraged to change and grow.
They are sometimes blocked and thwarted by the attitudes and actions of either those who are quite satisfied with the way things are or those who are
threatened by new ideas and unwilling to grow.

So far, we've scrupulously avoided the use of medical metaphors in this
book. We don't care much for the diagnosis and prescription of anything in
the schoolhouse, and we certainly don't want to hear about terminal students. As we've thought about this chapter and how we want to encourage
you to sustain personal and professional growth, however, the words *inocu-
lation* and *immunization* keep coming to mind. If you're going to nurture
thinking in your classes and keep your own mental edge, you may need to
fortify yourself against some rather insidious viruses that lurk in the workplace. This is a chapter to encourage you to transform your classroom, to ex-
hort you to work more toward the edges of your competence, to help you

think through what you want to do in your content area or grade level and how you might go about it. Curiously enough, such efforts are not particularly valued by everyone in the workplace. There are people out there who will work to defeat your efforts at growth: colleagues, students, administrators, and parents. These people may be carriers of viruses that will weaken your resolve and sap your strength for constructing a new learning environment. Thinking about them now may help you ward off these negative thinkers and avoid some of the pain they can inflict.

VIRUS #1:
THE "WE ALREADY-DO-THAT" STRAIN

You've read this book and tried out some of the ideas in your classroom. You're excited and want to share your experience with the teacher next door. You give him this book with an enthusiastic recommendation and ask him to read it over the weekend and tell you what he thinks. On Monday he passes you in the hall between periods, hands you the book, and says, "I'm already doing all of that stuff." Just like that he dismisses the book, the ideas, and your enthusiasm. Hard to take. You wonder if maybe you've gone a little overboard with this thinking pitch. Or you explain some of the things you're trying in your class to a group of grade-level colleagues at lunch. They listen awhile, and then one says, "Oh, we had an in-service on higher-level thinking skills last fall." "Yes?" you say in anticipation. "I got a couple of good worksheets that I use with my kids. That's the kind of stuff we're already doing in reading and math." Your own students have a version of the same virus: the "we-did-this-last-year" bug.

Everyone in the schoolhouse has a little healthy skepticism about "revolutionary new ideas." A lot of educational innovations are hot today and gone tomorrow. That's one reason we suggest being careful how you talk about what you're trying in your classroom. Be tentative. Talk more about the questions you have than how well everything's working. Share your experiments and your questions with colleagues. Avoid an "I-know-more-than-you-do" attitude. Some cynical colleagues may co-opt your new thinking by calling it "old" or "same-old." Some colleagues may resist the pressure for change by refusing to examine their own teaching. Some may have a cynical disregard for new ideas. But many of your colleagues do want to improve their teaching. These are people who can grow and change if you don't threaten them through arrogance.

You need a colleague or a confidante who is interested in your growth and who wants to listen and share ideas. Try again. Choose carefully the people you talk to. The ditto buff next door isn't going to like this book. But then maybe your building administrator is interested. Maybe a district-level person is interested. Maybe your roommate is good at hearing you out. Maybe talking with your own students about what you're trying to do will help. In any case, talking about growth is important for you because you need to hear yourself talk to find out what you think. You need to try out ideas and talk yourself into new understandings. As you do so, we suggest that you use a tentative tone and ask honest questions. We also suggest that you stay away from those carriers of negative attitudes.

VIRUS #2:
THE "YOU-CAN'T-TEST-THAT-STUFF" STRAIN

Evaluation—especially testing—will always be a legitimate concern in schools. Taking a cavalier attitude toward it won't help you gain support for what you want to do. We've been helping you prepare an antidote for testing concerns in chapter 9. But even though the "you-can't-test-that-stuff" response is only partially true, it's difficult to counter. Testing intellectual growth using the standard assessment tools we're now using is difficult. Worse yet, you're afraid that by teaching kids to think, you may be depriving them of instruction in the skills and facts they'll need to do well on standardized tests. If you're a good teacher, you'll worry about whether their scores will go *down* on the Iowa or the California tests or, worst of all, the state department of education tests given each year, the scores of which are published in the paper and ranked by school. You don't want this emphasis on thinking to erode the other gains you've work so hard to achieve in your classes. Maybe your principal has already said, "I don't care if you add some thinking skills to your class, but be sure you work on the test of basic skills," and he means SKILLS! Chilling stuff. Deep in the heart of every teacher who reads this book and works to reform his or her teaching is a fear that it might not work or pay off in visible results. What do you do to cope with your uncertainties?

First, as we've already suggested, know what's on those tests. There's a lot of myth and misinformation out there about what standardized tests actually measure. Teachers frighten themselves with irresponsible talk about tests. Counter those myths with information. Study test manuals and sample test items. Assure yourself that you're preparing kids to do well on those instruments. Second, share those sample items with your kids, not to teach to the test but to show them how tests work. Show them multiple-choice items and teach them how to narrow down choices. Show them how test taking requires thinking and solving problems.

Here's another suggestion. Don't try to change everything you've been doing overnight, but do more than just tinker with assignments. Start by re-working a unit that hasn't worked very well anyway, or begin experimenting with concepts that have always been difficult for students to grasp. Above all, believe in what you're doing. We have yet to see or hear of a single class-room where a teacher actively worked to develop thinking and saw his or her students' scores decline on tests. Yes, testing for intellectual growth pre-sents different and more complex problems for evaluation and assessment, but we're convinced that the very process of designing new ways to under-stand how well students are learning will improve your own instruction. Trying out new assessment procedures will inform your instructional strate-gies.

VIRUS #3:
THE "TEACHING-FOR-THINKING-TAKES-TOO-MUCH-TIME" STRAIN

We guarantee you'll catch a little case of this bug at some point. You'll be rolling along teaching your kids to think like inventors or artists, or you'll be encouraging them to develop their own problems and solutions, and it will hit you: "I'm not covering as much ground as I did last year. I'm afraid I'm shirking my duty to the content. How do I teach thinking and still cover everything in the curriculum guide and the textbook?" Sound familiar?

Teaching in a rich context that allows students maximum amounts of time to plan and work cooperatively, revise and redo their work, and reflect on their processes will take a great deal of class time. You won't be able to as-sign as many stories to read or problems to work or reports to write as you have in past years. In fact, you may cover less ground than when you had a well-oiled, teacher-centered class. But look at what the kids *are* doing. Look at the quality of their work, how proud of it they are, and how much effort they put into their products. Look at your expanded role as coach and men-tor, and remember Ted Sizer's admonitions about how less can be more when students are deeply involved in the content.[1] Decisions about depth and breadth, tough choices about when to move on and when to stay with something another week because students are really learning—these are an essential part of teaching. Time limits will be more of a frustration for a teacher who thinks of teaching as covering ground or who measures learn-ing by the quantity of student products than for teachers who put thinking first. Time limits will become less of a frustration for you as you learn to build learning into larger, more inclusive frames. Learning to orchestrate in-tegrated classroom experiences is growth that can't be rushed. You may of-ten feel uncertain about how you've organized the learning environment, but experience will make you progressively better at planning and managing a more complex, more dynamic, and more *whole* classroom.

We're assuming that many of you reading this book have already been experimenting in your classes. Along with your new understandings have come, no doubt, a number of new and more complex questions. Others of you are reading this book and preparing to teach. Your notebooks are full of ideas and your heads are full of plans. This chapter speaks to both groups by focusing on the concerns of introducing thinking into a particular grade level or content area and by offering some very concrete suggestions for where to begin and how to proceed. We begin by suggesting that you engage in a personal synthesis of all these thoughts about thinking. We encourage you to collect yourself and decide what's important. Think of the metaphor of the pebble thrown into the pond; the first ring is your own classroom. As your expertise and confidence grow in your own classroom, you'll share your experience with colleagues, and perhaps the ripples of that effort will widen to your entire school or district. We've already seen that happen in many places.

Exploration

Take a few minutes to put your reading of this book into perspective— to stand back and scan the broad outlines of what you've been thinking and writing. Look back through your journal. What highlights come to mind? Try to recollect the thoughts and feelings you've had as you made observations and raised questions.

Stake out the territory with a mental map; reflect on your explorations. These questions may help you get started. Can you recall any

- struggle with an unresolved question or problem?
- breakthrough in your own thinking or teaching?
- big risk you took?
- confirmation for something you've known intuitively or done unconsciously?
- new connection made in your own mind?
- new discovery about yourself or your students?
- change in your assumptions about thinking, learning, or teaching?
- strong response to something you've read?
- ideas you hit on to try out with your students?

Take some time to a write a journal entry about what has happened to you as you've read *Mind Matters*.

Read the following journal entry by Barbara Elmore, a high school biology teacher you know from previous chapters. Do any of Barbara's experiences or insights parallel yours?

> When I came into this program, I thought I was pretty good at critical thinking skills. I knew Bloom's taxonomy; I had written curriculum for HISD; and I taught science. I knew I was going to be really good at teaching this thinking stuff. But it wasn't that easy for me. At first I felt like I was plunged into total darkness. I am a highly organized teacher, a real paper pusher, and this kind of teaching was asking me to let go, to let go of control. I'm the kind of teacher who knows where she wants every child to be at every moment. Finally in frustration, I just turned to my kids. "What can we do to make biology more stimulating, more creative? What can we do to make it more fun?" It didn't take long for me to realize that students really do know a lot about how they can best be taught.
>
> First of all, they liked being able to express themselves in class and do things their way. They wanted time to think. They didn't want me just shoving stuff down them—you know, quick, quick, quick, "you have fifteen minutes." They wanted less testing, less fill-in-the-blanks stuff, fewer handouts, more projects, more student-designed things, more say in decision-making. They wanted more interesting problems. They wanted fewer problems. They wanted *their* problems. They were sick and tired of cookbook labs. So I took all of their ideas and thought about it awhile, and it wasn't all easy to take. But I was sick of most of that stuff too, so we embarked on real research in which they were given something to observe and inquire about. They designed their own labs, basically, designed them their own way using the materials at hand. I just stopped dispensing information. It's more like an inquiry now. The students are the learners, and they are also the providers of their own learning. I'm the one who steers, but they have a big say-so in the route we take.[2]

WHAT KIND OF KNOWLEDGE IS IMPORTANT?

Barbara has done more than cosmetic surgery on her classroom. She has changed more than assignments and tests. She has altered the balance of power and reshaped the definition of knowledge and knowing. To begin a comprehensive restructuring of your own classroom as Barbara has done will take some courage.

We suggest that you begin by looking at your content and how you teach it. Ask your students what they think, as Barbara did. Is your attitude toward your content frustrating students? Are you teaching your content as material you know and they don't? Are you defining knowledge as facts in books and lectures or, worse yet, stuff on tests? That view of knowledge is the norm in many classrooms, and it's a hangover from the nineteenth century when people believed that the essential mysteries of the universe had been encountered and solved by smart people.

It's a view of knowledge as containerized commodity locked in libraries that locks up the act of teaching too. It leads teachers to do what Carl Rogers has called "the exposition of conclusions."[3] If you're presenting the central tenets of your content as issues already settled, as truth already known and uncontested, then your students aren't going to be inclined to interact with that content and raise questions of their own. They're going to feel locked away from content. "Knowledge must solve a problem or provoke inquiry for it to seem important," says Grant Wiggins.[4] Expository teaching has too often characterized major subject areas like science and social studies and English. Schooling has far too often been a kind of warehouse operation where teachers load trivial knowledge into kids. The term paper, the science report, the essay have often been mere copying exercises from other sources. If you're going to develop your students as thinkers, you must begin to look at knowledge and knowing in new ways.

Of course, as we discussed in chapter 1, what has passed for knowledge in schools has been strongly manipulated by the dominant culture—or the "liberal culture" or the "culture of influence." What has passed for knowledge in the American culture has been summarized rather neatly for us by Allan Bloom, E. D. Hirsch,[5] and others, who suggest that Western cultural values or "our own culture," as they call it, should be preferred and taught above all others. Such culturally elitist views of knowledge suggest that knowledge is finite, reduceable to lists, and essentially what adults in the dominant culture know. Such views have tended to favor linear thinking over recursive; Anglo over African-American, Latino, and Asian; masculine over feminine; rational over intuitive; deductive over inductive; and the teaching of knowledge as a canon, a body of revered texts by a collection of sacred writers and thinkers. As a late twentieth-century teacher, you're a product of that kind of thinking. Changing your own mind and the minds of your students about knowledge won't be easy. But if you're still with us in this book, you must be interested in giving it a try.

THE VALUE OF CONSTRUCTED KNOWLEDGE

How else can you view knowledge? What other ways can you teach domain-specific knowledge to kids? What does it mean to *know* something? Think back to the early chapters of this book when we were trying to define thinking. You remember how much trouble we had really pinning all of this down. We said we favored metaphors that depicted thinking as dynamic, on-going, constructive. We said that thinking is making meaning. Look back at chapter 1 to refresh your own thinking on that topic. Isn't it really the making of meaning that teaching and learning are all about?

We hope that you'll value old knowledge and respect current truth but place a strong emphasis in your teaching on constructed knowledge, the kind of knowledge students author for themselves, the kind of understandings they come to by proposing and solving problems of their own making. The explosion of questions and problems about our universe should convince us that old knowledge, while it's the basis of new knowledge and valuable as reference point or point of comparison, will not be enough to educate students to solve current and future problems. Exclusive attention to particularized knowledge—the kind that schools are so fond of testing and teaching—has produced what David Perkins has called a "brittle knowledge,"[6] a fragile knowledge that fades quickly or goes out of date or crumbles in novel situations. As we write this last chapter, monumental social and political changes are exploding in Eastern Europe and in developing countries. Old answers and stock formulas are inadequate to explain and deal with these changes. Our foreign policies and economic plans and defense strategies must all be rethought. You can help prepare your students for a changing world by developing scenarios in your classroom that allow them to make their own discoveries, to develop their own theories, and—in effect—to personalize their own learning.

One other important understanding to stir into this stew of thinking about reform and change is that the knowledge thinkers can use is socially constructed. Personal knowledge is made powerful and permanent as it interacts with that of other knowledge makers. Meanings are negotiated and sharpened by learners as they talk and write about them in social contexts. There's not really any efficient way to shortcut or truncate the process of knowledge making. If students are to become authentic knowledge makers and acquire what Grant Wiggins has called "the habits of thoughtful inquiry,"[7] you'll have to provide a lot of time for them to talk—to you, to each other, and to themselves. That use of time will place a continuing emphasis on the importance of the classroom as community, a community where more speculative talk is encouraged, an environment where thinking-aloud talk and hypothetical talk and knowledge-building talk is ongoing. And more writing will be necessary. Not more encyclopedia writing and report writing but reflective, theory-building writing, student-owned writing like logs and journals that feed student thinking. All of this work will be grounded in your content and the central tenets of knowledge in your discipline, but you'll do less off-loading of textbook information, give fewer Scantron tests, and "tell" them far less. Dan testifies that when he first embarked on renewing his own classroom in those ways, as much as 80 percent of what he had been telling kids and having them do went by the wayside. So we really are talking about embarking on some major revisions of classroom activity.

Grace Beam, a seventh-grade life science teacher, began the school year by circling up the kids and placing a live hermit crab on the floor and letting it crawl around. As the kids oohed and aahed and sometimes screamed, she began to capitalize on their natural curiosity. She asked them what questions they had, and the talk began to focus on science. As they asked questions, she extended those questions and asked some of her own. Students jumped in to add personal knowledge and raise other questions. Within ten minutes or so, Grace had created an intense climate for inquiry and learning without telling the kids anything. Finally she said, "Class, this is how we're going to learn science this year. We're going to observe things and wonder about things and find answers and new questions. We're going to learn life science by thinking and acting like scientists."[8]

Grace began her year by signaling to students that their questions were important, that they were responsible for their own learning, and that they were going to function as a community of thinking scientists. Classrooms as communities is the key to that kind of learning. Communities offer modeling and support for individual thinkers to extend the thinking of others while offering opportunities for mutual criticism and self-correction. Communities build dispositions to think. Some naysayers have suggested that collaboration makes kids dependent learners, rendering them unable to think for themselves. We're convinced that quite the opposite is true. Collaborative learning contexts offer a protective environment in which kids develop independent ideas and feel free to try out unique and unconventional solutions. Of course, putting kids in groups to answer the questions at the end of the chapter is not the kind of collaborative learning we're talking about. When students are given opportunities to interact socially to construct knowledge, those opportunities must be truly open-ended and not overly teacher-directed and managed. As you reflect on your own approaches to your content, remember we're not talking just about pedagogy and methodology.

Reforming your teaching for thinking is not just doing new activities or offering students more freedom. As we've already suggested, what's at the heart of this reform is a new attitude toward knowledge and how it is acquired. Let us stress again that this new view of knowledge doesn't mean we have nothing to teach students or that textbooks are no longer important or that old knowledge is now no longer valuable. What it does mean is that we have to plan for and structure our classrooms in such a way that students construct their own versions of old knowledge in new and more personal ways. But there's even more at stake here than preparing kids to restructure what is already known. It's more than acquisition we're after. We want our students to create new knowledge in the future and be able to do something with it after they have it. Changing your class to make this happen may at first plunge you into an abyss of uncertainty, as Barbara Elmore related, but you can take courage from Donald Schön's writing on this subject. He says classrooms have always been uncertain places where student learning and student needs seldom conform to "what research tells us." He says classroom teachers rarely know what students need or which methodology is appropriate. In fact, he calls classrooms "indeterminate zones of practice." He sees classrooms as marked by uncertainty, uniqueness, and value conflict—places that escape the canons of technical rationality. Schön says every instruction we give our students, every assignment we construct for them is an experiment.[9] Perhaps we have fooled ourselves a bit by assuming that a well-oiled classroom is necessarily a place where all students learn. Failure to reform our teaching may be more risky than embracing change and growth.

Exploration

With your journal in hand, jot down some thoughts on these questions:

• What first steps have I already taken to build more opportunities for students to construct their own knowledge in my classroom?

• What changes do I need to make in the way I approach my content to give students more opportunities to develop thoughtful habits of mind?

• What experiments can I initiate to find out how students can best come to *know that they know* the essential content of my discipline?

CONSIDERING CONTEXT

After you've taken a good look at your attitude toward your content and your views of knowledge, you may want to look at how you organize that content for instruction: how your courses hold together and how well the ideas and areas of inquiry connect with one another. Compartmentalization and disconnectedness mark much of what we teach. Students often seem unable to connect ideas to form concepts and larger meanings. Oh, they're great assignment-doers. They love to complete work and hand it in and forget it. Have our course structures encouraged that factory-like mentality? Has organizing instruction around assignments encouraged kids to see the completion of an assignment as the end of that issue? The key to providing a climate for ongoing inquiry and knowledge making is to develop larger frames or contexts to hold the learning together, and in so doing to work to make sure that assignments don't mark the boundaries for learning in our classrooms. We need to work to ensure that our problems and assignments are not lifted out of larger frames like so many vocabulary words on the chalkboard.

When Dan worked with eighth-grade language arts and social studies teachers in Georgia a few years ago,[10] they voiced frustration with the way in which their students seemed to forget or fail to apply concepts and learning after a unit was completed. As a case in point, teachers mentioned the essays that students wrote for the Martin Luther King essay contest held each year in January. The papers students wrote were bad, mostly copied from the encyclopedia, and whatever students learned about civil rights and race relations seemed to leave them in February. Working together, the teachers decided to build a frame larger than just an essay for Martin Luther King Week. They decided to frame the inquiry with the issue of human rights around the world. Students wrote short pieces and held discussions and role playings dealing with human dignity and protest, and proposed solutions for breaking the race relations deadlock in this country. They researched the plight of a number of minority groups in our country, including Native Americans and new immigrants from Asia and Central America. They saw the "I Have a Dream" speech video and wrote eyewitness accounts of that day at the reflecting pond. They spent time in the library seeing what reference books and materials were available. They interviewed older people in the community about how things had changed and not changed in their own town. They wrote a piece to a younger sibling explaining the significance of the King holiday. They talked about changes they could make in their own school to improve race relations. Finally, each of them was asked to draw their inquiry together in an essay for King Week using any and all of the things they had thought and talked about during the three weeks.

Expecting students to accomplish such a synthesis was an ambitious goal, and teachers were patient and helpful as students struggled to express their new understandings and ideas in writing. The larger frame for inquiry had given students many more possibilities and themes to pursue. Many needed more time to accomplish the task. Teachers learned to be more flexible in planning time frames and deadlines. Dan remembers visiting the school about three weeks after King Week when a student rushed up to him in class and said "I got it. I got it. I finally thought of the opening to my King piece. It just came to me on the bus!" That assignment had not marked the end of learning for that student. She was still working on it (on the bus, no less) several weeks after it had been due. Teachers further reported that many of the issues and ideas they worked on during that three weeks continued to surface throughout the year. The teachers had created a frame large enough and interesting enough so that students forgot they were doing school assignments. The learning students were doing was situated in a rich context with many possiblities for individual and collaborative thinking.

Kathryn Timme teaches three levels of chemistry in Houston. In a regular Chemistry I class, she tried teaching electrolytes through their function in plants. "Now," she reported, "the students are growing their own plants and bringing them into the lab. They are feeding both through the roots and through the leaves. Students have to mix their solutions; we have special thermometers so they can check the concentration of those solutions, then feed their plants. If they miscalculate the concentration, it kills the plant, and they have to begin again. Sometimes that means tears of frustration, but you know they realize they have to reexamine their calculations."[11] Students are experiencing the joys and failures of scientific inquiry in Kathryn's class thanks to the kind of context she has created.

Kathy Mason teaches language arts in a middle school in an affluent Denver suburb.[12] She noticed that her students had very little understanding or concern for the problems of the homeless and the people who lived in the inner city, so she decided to use the city as a context for learning. Working with colleagues, she developed a four-week experience that took kids to downtown areas where they interviewed people, took pictures, and visited businesses, police, social service agencies, museums, and libraries to get a feel for the city. They pulled this experience together by developing their own ideas of what the people of the central city needed and what role suburban communities might play in satisfying those needs. In Kathy's case, the classroom just wasn't an appropriate place to learn about urban problems, so she took the kids to the city.

Another teacher in an inner-city high school saw her students grow upset as they listened to President Bush's speech on the drug problem. They thought he lacked an understanding of the inner city and that his "war on drugs" was wrongheaded. She rather spontaneously decided to lead the students in a series of inquiries into what the real problems of drug use were and what government should do about it. The young people began a serious inquiry into drug addiction and treatment alternatives, the role of hopelessness and alienation in drug use, and the economic factors involved in drug dealing. The students interviewed users, pushers, police, teachers, and medical personnel. The teacher reports that the inquiry was emotionally charged and students often challenged one another's ideas. Students pulled the ideas together by authoring their own "war on drugs" proposals and presenting them to their classmates. Side benefits of this kind of inquiry were that absenteeism was practically nil and student productivity was high.

What all of these stories have in common is that the teachers set learning in large frames. By creating contexts instead of assignments, they created spaces within which connections among and between ideas could take shape and be manipulated. Instead of teaching content in disconnected chunks, they used these frames to "hold the world together" while students pursued learning with abandon.[13] They set mandated curriculum and skills in meaningful contexts. Teachers had some ideas about where they wanted students to end up, but they let students map out their own routes to these destinations. They became the designers of occasions for student learning, and they coauthored these contexts with their students as partners.

Exploration

Continue to reflect on your efforts to teach for thinking by considering these questions:

- What are some units or topics or assignments I might reshape into larger, more inclusive, frames. How could my students help me do that?
- Are there parts and pieces of things I've been teaching that could be organized under a larger umbrella of ideas?
- Are there teachers in other disciplines and classes with whom I could work to build frames that might integrate topics into stronger contexts?
- How can I engage my students in coauthoring these contexts?

TRACKING PROGRESS IN THE THINKING CLASSROOM

How do you monitor the work of individual students as they find their own routes? Even organizing content around frames can still produce chaos if the teacher can't find a way to monitor what students are doing. In a classroom where the approach to content and instruction is dynamic, nonlinear, interdependent, and collaborative, there is much to keep track of. Managing such a classroom with a maximum amount of productivity and a minimum amount of chaos is a challenging goal. You'll find yourself using oxymorons to describe this experience to colleagues: "ordered chaos," "well-planned freedom," and "guided independence."

As discussed in chapter 9, students will need direction from you—markers, maps, guide posts, and reference points—to keep track of where they've been and where they're going. And you'll need similar kinds of data to know where you're going, how well students are doing, and what kinds of difficulties and roadblocks they're experiencing. If you wait to gather such information until students turn in finished products, you won't have ongoing information about how they approach problems, how they plan and implement those plans for solving problems, and how they feel about their work. You need to know how their minds are working while they're in the process of doing things if you're to coach and mentor their growth. That kind of information is largely invisible in the classroom, and unless you find ways to collect and monitor it, you'll miss most of the intellectual activity of your students.

THE STUDIO CLASSROOM

Something that has helped Dan restructure his classroom and think in new ways about what he's doing is to use a new metaphor. Here the work of Donald Schön has been particularly helpful.[14] Dan has adopted the term "studio" as one of the ways of expressing what he's trying to do. What comes to mind when you hear the word *studio?* Freedom, independent work, creativity, process, space, light, productivity? Those are things Dan wanted in his classroom. He wanted to work toward building what Lauren Resnick and others are calling "cognitive apprenticeships."[15] He wanted to build a work environment where students learn thinking as a trade. A studio is a place where learners work in front of each other and where the studio master is both mentor and artist. So Dan adopted the metaphor of classroom as studio to see how that might open his mind to new roles for him to play and help him place more of the responsibility for learning on individual students.

Dan's classes don't look much like real studios; they have desks in rows and far too many bodies to feel spacious. It's not interior decorating he's after, but the values and principles of a studio classroom. It's the psychological environment that's critical. In the studio, repeated practice and experimentation are the norm. Students don't expect to get it right the first time; getting it right may not be a primary value at all. Individual visions and versions are what's important. And thinkers come to those versions by experimenting, by trying out ideas. The teacher's role in the studio is to stay out of the kids' way, but not too far out of the way. Studio teachers are highly selective with their instruction. They might respond to students' questions like "What do you want?" with "I want to see your view of this" and to "Does this look right?" with "What do you think?"

Studio teachers often work in front of their students and share their own processes and quandaries. When studio teachers do give specific coaching suggestions, they try to give them while the student is at work. They abandon speeches to the whole class, such as the "Before you do this ..." speech and the rules and guidelines speeches. They try to build a comprehensive frame for learning by giving students a sense of how they're going to proceed; then the students set the whole thing in motion and go to work. Dan says he does his best teaching over-the-shoulder as he listens to the questions and problems of individual students. Students who need more help and support are encouraged to find it within the classroom community by consulting with partners and group members. "See what your partner thinks about that" is Dan's typical response to a student in dire need of direction. "Isn't that cruel?" you ask. "Isn't he abdicating his teacher role?" "Shouldn't he be telling kids what they need to know?" Our sense is that we've been entirely too willing to do just that in the past, too quick to give our own solution or help kids out of thinking quandaries they might well work their way through by themselves. If the kids are not in imminent danger of giving up, we try to encourage them to fashion their own answers by withholding ours. In a classroom that highlights thinking, teachers will be slower to give advice and opinions, allowing students time to work things out for themselves. Feelings of individual responsibility and community support grow as a teacher is able to avoid dominating the learning process and to act in more coach-like ways.

A TENTATIVE MODEL

How do you plan for a studio classroom, and how do you collect and use the invisible information about what's going on? First let's offer a picture of what the teacher needs to know and then suggest some ways to track student progress and keep the class moving toward thinking and learning. There are important kinds of information the leader of a studio needs to know at all times:

WHAT AM I DOING?

First, like any other job, teaching can become repetitive and habitual. The longer we teach, the less likely we are to monitor and reflect on our behavior in our own classrooms. As you already know, the thinking teacher has many strategies to work on: less text-pounding, less talk, better questions, more coachlike comments. You'll need to keep track of what you try and how well it works. Draft concrete plans. Keep good records. As a good teacher, you've been doing this forever. In the complexities of the thinking classroom, you'll need to know even more than the day-to-day activitities. You need to ask yourself, "What do I think I am doing?" You'll need to examine your motives and intentions and goals as well as your actual behavior. Reflecting on paper about your own ways of thinking and working can help, especially if you have students who do so as well.

Exploration

Begin keeping a log or a teaching journal. Keep it out on your desk and jot down your ongoing observations of your students at work; keep track of your own thoughts as they occur. Take your log home at night, write a review of the day and your actions in it, and engage in what Schön has called "reflection in action."[16] Maybe make this a double-entry journal and write notes on your notes. Keep asking yourself, "What am I trying to do here?" Consider inviting another colleague into your class to observe you at work and give you some feedback. Try tape-recording a class or two to monitor your talk and the amount of time you're running the show.

WHAT ARE STUDENTS DOING?

In the complex studio classroom, you'll need a plan for monitoring student progress and problems. Since you're going to give students a lot of time to work independently in class, in groups, and with partners, you'll want to be sure they're using that time well. Giving students three or four weeks to complete a project and then finding out that half of them haven't done very much won't do. You need to monitor their work with regular reports. The following strategies have helped Dan keep track of each student even when he has had ninety-five in three classes going at it.

A Thinker's Log

Dan has found it helpful to ask students to keep a log or journal as they work their way through a frame. Sometimes he assigns specific log entries like, "Read this article and talk back to it in your log." Sometimes he just asks students to give him a free-form response to something they did or talked about in class. He doesn't collect the log very often, maybe a sample page each week, and he doesn't try to structure it very much. He wants the log to be the student's own collection of reponses to readings and class experiences. But he learns how that's going by sampling it and keeps students on track by responding with encouraging comments.

A Portfolio

Students need a place to work and keep that work together. Dan has found a portfolio to be an invaluable tool in the studio classroom. Portfolios are somewhat in vogue now as tools for evaluation. As we discussed in chapter 9, a portfolio may contain samples of a student's best work which are submitted for grading or assessment. The kind of portfolio Dan uses is quite different. This portfolio is the place where students keep *all* their work: trials, experiments, drafts, sketches, experimental notes, observations, and musings. He tells his students that their portfolios are the tracks of their work, the visible evidence of their minds at work. And when he grades their performance, he gives the portfolio equal weight with their finished products, whatever those are. The portfolio is the record of process, and we view it as every bit as important as the completed products.

A Working Plan

Try to have students develop a working plan at the very beginning for how they think they'll proceed. This plan will vary depending on the frame you've developed and what kind of work they're going to get done. This plan can be a map, a series of drawings, a list of steps, a time line, a list of concerns or obstacles, even a log entry on how they feel about the project before they launch into it. The plan is not a straightjacket, a rigid outline, or a pressure-packed deadline. It's a way of getting students to think about where they're going even before they know what they're doing. And it gives you information about what kind of problem solvers they are and how their minds are already working. As students proceed through the frame of experiences you've developed, have them revise and alter their plans. Discuss these documents with the whole class and with individuals as they unfold.

Auditing

Devising some procedure for getting a progress report from each student each week is almost essential. Dan uses something he calls "audits." In the previous chapter, we spoke of them as windows into minds. Dan's students prefer to give him these reports on Mondays. They know when they come to class that he's going to ask them to document how the work is going. Since he teaches writing, his audits have to do with how that's going, but yours could focus on any specific task students are working on. Here are some sample questions from Dan's weekly audits:

- *What's in stock?* How many pieces do you have in the portfolio and in what shape are they?
- *What's on back order?* What is still in your head? What pieces are you thinking about and planning to write?
- *Which pieces are working?* Do you have any really solid pieces that may grow into longer ones? Do you have any pieces worth elaborating on?
- *How are your work habits?* How much time are you spending on your writing? Are you jotting notes and ideas? Working at the computer? Reading?
- *What problems are you having?* Is there anything I can do to help?

What's amazed Dan most about the audits is how honest kids are about their own production, and how much useful information he gains from reading them. Here's a typical example from a college student several weeks into the frame:

> Dan,
> I now have five pieces in my writer's portfolio; the first being our first write starting with "My family is …" and it's in okay shape. It's rough, I did it in a hurry. It'll do, but I could fix it if you want me to. Then I have the summary of my "Life Parts," and that may as well be in Greek because only I could understand it. I thought we were just going to discuss it and not read it. My third piece is the first of a trilogy of memoirs. I am quite proud of it, in fact. I spent much time and thought on the piece and, although none of my group liked it, I still can't wait for *your* feedback. It's my best piece. The second part (4th piece) is written out and not bad, but I'd like to develop it more. The final work I have in my possession is that which I wrote last night; it is weak and I'm getting discouraged. To get something pulled together for next Thursday, I must really concentrate on my love of writing and the important, positive first impression I want to make. I will probably compile the three pieces for a large synopsis (I'll have to play around with them.), I have to purchase some typewriter ribbon, and you can count on a finished project I will be proud of.
>
> > Have a good weekend,
> > Ruthie[17]

Ruthie's audit, like most of Dan's other student audits, is honest and informative. He learns that she has five pieces in the portfolio, and she gives him a status report on each. He learns that she's still trying to please the teacher even though he's been emphasizing the importance of pleasing one's self: "I can fix it if you want me to," and "I still can't wait for *your* feedback." But she closes with the line, "a finished project *I* will be proud of," a hint that she really is beginning to see the work as her own. She also gives an updated plan for pulling the writings together by the deadline. As a teacher, Dan feels like he knows exactly where Ruthie is and how her work is going, and he has the feeling that Ruthie knows that too.

Reflecting

The most helpful and valuable information we're getting from students is coming from the reflections they write when the inquiry has drawn to a close and the final products and portfolios are ready for evaluation. This powerful information about how things went and how we can revise and change what we did is something most of us have been missing for all our teaching lives. We've asked students to evaluate a unit or even complete a self-evaluation, but those documents were almost always perfunctory and useless. Students either told us what we wanted to hear or didn't have much to say at all. It wasn't until Dan began the studio classroom approach that he realized his own mistake. If students do only teacher assignments to teacher specifications, there really isn't much they can say about their processes: "I did what you wanted; here it is." But if they do have freedom to make individual decisions about how to proceed, they have important things to tell us about how it went. If they have to find their own ways through a problem, devise and think through alternatives, and consult with other class members, they can be quite articulate about the circuitous route that inquiry took.

Dan reserves some class time at the end of a frame of experiences for students to write these reflections. He's been amazed at how seriously and thoughtfully students approach these reflection times. For the first time in his teaching, he knows *what students think they are doing,* as well as what they have been doing. See chapter 9 for sample reflection questions, and consider this student example from Mark:

> Dr. Dan,
> I am taking this time to respond about a few things I have had on my mind. The first item I would like to talk about is the nature piece. I have been wondering why I do not have the motivation I did for the memoir piece. Part of the reason must be the winding down of the quarter. But I think there is more. I love being out in nature. I especially love going camping in the mountains with my friends, or going fishing (saltwater) in Florida. In both instances, I feel a sense of awe, and a sense of smallness?? It is a great feeling. I am not sure if I always feel a part of nature. Sometimes I feel like I belong, and at other times I feel I am an outsider. I do not know if I can find universal truths in nature; I guess I have tried such things in this class. But it is difficult to go out, observe nature, and rattle off truth. It is difficult to always compare nature to my life. Perhaps I didn't always have to do this, maybe I'm looking, and writing the wrong way. In any case, the writing is unnatural. It is too forced, thus it lacks emotion, fire. I think it is dull. Still, explorations benefitted me.
>
> First of all, even though my writing was scarce and poor, I believe my powers of observation improved. Often, I would be driving somewhere and I would just stop and think of how I would describe that field, or that sunset, and why. Why do I want to write about the sunset? I *know* that this is where my

nature piece should start. An enforced observation is the beginning. (I suppose I do have a basic understanding of what I'm supposed to be doing, but still it isn't easy.) The second benefit is the crafting of the language. I enjoyed experimenting with the form, and I liked my Shakespeare piece because of this reason. It was fun to try new things. Sometime, I really want to write a great nature piece like Annie Dillard, but first I really need to get motivated; I need to feel that the piece is important, relevant, and natural. I'm hoping I'm developing this sense....[18]

Mark's reflection comes after a demanding frame centered around observing and writing about nature. Obviously Mark is not satisfied with his writings, but he has come to learn some things about himself as an observer, thinker, and writer. If Dan doesn't collect this information, he may look at Mark's work and think the student just wasn't interested or didn't work hard enough. Dan may think the nature frame itself was the problem. He may blame himself or the readings or the explorations he chose. Worse, he may jump to all the wrong conclusions about Mark as a thinker if he only grades Mark's work. But in this reflection Dan learns that Mark really has wrestled with important ideas about observing nature. Mark has a strong sense of what worked and didn't work for him in his writings and in this inquiry. He gives Dan some specific clues as to what he might do next time with this frame: play with the outsider/insider dichotomy, continue to emphasize observation activities, encourage experimentation with form.

But Mark is only one student in the class. Dan needs to know *what triggers thinking* for each student in his class. He needs to know which explorations worked for which kinds of thinkers and whether his coaching and handouts were helpful. He needs to know how well groups and collaborative time functioned. He needs to know the effectiveness of his own attempts to coach thinking. Dan must ask himself, *What triggers my own thinking?* He needs to compare his teacher notes and observations and feelings with those of his students. When he collects and studies the portfolios, audits, and reflections from everyone in the class, he gets a powerful composite picture of thinking and learning, information rich with potential to inform and improve his teaching.

The key to getting thinking about thinking flowing in your classes is to emphasize and value it from the very beginning. Give students frequent opportunities and invitations to talk about how their minds work and how they went about solving problems or finding answers or creating artifacts before, during, and after the process. Value speculative, tentative talk, encourage risk taking and hypothetical solutions. Engage in this kind of thinking yourself and in front of your students. And remember, students will make authentic observations of their minds at work only when they engage in real tasks and make independent decisions about how to pursue those tasks.

Exploration

We ended chapter 2 with an exploration that asked you to rate how your classroom looked based on those six essential conditions for thinking. For this last exploration, you're asked to work through a more elaborate version of the same continuum, shown in the form on pages 222–225.

A TALE OF TWO CITIES

Think of teaching and learning in terms of the pebble in the pond metaphor, with your class and the work you do as the first ripple. For many of you, that one ripple may be enough. You may prefer to work quietly on your own teaching without reaching out to colleagues. But for those of you who want to create larger ripples, maybe even make a few waves by extending the reforming of teaching and learning to your school and district, this following two-city story is for you.

Sioux Falls

Sioux Falls is a little off the beaten track. Sitting on the plains at the eastern edge of South Dakota, it's a quiet, conservative, friendly town. Many of its teachers have grown up in the area around Sioux Falls, across the border in Minnesota and Iowa, on farms and in small towns. There isn't much teacher turnover here. Most of the teachers have been working here long enough to sport a little gray hair. The schools still work in Sioux Falls; the community is interested in quality education and supports the schools with its taxes and goodwill. But times have been hard on the farms around Sioux Falls, and despite goodwill, there simply isn't the money available to pay teachers what they're worth. Salaries in South Dakota are some of the lowest in the nation, and many of Sioux Falls's teachers work at extra jobs and summer jobs to make ends meet. Not a place you might go looking for leadership when it comes to teaching for thinking. About five years ago, a couple of middle school language arts teachers who had been in the South Dakota Writing Project were trying to change the way they taught writing in their classrooms. They found that as they acquainted their students with the processes writers use to complete texts and placed less emphasis on finished products, their students grew as writers and readers. What's more, they noticed that when they offered students more freedom, more room for decision making, their students began taking more responsibility for their own writing and making some very intelligent editorial decisions about texts. These two teachers wondered if what they were doing was actually improving the quality of their students' minds as well as making better writers of them.

(Text continues on page 226.)

The Thinking Teacher:
A Self-Evaluation

Each item below represents a continuum of classroom activities that can inhibit or nurture thinking.

Play back mental movies of your own classroom as it was when you first began to read this book. Using a pencil or ordinary pen, circle the letter that most accurately places that classroom of the recent past on each continuum.

Then think of your classroom as it has evolved since that time—indeed as it was today and will be tomorrow. Use a colored marker to place that classroom of the present on each continuum below.

In the space that follows each item, give at least one example of any change. Then set one goal for further change.

1.

Setting is orderly but sterile. Routines vary little, and students are reinforced for right answers. Atmosphere is impersonal, and the teacher is in tight control.

Setting is vibrant and various. High expectations challenge students and encourage risk taking. Teacher maintains atmosphere of trust, poses stimulating problems,

A	B	C	D	E

Example of change:

Goal for further change:

(continued)

2.

Teacher talks; students listen. Teacher asks questions; students answer. Independent work is strictly solo and usually competitive.

Students talk to each other as well as the teacher; they ask as well as answer questions. Work with partners and groups is a way of life. A spirit of community rather than competition prevails.

A	B	C	D	E

Example of change:

Goal for further change:

3.

Textbooks dominate. Students have little opportunity to express their own ideas in their own words and their own ways.

Students are awash in all forms of language. They use their own words and find their own forms for responding to what they read and hear in a language-rich environment.

A	B	C	D	E

Example of change:

Goal for further change:

(continued)

4.

Students are passive, doing what they are told and little else. Rote learning, drill, and practice abound. Learning has little connection with life outside school.	Students are actively engaged. They do things with their hands as well as their heads. Practice is authentic, grounded in a meaningful context.

A   B   C   D   E

Example of change:

Goal for further change:

5.

Teacher rushes to cover material. Students are rewarded for quick, one-shot answers. There is little time to consider alternative ways of solving problems.	Work is sustained and deliberate; it proceeds step-by-step with time for planning and considering options.

A   B   C   D   E

Example of change:

Goal for further change:

(continued)

6.

| Students seldom retrace their own steps in solving a problem or working through a task. There is little thinking about thinking. Self-evaluation is minimal. | Students pause frequently to plan, monitor, and evaluate their own ways of thinking through a task. They explore their own mental processes on paper and compare their ways of thinking with those of other thinkers. |

A   B   C   D   E

Example of change:

Goal for further change:

They wondered what else they might do to encourage the growth of thinking in their classrooms.

The teachers began to explore together what this thinking business is all about. They read articles in *Educational Leadership,* the journal of the Association for Supervision and Curriculum Development (ASCD), and they began to order books on thinking. They also began to discuss their interests with other colleagues. Before long, a study group of nine or ten teachers was meeting monthly to discuss current books and articles on intellectual development. After a year of reading and talking, they decided to take up the issue with administrators in the central office. They asked if a Committee on Thinking could be formed for the district, a committee of teachers from each school, kindergarten through twelfth grade. The committee was formed; and as they met on a regular basis, they began to debate how best to develop their knowledge base on thinking and how they might influence the district curriculum. They looked at materials on thinking from publishers and were disappointed. They went to conferences and heard presentations on teaching for thinking that left them cold. Finally, they decided to develop their own knowledge by trying things in their classes and sharing how it went. They also proposed a voluntary, district-wide in-service workshop on teaching for thinking to be held in the fall.

Over fifty teachers and several principals showed up for that workshop. Dan led them through a variety of activities in that first meeting—activites designed to help them examine their own teaching, activities that we eventually wrote into the early chapters of this book. Most of the folks who attended that workshop were not sure what this thinking business was all about, but they were united in their desire to do more in their own classrooms to develop thinkers. The group met several more times that year and eventually planned and directed workshops in their own buildings. They wanted to see if they could entice their colleagues into reforming their own classrooms and join them in learning more about teaching for thinking.

What's remarkable about the Sioux Falls story is that from the beginning to the present, the vision and energy and enthusiasm for growth and reform came from the teachers themselves. Dan hasn't been back there in a while. Maybe the teachers' enthusiasm for teaching thinking has waned. But we doubt it. The thinking project in Sioux Falls was teacher owned and operated from the beginning, and we suspect that the ripples from the pebble those two language arts teachers tossed into the pond are still spreading.

Houston

Houston, Texas, is a difficult city to classify. In this sprawling, fast-moving metropolis, change is a way of life. As the economy rebounds from the hard times of boom-town-gone-bust, Houston becomes more and more international. Its people have not one culture but many. The city itself is a collision of contrasts: conservative and liberal politics, skyscrapers and green spaces, country-western music and grand opera, high-tech industry and ethnic enclaves.

Unlike most major cities, Houston has not written off its school system. The Houston Independent School District—geographically larger than the state of Delaware—enjoys strong support from local universities as well as businesses and civic organizations. Its 234 schools serve more than 190,000 students, who are roughly 43 percent Hispanic, 40 percent African-American, 15 percent Anglo and 2 percent Asian. Though as diverse as the city itself, Houston's schools have all been subjected to at least a decade of such Texas-sized pressures as back-to-basics, overzealous testing, and a state-mandated teacher appraisal system that should make even Madeline Hunter blanch. Add in all the social problems that come with poverty, plus a 40 percent student mobility rate, and you see why morale among the district's more than ten thousand teachers is often low. You also understand why it's so difficult but so crucial to infuse those schools with thinking. Having been a teacher in Houston schools before coming to the Central Office as an Assistant Superintendent, Carol is deeply concerned with all of the above. Several years ago, she wanted to find a way of rewarding good teachers and helping them renew themselves by forming a community of dedicated soul mates. Beginning with a modest budget and an outline that has since become the table of contents for this book, Carol initiated the "Growing Thinkers" program. Rooted in the premise that only thinking teachers can develop thinking students, this program takes twenty-four teachers a year through approximately sixty hours of activities that look a great deal like what we hope you've done on your own as you've worked your way through the preceding chapters. Carol likes to describe "Growing Thinkers" as one-part doctoral seminar, one-part action research, and one-part summer camp. That's because each year's participants read and discuss many scholarly works, devote much effort to becoming researchers in their own classrooms, and share many Saturday adventures as they explore various contexts for thinking. Because each year's participants are supported in conducting their own campus-based activities, the program annually spins off little colonies of thinkers. After a couple of years, principals and other central office administrators demanded their own cycle of "Growing Thinkers." After five years, several hundred teachers and a more modest number of administrators have been touched by the program. Furthermore, Carol is convinced that "Growing Thinkers" has provided the seedbed for Project ACCESS, a sweeping curriculum renewal project run *by* teachers *for* teachers, which places thinking at the center of all classrooms.

Have morale problems become a thing of the past in Houston schools? Have most classrooms been infused with thinking? Certainly not. Houston is still a tough place to teach, and many students have not yet begun to learn as well as we'd hope. "Growing Thinkers" has provided a start but nothing more.

As chief architect of the program, Carol is deeply gratified by the way it seems to have taken on a life of its own. As leader and mentor for its participants, she's unabashedly proud of the teachers with whom she has spent so much time and whose stories are woven into the pages of this book. Together they confirm everything we've said about the importance of having close, long-term collaborators and the importance of belonging to a community of thinkers.

On the surface, these case studies of Houston and Sioux Falls would seem to be more different than alike. In Sioux Falls, the impetus for growth came from the teachers themselves who rejected "*They* won't let us do that" for "We need to do this for ourselves." In Houston it was "They" who initiated, but in this case "They" were not out to coerce or manipulate or manage teachers but to excite and guide them. In both environments, however, teaching for thinking is alive and flourishing. Top-down or bottom-up seems not to be the issue in reforming teaching and learning. What matters is minds. Reforming classrooms and restructuring schools begins with teachers renewing their own minds. We hope this book has helped you begin a renewal process in your own thinking about teaching and learning, as it continues to do for us.

NOTES

1. Theodore Sizer, *Horace's Compromise: The Dilemma of the American High School.* Boston: Houghton Mifflin Company, 1984.
2. Barbara Elmore teaches biology at Jones High School in the Houston Independent School District.
3. Quoted in Donald Schön, *Educating the Reflective Practitioner.* San Francisco: Jossey-Bass, 1987.
4. Grant Wiggins, "The Futility of Trying to Teach Everything of Importance." *Educational Leadership* (November, 1989).
5. Allan Bloom and E. D. Hirsch certainly didn't invent the elitist intellectual tradition in this country, but popular books such as *The Closing of the American Mind* (Bloom) and *Cultural Literacy* (Hirsch) have rekindled old American fears that cultural pluralism and multicultural educational perspectives might somehow hasten the decline of Western civilization.
6. David Perkins and Gavriel Salomon, "Are Cognitive Skills Context-Bound?" *Educational Researcher* (January/February, 1989).
7. See note 4 above.
8. Grace Beam is a seventh-grade science teacher at Pershing Middle School in the Houston Independent School District.

9. Peter P. Grimmett and Gaalen L. Erickson, *Reflection in Teacher Education*. New York. Teachers College Press, 1988.

10. Teachers at Glynn Middle School in Brunswick, Georgia, shared their classes with Dan. Particularly helpful was Susan Lee, an eighth-grade language arts teacher.

11. Kathryn Timme teaches three levels of Chemistry at Lee High School in the Houston Independent School District.

12. Kathy Mason teaches language arts at West Middle School in the Cherry Creek School District, Denver, Colorado.

13. Dan Kirby, Dawn Latta, and Ruth Vinz, "Beyond Interior Decorating: Using Writing to Make Meaning in the Elementary School." *Phi Delta Kappan* (June, 1988).

14. See note 3 above.

15. Lauren Resnick, *ASCD Update* (February, 1990).

16. See note 3 above.

17. Ruthie Escalante was a student in Dan Kirby's class in Santa Barbara, California, in 1988.

18. Mark Mester was a student in Dan Kirby's class in Athens, Georgia, in 1989.

A Brief Bibliography

Arnheim, Rudolph. *Visual Thinking*. Berkeley: University of California Press, 1969.

Though more than twenty years old, this book remains timely in its treatment of perception as the basis of thinking and the role of the arts in all fields of learning.

Barell, John. *Playgrounds of Our Minds*. New York: Teachers College Press, 1980.

This book makes a compelling case for educating the imagination, which Barell believes to be fundamental to all learning. Fictitious characters illustrate how imaginative learning might look in the various academic subjects.

Bruner, Jerome. *Actual Minds, Possible Worlds*. Cambridge: Harvard University Press, 1986.

Extending a forty-year inquiry into questions of thinking and learning, this work reflects a thoroughly constructivist view of mind. As in his earlier book, *Beyond the Information Given,* Bruner sees the mind as a maker rather than a mere perceiver of worlds. Further, he epitomizes the workings of mind in two functions, one narrative and the other paradigmatic—an elegant analysis that has powerful implications for work with thinking in schools.

Clifford, James, and George E. Marcus. *Writing Culture: The Poetics and Politics of Ethnography*. Berkeley: University of California Press, 1986.

This book about the making of ethnographic texts has implications for the teacher as well as for the anthropologist. Both are concerned with the making of meaning and the expression of that meaning so that others can understand and construct their own meaning.

Csikszenmihalyi, Mihaly and Isabella S. (Eds.). *Optimal Experience*. New York: Cambridge University Press, 1988.

This book reports research on the nature and nurture of intrinsic motivation.

It focuses on the intense motivation demonstrated by highly creative people and identifies key factors as being the absence of both boredom and anxiety.

Donaldson, Margaret. *Children's Minds.* New York: W. W. Norton, 1978.

Donaldson examines the reasons children so often begin school seemingly bright, eager, confident learners only to become less so with each passing year. Though the book focuses on the kinds of experiences children need in order to learn at the elementary level, principles are applicable to learners of all ages.

Edwards, Betty. *Drawing on the Artist Within.* New York: Simon and Schuster, 1986.

In this highly readable book, the author applies the creative processes of the artist to everyday problem solving. She recommends a number of techniques for developing creative abilities and includes practice activities.

Gardner, Howard. *Frames of Mind: The Theory of Multiple Intelligences.* New York: Basic Books, 1983.

Arguably the most influential of current works on intelligence, this book sets forth Gardner's theory that intelligence is too complex to be measured as a single-number IQ. To the contrary, the author argues that each person possesses at least seven intelligences—linguistic, logical-mathematical, musical, spatial, bodily-kinesthetic, interpersonal, and intrapersonal—each of which follows its own trajectory of development to produce a unique cognitive profile.

Gardner, Howard. *The Mind's New Science: A History of the Cognitive Revolution.* New York: Basic Books, 1985.

Besides placing emerging theories of mind in historical context, this highly readable book offers a guided tour of wide-ranging research into the workings of the brain and the nature of thought.

Geertz, Clifford. *Local Knowledge: Further Essays in Interpretive Anthropology.* New York: Basic Books, 1983.

By examining the particulars of local knowledge and the understandings that underlie divergent cultures, Geertz demonstrates the power of anthropological thinking—the workings of mind that seem most fundamental to all human beings of all ages and all places.

John-Steiner, Vera. *Notebooks of the Mind: Explorations of Thinking.* Albuquerque: University of New Mexico Press, 1985.

In her study of how creative people think, John-Steiner draws upon her own interviews with more than fifty distinguished artists and scientists as well as from personal journals, letters, and autobiographies of such gifted thinkers, living and dead. Besides analyzing the processes and characteristics of creative minds across a wide range of fields, the author pays special attention to the development of creativity.

Neisser, Ulric. *Cognition and Reality.* New York: W. H. Freeman, 1976.

This book debunks information-processing theories of mind and focuses instead upon the fundamental role of perception in thinking, which Neisser sees as the making of personal meaning by interaction with the given world.

Neisser, Ulric. *Memory Observed: Remembering in Natural Contexts.* New York: W. H. Freeman, 1982.

This book explores and illustrates with highly readable case studies the workings of memory, both short- and long-term.

Perkins, David N. *The MInd's Best Work.* Cambridge: Harvard University Press, 1981.

In this study of creativity, Perkins frames each real-life illustration with hypotheses, which accrue to offer rich insights into imaginative thinking across widely diverse fields.

Resnick, Lauren B., and Leopold E. Klopfer. *Toward the Thinking Curriculum: Current Cognitive Research.* Alexandria, Virginia: Association for Supervision and Curriculum Development, 1989.

This book focuses on the centrality of knowledge to thinking. Following a quick review of research into cognition, each chapter applies these findings to the role of thinking in a particular content area.

Sacks, Oliver. *The Man Who Mistook His Wife for a Hat.* New York: Harper and Row, 1987.

This collection of "clinical tales" focuses on the power of the arts to organize and activate otherwise dysfunctional minds. Sacks, a practicing neurologist, draws from his extensive experience with impaired thinking a rich set of insights into the workings of "normal" minds.

Schön, Donald A. *Educating the Reflective Practitioner.* San Francisco: Jossey-Bass Publishers, 1987.

This influential work presents the design studio as a model for professional education. Schön sees teacher education as a process that allows novices to interact with experts and reflect on their own evolving practice. Discussions of knowing-in-action and reflection-in-action offer powerful new ways of looking at teaching as decision making and at thinking itself.

Smith, Frank. *Insult to Intelligence.* New York: Arbor House, 1986.

The title of this book is Smith's irreverent comment on schools. In an entertaining but highly substantive way, the author takes on the "nonsense industry" that has made so many schools mindless places that depress the thinking of both students and teachers.

Sternberg, Robert. *Beyond IQ.* Cambridge: Cambridge University Press, 1985.

Rejecting the concept of the the fixed, monolithic IQ, Sternberg proposes a theory that looks at intelligence as having three parts: componential, experiential, and contextual. In supporting this theory, he focuses on people's ability to succeed in the real world rather than merely to answer questions on a test.